GRANDMA MOSES

AMERICAN MODERN

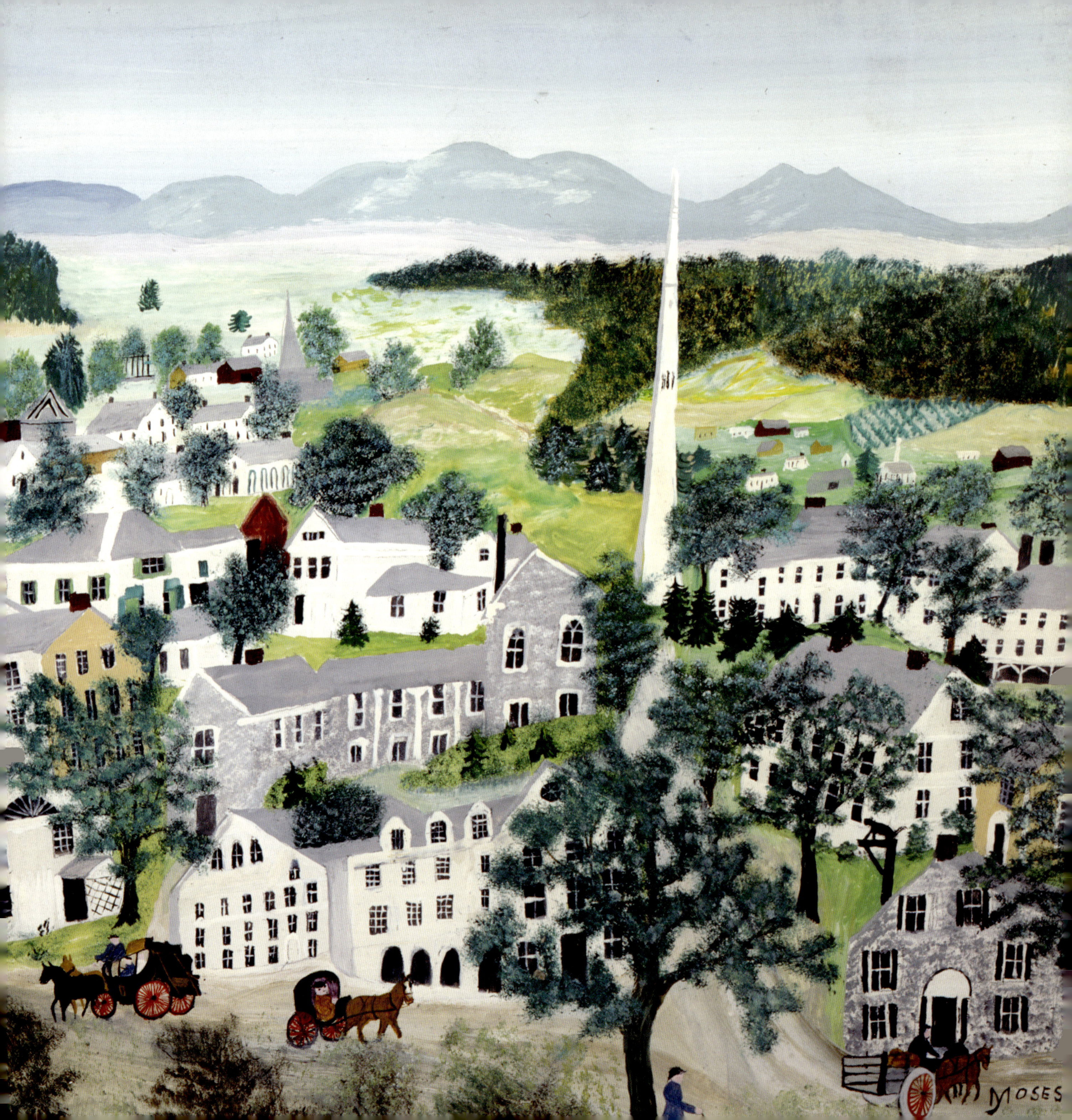
MOSES

GRANDMA MOSES
AMERICAN MODERN

SHELBURNE MUSEUM BENNINGTON MUSEUM

Skira Rizzoli
NEW YORK

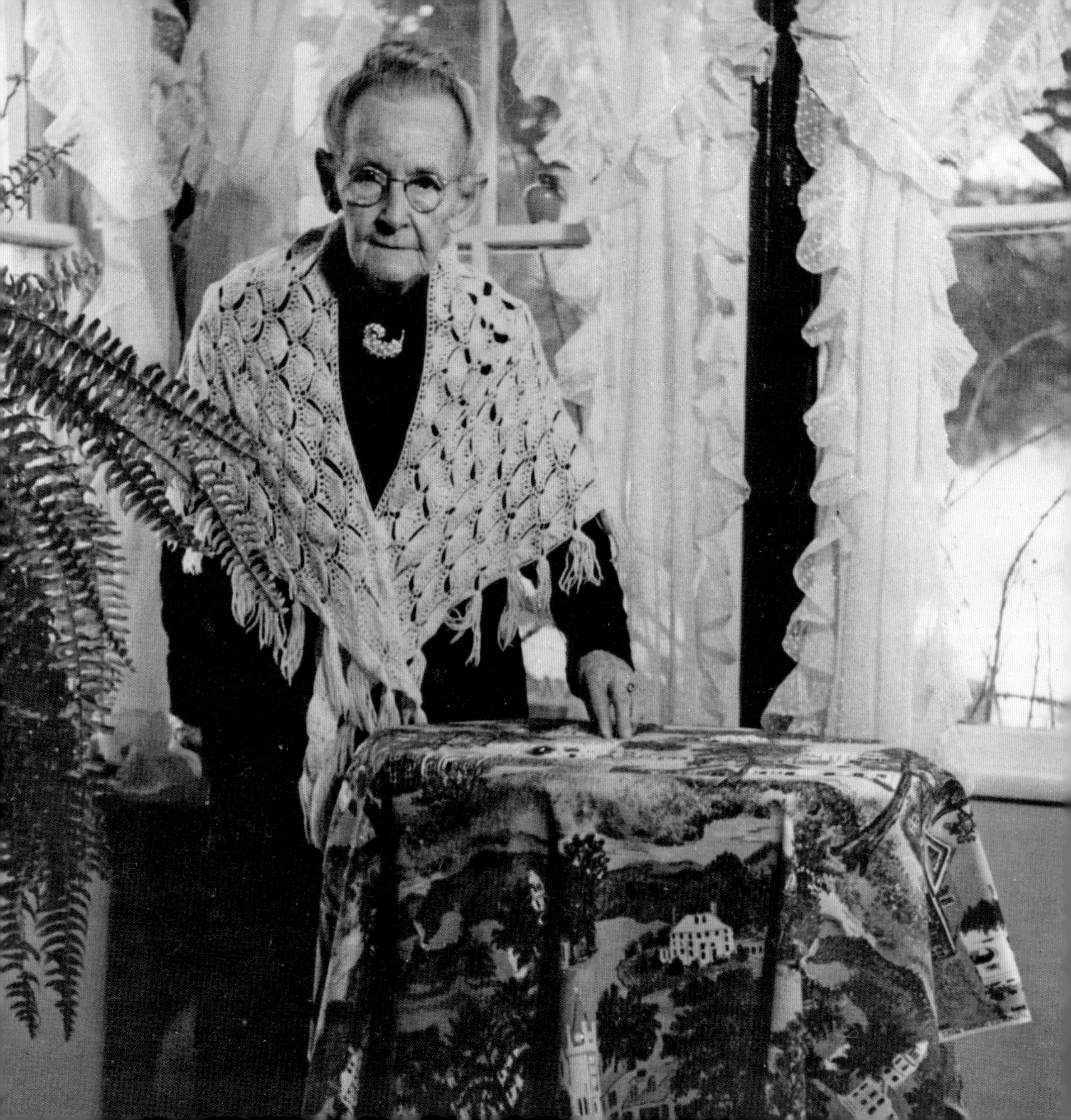

CONTENTS

FOREWORD

THOMAS DENENBERG AND ROBERT WOLTERSTORFF

FEW AMERICANS NEEDED A MAP to locate "Grandma Moses Country" in the 1950s. For the literal, it could be plotted as that corner of the United States where New York adjoins Massachusetts and Vermont. For most people, though, it was a landscape of the imagination—an idealized and geographically indeterminate place of hill and dale planted with tidy houses and barns and populated by hardworking yeoman families. It proved easy to find. Grandma Moses images were ubiquitous in post–World War II America, appearing in her paintings, housewares, greeting cards, magazine advertisements, on television, and in the movies. Grandma Moses herself served as a national icon. Her public image as a farmer's wife, all but preserved in amber, amplified popular understanding of her work and lent authority to her vision of a rural past for an increasingly modern nation.

The relationship between Grandma Moses, Shelburne Museum, and Bennington Museum is long-standing and intimate. Shelburne Museum founder Electra Havemeyer Webb (1888–1960) developed a warm personal relationship with Moses, repeatedly hosting the artist at her Vermont house, and organizing an exhibition of her work in 1960. Bennington Museum's close identification with Grandma Moses took longer to develop, even though the world she painted lies a scant fifteen miles from the museum. In 1963, two years after her death, Otto Kallir and Galerie St. Etienne created the first of several temporary exhibitions at the museum. These led to the "Grandma Moses Gallery," where at times up to eighty paintings were on loan all through the 1970s. Eventually the museum's interest in Moses led to gifts and purchases. Today the museum holds the largest public collection of her work: more than forty paintings, needleworks, the eighteenth-century tilt-top table she decorated with landscapes and then used as a painting table, her iconic apron, photographs, documents, and even the schoolhouse she studied in as a little girl. The work of Grandma Moses has come to be as deeply identified with these two Vermont museums as with the region itself.

This exhibition and catalogue regard Grandma Moses in new light. To this day she is viewed as a naïf: self-invented, without precedent, context, or connections. In fact, her work emerged out of nineteenth-century artistic practice and was discovered and championed by collectors of modern art in the 1930s who created a canon of folk art to serve as a branch of modernism's family tree. The four essays here show how her work grew out of nineteenth-century art pedagogy and art-making practices; place it in the context of American Modernism from the 1930s to the 1950s; connect it to suburbanization and the creation of a mythology of rural, small-town, New England in the years after the war; and draw parallels between her work and the short stories of Shirley Jackson, who had a very different take on small-town life, developed in North Bennington, Vermont, at midcentury.

Books and exhibitions are the work of many hands. We are grateful for the contributions of Jamie Franklin, Curator of Bennington Museum, and Carolyn Bauer, Assistant Curator of Shelburne Museum. Coauthors Diana Korzenik and Alex Nemerov defined collegiality. In the myriad logistics of realizing such an undertaking, we have been assisted by Callie Stewart, Barbara Rathburn, and Kate Owen. The staff at Rizzoli produced a beautiful volume, and also shaped our understanding of Grandma Moses and her world. Finally, we express our special thanks to Galerie St. Etienne and to Otto Kallir, Jane Kallir, and Hildegard Bachert for forging a relationship with these two museums that has extended for well more than half a century and continues, fruitfully, to this day.

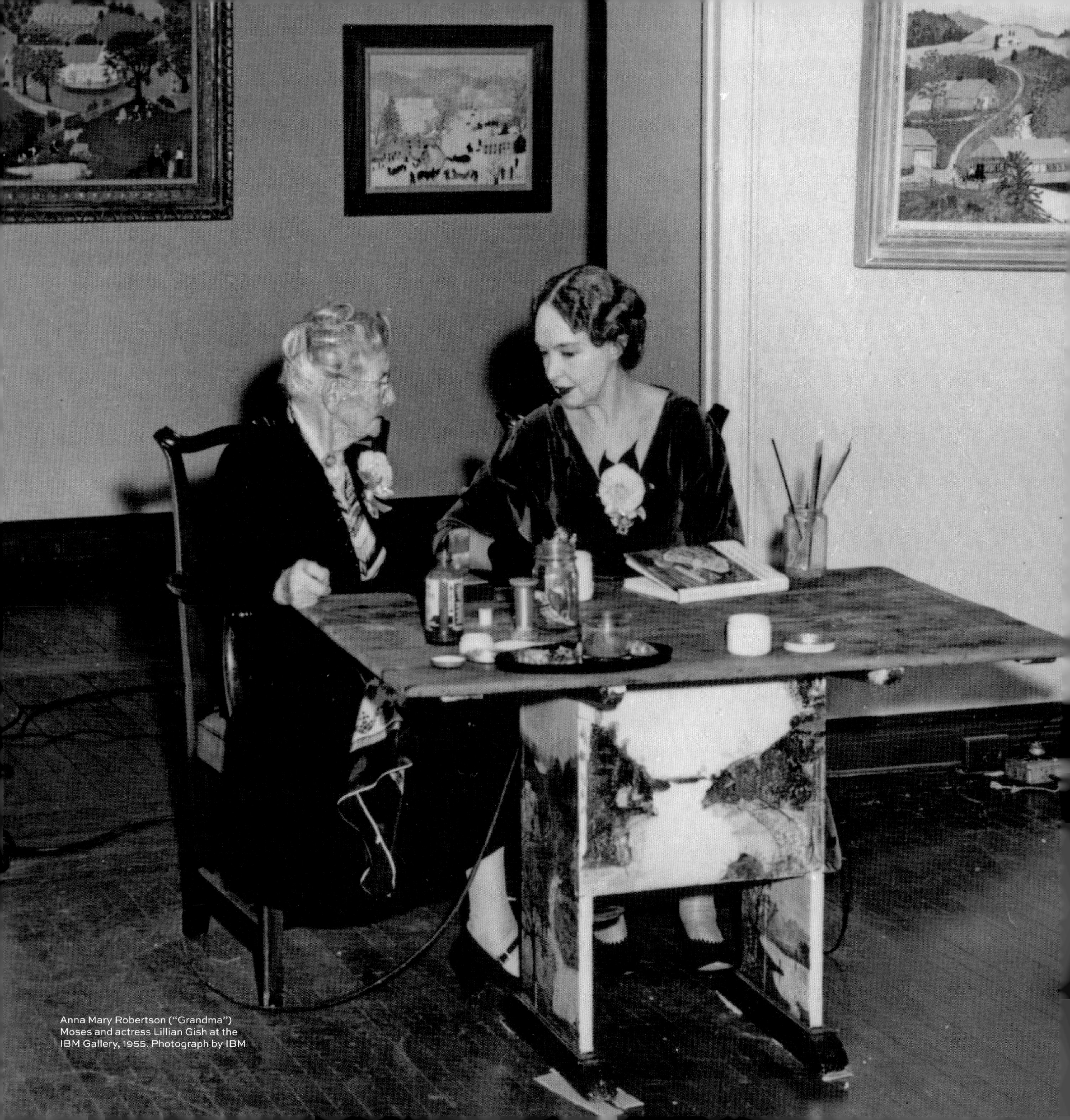

Anna Mary Robertson ("Grandma") Moses and actress Lillian Gish at the IBM Gallery, 1955. Photograph by IBM

MOSES, MoMA, AND THE MODERNIST NARRATIVE

JAMIE FRANKLIN

BETWEEN 1936 AND 1938, the Museum of Modern Art in New York, under the directorship of Alfred H. Barr Jr., organized three exhibitions—*Cubism and Abstract Art*; *Fantastic Art, Dada, Surrealism*; and *Masters of Popular Painting: Modern Primitives of Europe and America*—in a series that was intended, in Barr's words, "to present in an objective and historical manner the principal movements of modern art."[1] The first two exhibitions in the series represented such undisputed masters of modernism as Pablo Picasso, Wassily Kandinsky, Marcel Duchamp, and Paul Klee. *Masters of Popular Painting*, on the other hand, featured the work of mostly little-known painters—from both Europe, such as Camille Bombois, Séraphine Louis, Henri Rousseau (by far the most famous of the group), and Louis Vivin, and America, including Edward Hicks, John Kane, Joseph Pickett, and Horace Pippin—all of whom who had little or no formal training in the arts and created their work beyond the boundaries of the "art world" of their time and place (at least prior to their "discovery" by art world insiders). The current reputations of the artists surveyed in these three exhibitions aside, it is hard not to take issue with Barr's claim that his attempt to codify the history of modern art was "objective" in any sense of the word. He even created a chart—the most tantalizingly objective of visual formats—attempting to trace the interconnections and development of the various "isms" of modern art, which graced the dust jacket for the catalogue to *Cubism and Abstract Art* (fig. 1). In its visual convolution this chart makes clear just how complex a topic Barr was tackling. Eighty years later it seems perfectly clear that the divisions, bifurcations, and linkages that Barr was attempting to codify begin to break down at even the simplest of queries. What, for example,

FIG. 1
Alfred H. Barr. Cover of the exhibition catalogue *Cubism and Abstract Art*, New York, The Museum of Modern Art, 1936. Offset, printed in color, 7 3/4 × 10 1/4 in. Alfred H. Barr, Jr. Papers, 3.C.4. The Museum of Modern Art Archives, New York © The Museum of Modern Art/ Licensed by SCALA/Art Resource, NY. Digital Image: Middlebury College, Middlebury, Vermont

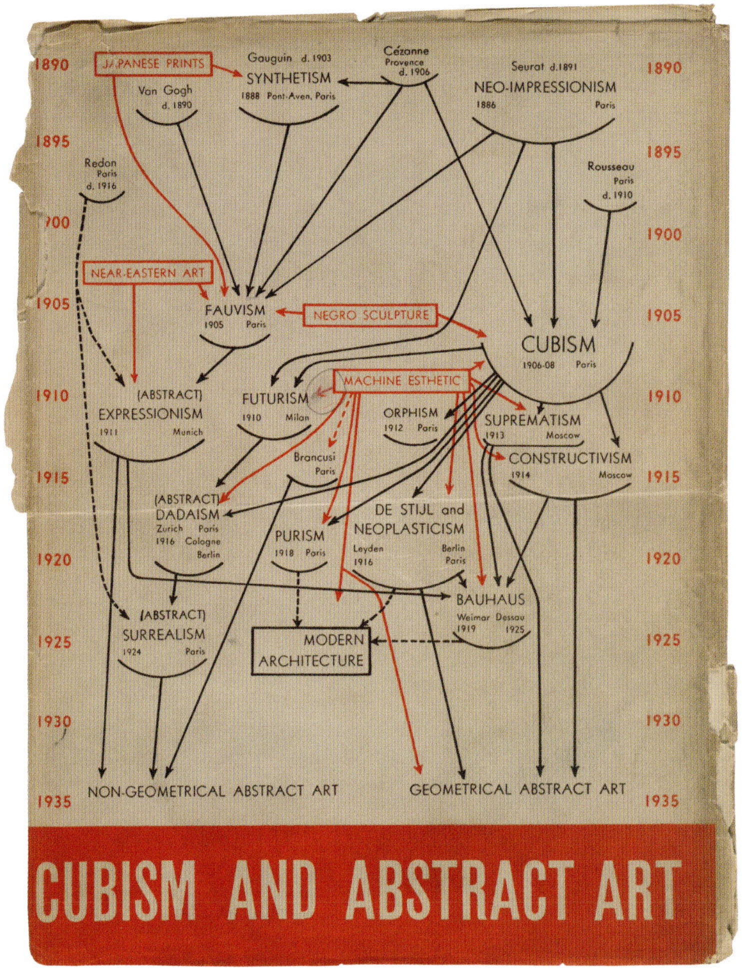

makes Rousseau's paintings a precedent for cubism, beyond the fact that Picasso and other progenitors of the style admired his work? Barr himself, despite his claim of objectivity, acknowledged that the reality of modernism, only a few decades old at the time, was far more complex than he could possibly encapsulate in a single exhibition or chart. This is evidenced by the fact that he made his survey serial in nature, continued to make revisions over time to his chart, which he never considered definitive, and noted, for example, that by 1936 an artist such as Picasso was creating works that could be classified as both cubist and surrealist, or both simultaneously.[2] Just as Barr recognized that the boundaries between cubism and surrealism were permeable, so, too, did he make clear that the distinctions between so-called folk artists and their counterparts who worked within the context of the mainstream art world were equally tenuous, stating in his introduction to *Masters of Popular Painting*, that "the purpose of this exhibition is to show, without apology or condescension, the paintings of some of these individuals, not as folk art, but as the work of painters of marked talent and consistently distinct personality."[3] Despite the flaws and inconsistencies in Barr's larger agenda, his statement of purpose for *Masters of Popular Painting* is still relevant today, eighty years later, as we continue the art historical struggle to break down such deeply rooted biases as the false dichotomies between "high" and "low" art or artists that are classified as "insiders" or "outsiders."

Masters of Popular Painting was far from an anomaly in MoMA's early exhibition programming. From its inception in 1929, MoMA had what the art historian Thomas Crow has recently called "a dual commitment" to European modernism and the art of the "common man" in America.[4] This agenda was particularly strong between 1932, when acting director Holger Cahill organized *The Art of the Common Man: American Folk Art, 1750–1900,* which consisted almost solely of works of early American folk art from the collection of MoMA founder Abby Aldrich Rockefeller, and 1943, when Barr was dismissed from his position as director in no small part due to his enthusiastic support of "self-taught" artists, including a solo exhibition of Morris Hirshfield's paintings. It was from within this complex historical nexus of "folk art" and modernism that Anna Mary Robertson "Grandma" Moses was catapulted to international fame. Today, Moses is the best-known artistic autodidact of the twentieth century, and her work is often perceived as exceptional, somehow operating outside the mainstream of art history and certainly distinct from the productions of such modern artists as Picasso and Jackson Pollock. Yet, I would argue that Moses's art and its reception are integral to a full understanding of the history of modern art in America. In 1939, the year after *Masters of Popular Painting,* MoMA presented two exhibitions that are revealing in their rather startling juxtaposition. From October 18 to November 18, the museum debuted three of Moses's paintings to an art world audience in an exhibition, *Contemporary Unknown American Painters,* curated by the influential collector and dealer Sidney Janis. This was an exclusive "members only" show, then a common practice at MoMA, which writer and collector Diana Korzenik has compared to "insider trading."[5] Overlapping slightly with this exhibition was a much more public one, *Picasso: Forty Years of His Art,* on view November 15, 1939, through January 7, 1940, the largest retrospective of Picasso's work to date, featuring more than three hundred works. While the overlap of these two exhibitions may have been purely coincidental, the relationship between the work of Moses and Picasso, as well as other modernists, was definitely not inconsequential or superficial. Moses's work and the debates that have surrounded it since her first outing at the Galerie St. Etienne in New York serve as a nearly perfect litmus test for understanding the complexity, politics, and contradictions of modern art in America from the late 1930s until her death in 1961.

MODERN/PRIMITIVE

In the decade after her introduction to the art world, Moses went from being an unknown farm wife in rural upstate New York, who happened to paint, to an international artist celebrity. In 1950 an exhibition of fifty of her paintings, organized by Otto Kallir, the director of the Galerie St. Etienne, under the auspices of the US Information Service, made her work available for the first time to a hungry European public.[6] The tour began in Vienna at Kallir's former Neue Galerie, where he had been one of the earliest champions of Austrian Expressionists such as Gustav Klimt, Egon Schiele, and Oskar Kokoschka, before traveling to the Netherlands, Germany, and Switzerland, and finishing up in Paris, the "birthplace" of modern art (if we are still willing to believe Barr and his cohorts), at the Musée National d'Art Moderne. While Moses had entered the art world through no less an arbiter of taste than MoMA, over the course of the 1940s her exploding popularity outside the marble halls of museums and her overwhelming commercial success made her work suspect to the majority of American art critics, who by and large bemoaned the European tour of Moses's works.[7] As the cultural critic Lucy Lippard later pointed out, this practice of negating work that "communicates to a dangerous number of people . . . is a blatantly classist attitude."[8] By 1950 American critics had widely embraced abstract expressionism, claiming it to be the first American victory in an international war over artistic supremacy. However, in the aftermath of the horrors of World War II, which Europe experienced much more directly than America, the French critics and public ate up Moses's pictures. As one American in Paris summarized the French response to Moses's work: "She is bound to mean the most to everyday people living in an unhappy world who, during the few minutes they look at Grandma's pictures, drink in her memory of a happy world."[9] The Musée National d'Art Moderne acquired Moses's painting *The Dead Tree* (a decidedly unhappy subject, it must be noted, even if set in a bucolic landscape) after the exhibition, making it the first painting by a contemporary American artist to enter that prestigious institution's permanent collection.

Most critics—whether in America or abroad, positive or negative—put Moses and her work in stark contrast to the darker, angst-ridden strains of modern art, notably abstract expressionism. Yet, she still served in many ways as the perfect symbol of a modern artist, unshackled by the expectations of the art world. It could be argued that her insistence on painting "happy" pictures was unexpectedly bold in the context of a morose postwar world. Exemplifying this attitude is a cartoonlike caricature of Moses, sent to her by an admirer from Paris, presumably around the time of her debut there in 1950 (fig. 2). In the drawing, Moses's body is grossly contorted and she confrontationally, though with a smile on her face, stands before a bed that has been stood on end. With a

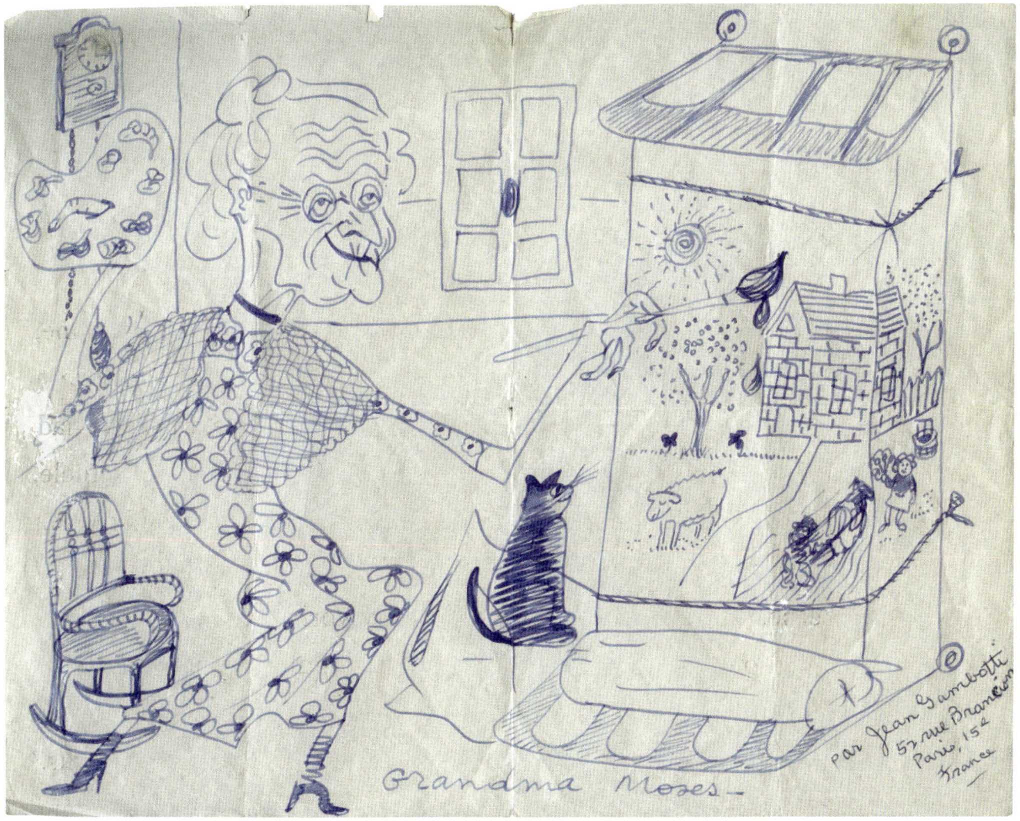

FIG. 2
Jean Gambotti. *Grandma Moses*, ca. 1950. Ink on paper, 8 1/8 × 10 ½ in. Bennington Museum, Museum purchase, Bennington, Vermont, 2005.62

traditional artist's palette in one hand (she actually used repurposed jar lids to mix her colors) and a dripping paintbrush in the other, she seems to be attacking the picture plane, in this case the bedsheet. The imagined painting is a stereotypical (though not very Moses-like) rural scene, with a sun shining down upon a prim little farmhouse surrounded by a smiling sheep, a horse-drawn plow, and a young girl holding flowers. The drawing mythologizes Moses as a cross between a benign farm wife and a wild woman who painted on any surface she could find. Prior to her "discovery," she did, in fact, paint on a variety of found objects, including the base of a tilt-top table that had been passed down in the family since the eighteenth century and served as Moses's improvised easel (figs. 3 and 5). The admirer, Jean Gambotti, has depicted Moses as the quintessential *peintre naïf*, the embodiment of the American rags-to-riches, hardworking ideal. Paired with one of Hans Namuth's iconic photographs of Pollock (fig. 4), the "other" American artist taking the world by storm in 1950, I cannot help but think that we are looking at the King and Queen of Modern Art. Pollock was born in Wyoming, grew up in the American West, and found inspiration in the ephemeral sand paintings created by the indigenous peoples of the American Southwest. Dancing around an unstretched canvas spread out on his studio floor, he flings skeins of house paint directly out of the can,

FIG. 3 (BOTTOM)
Anna Mary Robertson ("Grandma") Moses painting in room behind kitchen, 1952. Photograph by Ifor Thomas

FIG. 4 (RIGHT)
Jackson Pollock, 1950. Photograph by Hans Namuth. Courtesy of Center for Creative Photography, University of Arizona. Copyright © 1991 Hans Namuth Estate

FIG. 5
"Tip-up" Table, c. 1773. Attributed to John Whiteside. Painted by Anna Mary Robertson ("Grandma") Moses, c. 1920. 27 × 45 × 31 ½ in. Bennington Museum, 1984.516

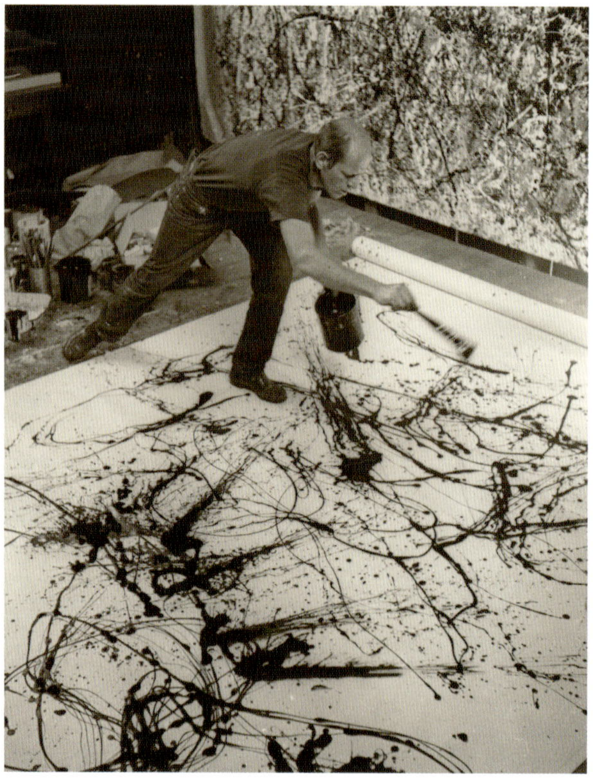

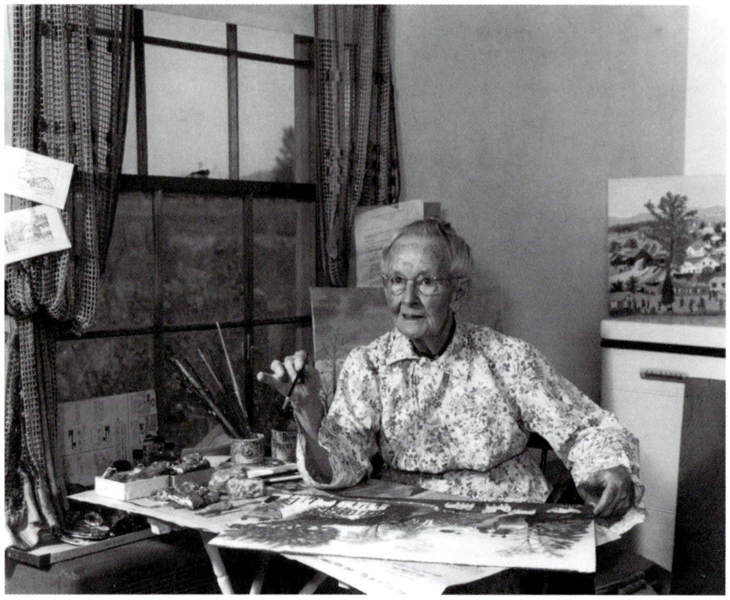

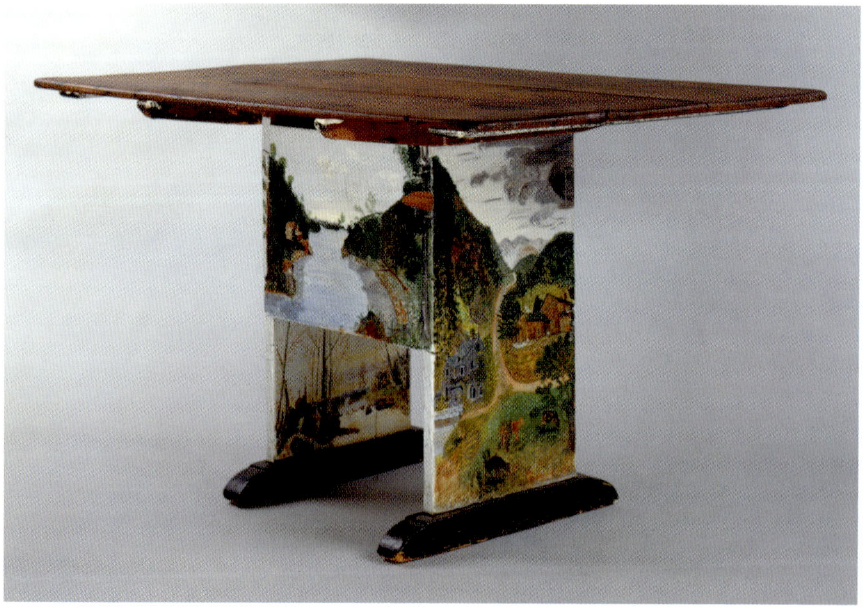

exemplifying the wild and woolly modern artist as primitive "other." Moses and her work were commonly referred to as "primitive," a term she personally loathed.[10] It was a label used during the period to describe pretty much any artists who weren't part of the modern artistic establishment in Europe and America (unless to describe the nature of their inspirations), from makers of African masks to medieval sculptors to little old ladies who lived a few hours' train ride up the Hudson River from New York City.

MELDING MEMORY, IMAGINATION, AND INTUITION

At the core of Moses's artistic success was her personal, deeply felt approach to landscape painting. In her autobiography, Moses spent far more time describing childhood memories than her more recent artistic fame. These recollections are filled with metaphors connecting life to earth's natural rhythms and detailed, almost transcendent descriptions of her experiences in nature: "In the springtime of life there is plenty to do. Oh, those damp snowy days, early in spring, when we loved to go to the woods, and look for the first blossom of the trailing arbutus, which sometimes blossoms beneath the snow, or gather the pussy willows. Feeling nearer to God's intentions, nearer to nature."[11] Moses also provides us with a basic outline of her artistic mind-set. Following a matter-of-fact description of the mechanical process of preparing a Masonite board for a picture—"I go over the board with linseed oil, then with three coats of flat white paint"—Moses dives into an evocative description of her approach to divining an image: "Now the board is ready for the scene, whatever the mind may produce, a landscape, an old bridge, a dream, or a summer or winter scene, childhood memories, but always something pleasing and cheerful, I like bright colors and activity."[12] I am particularly struck here by the phrase "whatever the mind may produce." Moses's paintings have often been discussed as if they are factual visual records of her lived experience. It is usually forgotten that Moses was, first and foremost, an artist, not a historian or documentarian. Her mind was occupied by the unlimited possibilities of the imagination, and she felt very little obligation to record "facts" in the traditional sense of the word. In an interview she clarified that while she did make careful observations of nature, her basic approach to landscape painting was deeply intuitive: "I look out the window sometimes to seek the color of the shadows and the different greens in the trees, but when I get ready to paint I just close my eyes and imagine a scene."[13]

Helen Frankenthaler emerged on the national stage a few years after Moses, sharing her close ties to Bennington. Her lyrical, highly emotive abstractions of atmosphere, personal associations, and place are often cited as the next step, after Pollock, in the supposedly linear progression of modernism. Frankenthaler herself noted that while you could only ape most abstract expressionists, "you could depart from Pollock," and her fellow painter Morris Louis claimed that Frankenthaler's work was the "the bridge between Pollock and what was possible."[14] Frankenthaler's approach to landscape, particularly during the 1950s, her first decade as a mature artist, was not all that different from Moses's, even if the end products are markedly different. Describing the creation of her seminal masterpiece from 1952, just three years after graduating from Bennington College, Frankenthaler recalled, "I painted *Mountains and Sea* after seeing the cliffs of Nova Scotia. It's a hilly landscape with wild surf rolling against the rocks. Though it was painted in a windowless loft, the memory of the landscape is in the painting," finishing with the caveat, "but it has also equal amounts of cubism, Pollock, Kandinsky, Gorky."[15] Much like Moses, Frankenthaler held the landscape inside herself and simply let it pour out, literally in her case, splashing thinned oil paints directly from a coffee can onto unprimed canvas. Unlike Moses, Frankenthaler was deeply knowledgeable about the history of art and contemporary artistic trends, recalling Salvador Dalí's famous painting *Persistence of Memory* as the first she ever stood in front of and talked about, with her sister Marjorie.[16] On a separate occasion, she noted, "I've been touched . . . by a Surrealist—by Surrealist I mean 'associative'—quality. It's what comes through in association after your eye has experienced the surface as a great picture; it is incidental but can be enriching . . . I leave it out of my own pictures more and more as I become increasingly involved with colors and shapes. But it is still there."[17] As much as her paintings might be built upon the memory or evocation of a specific landscape, they were equally tied up with the formal elements of art. For Frankenthaler the most successful paintings walked a tightrope, balancing pictorial depth with the flatness of the canvas. "The 'why' of how a picture works best for me involves how much working false space it has in depth. . . . It's a play of ambiguities."[18] While Moses may not have been familiar with terms such as "perspectival space" or the critic Clement Greenberg's ideas about the integrity of the picture plane, her best landscapes demonstrate that she intuitively came to similar conclusions as Frankenthaler. Moses noted, "I like to paint something that leads me on and on into the unknown, something that I want to see away on beyond," simultaneously expressing her interest in drawing the viewer into a false pictorial space while emphasizing an overriding desire to convey a sense of mystery or, as Frankenthaler may have put it, ambiguity.[19] In paintings like *White Creek* (plate 20) and *Hoosick Valley (From the Window)* (plate 31), Moses's delicate, atmospheric transitions of color, from rich forest and vivid grassy greens in the foreground to softer minty and sage greens in

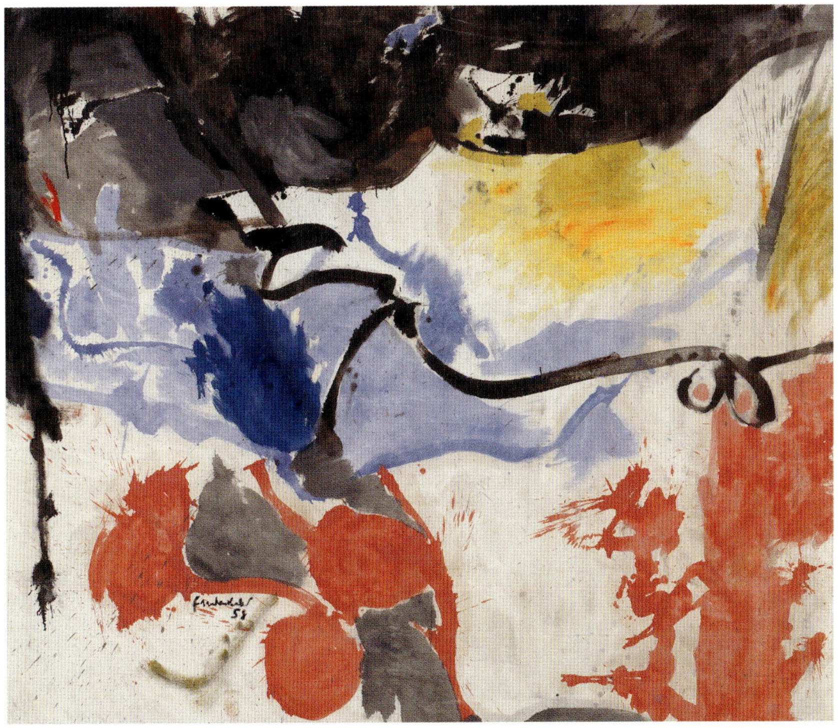

FIG. 6
Helen Frankenthaler. *Hotel Cro-Magnon*, 1958. Oil on canvas, 68 × 81 in. Milwaukee Art Museum, Gift of Mrs. Harry Lynde Bradley M1966.153 © 2010 Helen Frankenthaler / Artists Rights Society (ARS), New York

the middle ground, melting into the soft blues of the background hills and sky, combine with the complex topography of Washington County's rolling hills that drop steeply downward into the river valley below before rising precipitously to a relatively high horizon line, creating a complex, slightly baffling effect of simultaneous depth and flatness. A similar effect of push and pull can be found in Moses's *The Baker Home* (plate 34). The snow-covered banks framing the left and right foreground, along with the trees in the foreground and middle ground, flatten the pictorial space, as does Moses's typically scumbled, highly textural surfaces, while the bands of starkly contrasting color that form the bold curve of a road, shadowed snowbank, and glistening reflection pull the viewer into the typically expansive scene. The subtle overall blue-gray tonality of the painting brings everything into unity.

Moses often drew on memories of places or events that she had experienced as much as eighty or ninety years prior or passed down stories of "old-timey" things from an even hazier past. Yet, those recollections or borrowed stories were almost always heavily colored by her relationship to the same landscape in which they had taken place, which she continued to experience on a daily basis. Take for example Moses's *The Battle of Bennington* (plate 25), from 1953, which depicts the historic Revolutionary War conflict of August 16, 1777, as if it were taking place before our eyes, yet includes the monument built to commemorate the battle over one hundred years later in the upper right-hand corner, its reflection shimmering on the surface of the Walloomsac River that winds its

FIG. 7 (TOP)
Anna Mary Robertson ("Grandma") Moses. *Bennington*, 1945. Oil on pressed wood, 17 3/4 × 26 in. Bennington Museum, Museum purchase, Bennington, Vermont 1986.310

FIG. 8 (BOTTOM)
Unknown photographer. "Bennington, VT" ca. 1910. Halftone printed postcard, 3 1/2 × 19 1/2 in. Bennington Museum, Gift of Mrs. George Atwood, Bennington, Vermont, 1983.12.1

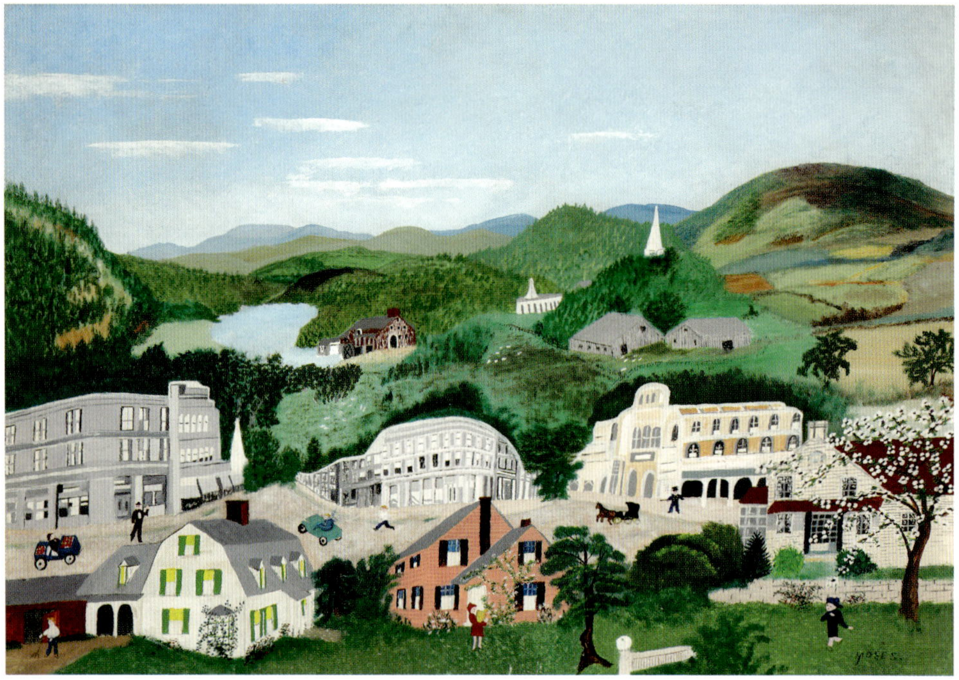

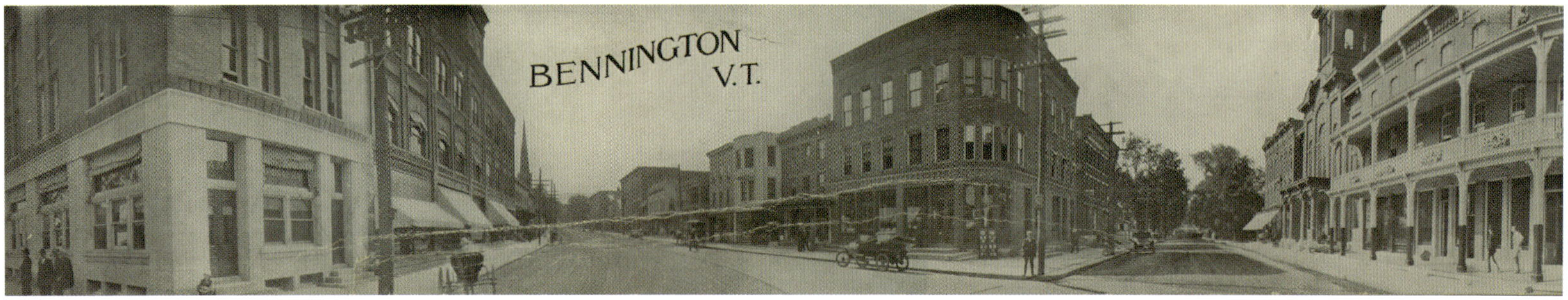

way below. Moses lived most of her adult life only a few miles from the site of the battle and had lived even closer to the monument itself, located ten miles away in Bennington proper, between 1932 and 1935 while caring for two granddaughters. Understandably, she associated the monument with the battle and it made sense to her to include it in her painting, not just as an anachronistic symbol but on artistic grounds as well. In a 1955 television interview, the newsman Edward R. Murrow slyly asked Moses why she had included the monument in the painting, and she answered, quite simply, "Well, I put the monument in because it looked good, I guess."[20]

The temporal relationship between the experience of a place and the translation of that experience into a painting was fluid for Frankenthaler as well. In 1958 Frankenthaler created a small group of paintings inspired by her personal encounters with the prehistoric cave paintings in Altamira, Spain, and Lascaux, France. She recalled her initial experience of encountering the paintings at Altamira in 1953 in a postcard to Greenberg—"It all looks like one huge painting on un-sized canvas; it all reminded me a lot of my pictures"—drawing a direct link between herself and the prehistoric painters, taking on the mantle of modern as primitive, as Pollock had before her.[21] Yet it wasn't until five years later, working with what the curator John Elderfield has described as "anticipatory imagination," that she executed her first paintings inspired by the prehistoric images and their subterranean context.[22] *Before the Caves* was created shortly before Frankenthaler's 1958 honeymoon to France and Spain with the artist Robert Motherwell, when she revisited Altamira and experienced the caves in Lascaux for the first time. During that trip she executed *Hotel Cro-Magnon*, named after the hotel where she was staying and inspired by a famed depiction of a horned bovine at Lascaux (fig. 6). A year later came the painting *Cave Memory*. Despite having been executed in the closest temporal proximity to her actual experience of the caves, *Hotel Cro-Magnon* may well have drawn inspiration from a postcard depicting the famed Lascaux bull, with its distinctive undulating black outline, a copy of which she sent to a friend.[23] It seems memory wasn't the only resource Frankenthaler was able or willing to draw from.

ARTISTIC PROCESS: "STEALING" POPULAR IMAGERY

> "When there's anything to steal, I steal."
> —Pablo Picasso[24]

Drawing inspiration from commercially produced images such as the postcard of the cave painting wasn't standard practice for Frankenthaler, though she frequently payed homage to her art historical heroes in compositions that were based very directly on favorite paintings from the past. Moses, on the other hand, was outright omnivorous when it came to stealing already existing imagery for her work. A postcard featuring a panoramic fish-eye photo of prominent buildings in Bennington's commercial center (fig. 8) serves as the compositional spine for Moses's *Bennington* of 1945 (fig. 7), in much the same manner as the image of the bull serves as the anchor of Frankenthaler"s composition. Though the buildings are heavily distorted by the fish-eye effect of the photograph, difficult to identify even for longtime Bennington residents, Moses nonetheless transferred the image quite directly to her painting, even partially maintaining the black-and-white postcard's grisaille color scheme. She seemingly improvised the rest of the scene, undoubtedly drawing heavily on other

FIG. 9 (LEFT)
Currier & Ives. *Home to Thanksgiving*, 1868. Chromolithographic print, 16 1/2 x 26 in. Bennington Museum, Collection of the Cleveland E. Dodge, Jr. 2005 Trust

FIG. 10 (RIGHT)
Currier & Ives. *American Homestead–Summer*, 1869. Hand-colored lithograph, 10 1/16 x 13 7/16 in. Collection of Shelburne Museum, gift of Rush Taggart, Shelburne, Vermont, 1985-58.7

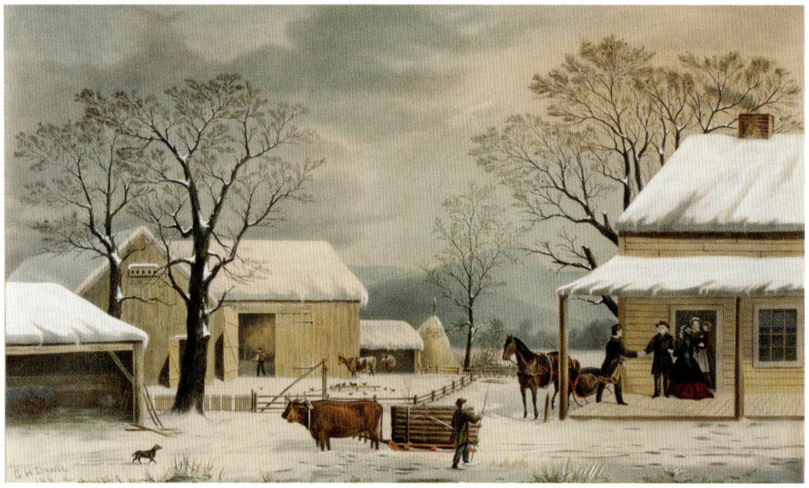

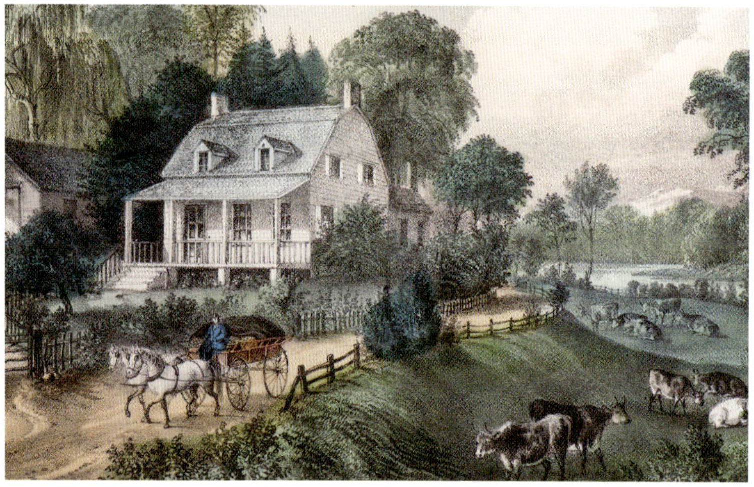

unidentified sources, making it even harder to decipher as Bennington except for a few potentially identifiable landmark structures, such as the Old First Church and the Battle Monument (the two white spires right of center in the midground). While it has long been recognized that Moses drew inspiration from Currier & Ives chromolithographs, redolent of old-timey Americana, and the art dealer Jane Kallir has documented her use of other popular imagery, the full extent of this practice in Moses's work is difficult to fully grasp, as this aspect of her artistic process is nearly invisible in the finished product and it is difficult to pin down all her original sources.[25] However, thanks to the survival of at least two substantive caches of her "secret" source materials, now in the archives of Galerie St. Etienne in New York, we can begin to cobble together a picture, much as Moses herself did, of a sophisticated process. It is impossible to say exactly what percentage of the artist's paintings are based on her voluminous collection of clippings, but given the surviving evidence it is safe to say that the majority of her figures, animals, and buildings—and even a large percentage of her landscape elements—were directly traced or adapted in some form from preexisting imagery. The complexity and sophistication of the various ways in which she incorporated these sources into her paintings is astounding.

Some Moses paintings, such as *The Old House at the Bend of the Road* (plate 2) and *Thanks Given Day* (plate 3), are based directly on Currier & Ives lithographs with expected adjustments to

FIG. 11 (RIGHT)
Source materials (unknown origin) for Anna Mary Robertson "Grandma" Moses's *In Harvest Time* (plate 12)

FIG. 12 (BELOW)
Clipping from the cover of the *Saturday Evening Post*, August 18, 1951, *Evening Picnic* by John Falter. Source material for Anna Mary Robertson "Grandma" Moses's *Catchin' the Turkey* (plate 1)

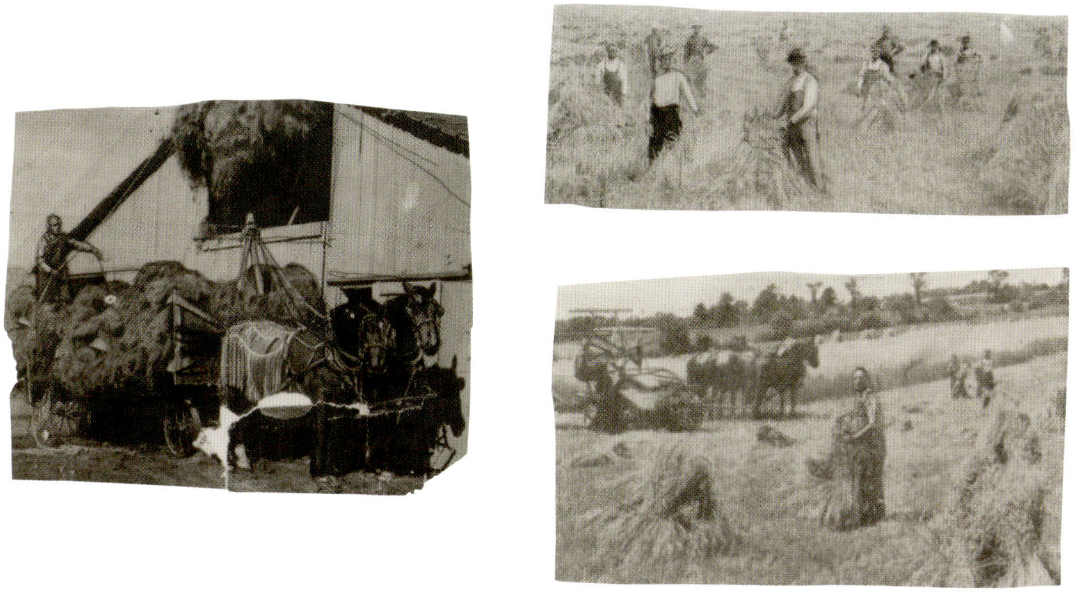

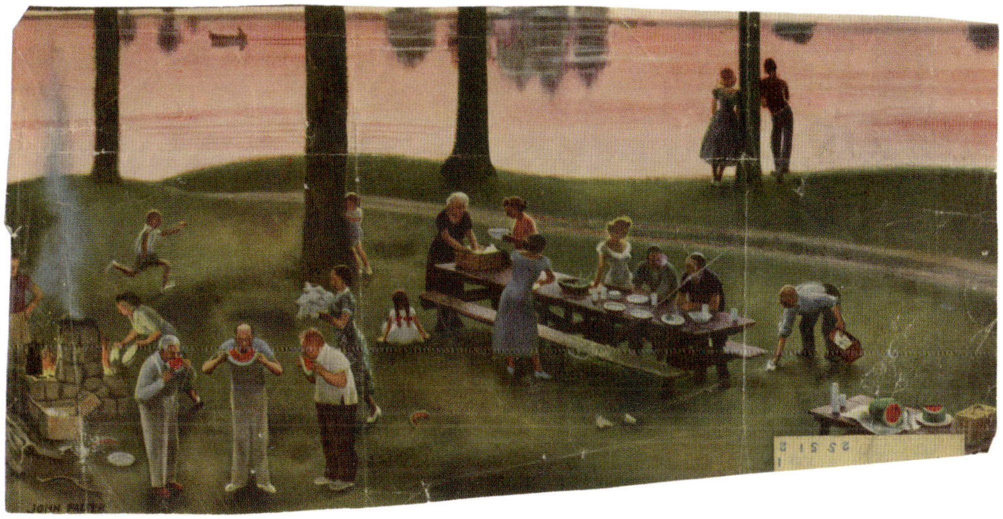

color and the substitution or addition of a new figure or tree here or there (figs. 9 and 10). Even in these direct, uncomplicated borrowings, Moses improves upon the originals. Her lively, unhackneyed application of paint, luminous color, and expansive compositional sensibility bring the otherwise traditional images to life. Though I wonder what Duncan Phillips, one of the leading modern art tastemakers in America, would have thought if he knew that the first Moses he acquired (he purchased *The Old House at the Bend of the Road* in 1941) was based on a Currier & Ives lithograph. Far more interesting and aesthetically successful was Moses's more common practice of cobbling her paintings together from many sources, rarely identifiable, into cohesive, balanced wholes. It would be hard to convey just how extensively Moses's work depended on sources clipped or otherwise borrowed

FIG. 13 (LEFT)
Anna Mary Robertson ("Grandma") Moses. *Sugaring Off* (detail), 1943. Oil on pressed board, 23 × 27 in. Private Collection, courtesy of Galerie St. Etienne, New York

FIG. 14 (RIGHT)
Anna Mary Robertson ("Grandma") Moses. *Over the River to Grandmother's House* (detail), 1944. Oil on pressed wood, 20 × 36 in. Collection of Carol Wakefield and Sharon Curry

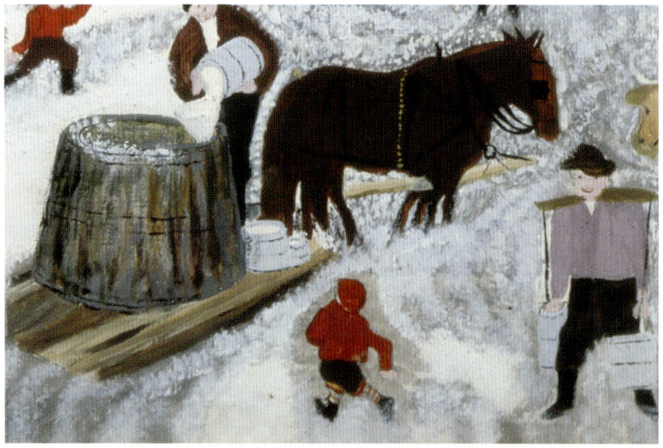

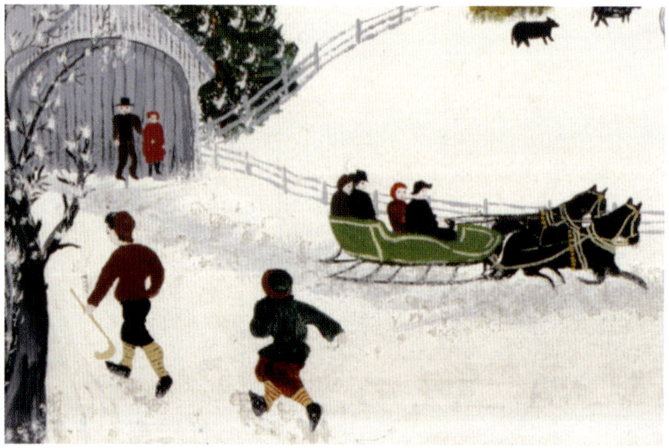

from popular periodicals such as *The Saturday Evening Post, Time* and *Life* magazines, farmers' almanacs, greeting and holiday cards, postcards, photographs, chromolithographs, and just about any other image that passed through her hands. And she didn't just borrow from generic commercial illustrations, as she seems to have made little distinction between "high" and "low" sources. All that mattered to Moses was that the image carried an associative quality that stirred her memories and imagination. Surviving clippings in her archives include reproductions of paintings by such well-known artists as Luigi Lucioni and Norman Rockwell, both of whom lived in nearby Vermont and were acquainted with Moses personally. And claims of the similarity of Moses paintings to seventeenth-century Dutch old masters such as Bruegel, which have often been brushed off with an insistence that she had never seen them, should be reconsidered.[26] Among her archived clippings is at least one reproduction of Pieter Bruegel the Younger's *Winter Landscape with Skaters and Bird Trap*, with its depiction of wintertime recreation, a subject dear to Moses. There are even clippings of reproductions of her own paintings with pencil outlines, indicating that she stole from herself! While Moses's use of popular, commercially printed imagery might seem anathema for a "folk artist," valued for her highly personal, supposedly "authentic" depictions of a bygone era, such a practice of appropriation was the norm for many modern artists. These "stolen" images were simply another tool in Moses's artistic arsenal.

Moses's painting *In Harvest Time* (plate 12) serves as a good example of the artist's practice of appropriation. The overflowing wagon in the lower right foreground, the stacks of hay and figures

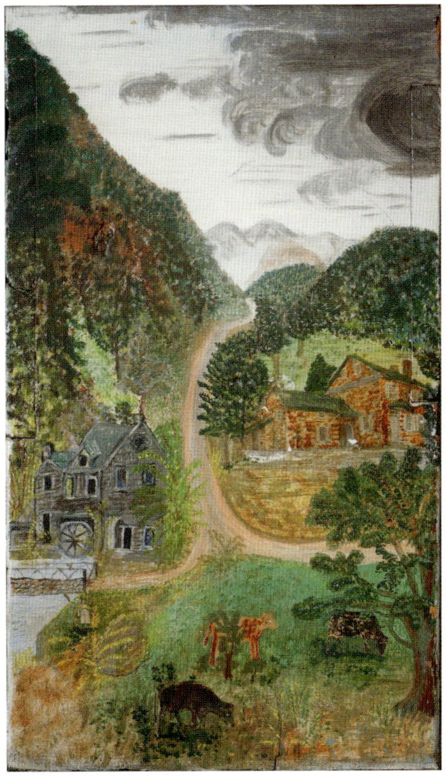

FIG. 15
"Tip-up" Table (detail), c. 1773. Attributed to John Whiteside. Painted by Anna Mary Robertson ("Grandma") Moses, c. 1920. 27 × 45 × 31 ½ in. Bennington Museum, 1984.516

at right center, and the horse-drawn threshing machine to the left of the tree in the upper right quadrant are all drawn from separate clippings that originally had no relation to one another (fig. 11). Not only did the individual borrowed elements within a single picture have no direct relationship with one another to begin with, Moses often pulled figures completely out of context to suit her artistic needs. A figure of a young boy running after a turkey in *Catchin' the Turkey* (plate 1), for example, is taken from a *Saturday Evening Post* cover of a family picnicking, the boy in this original context frolicking playfully with the other children (fig. 12). Moses had a knack for finding images of figures that powerfully convey abstract visual information via posture and body language. When she found a figure that she particularly liked, she would reuse it in multiple paintings, such as a child with his back to the viewer running into the fictive space of the paintings in the center right foregrounds of *Sugaring Off* and *Over the River to Grandmother's House* (figs. 13 and 14).

It is often claimed that Picasso and Georges Braque "invented" collage, or the direct pasting of printed paper scraps onto the picture plane, in 1912. More accurately, they simply introduced the technique, long popular among amateur art makers, especially women, into the fine art realm, as feminist artists and theorists were quick to point out in the 1970s. Moses's collage-like practice grows directly out of artistic strategies common among children and nonprofessional artists during the second half of the nineteenth century, as seen in the dozens of late nineteenth-century tracing

FIG. 16
Joseph Cornell. *View* (New York, 1940–47), Second series, no. 4, January 1943. "Americana Fantastica," edited by Charles Henri Ford; cover design by Joseph Cornell. Sterling and Francine Clark Art Institute Library, Williamstown, Massachusetts. Photo by Michael Agee/VAGA

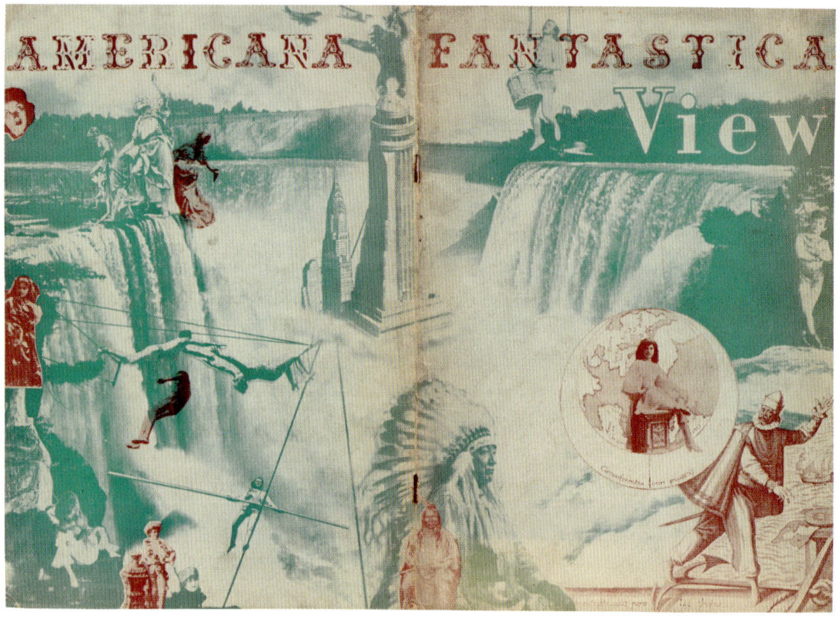

books in Diana Korzenik's collection of art education ephemera, now part of the Huntington Library collection in San Marino, California (fig. 23). The painting Moses made on the eighteenth-century tilt-top table that descended in her family is the only extant example of direct collage technique in the artist's oeuvre (figs. 3 and 5). A group of sheep, a stone house, a small figure, and three cows have all been pasted directly to the painted surface and painted over (with the exception of the sheep, whose tonality already worked with the composition) to integrate them into the scenes. Moses's *The Old House at the Bend of the Road* (plate 2) shows evidence that two cows were collaged in the right foreground and removed before the painting was finished. Moses consciously tried to hide her practice of borrowing imagery, and it was little known outside her family or close circle of friends and rarely mentioned in discussions of her work during the artist's life. The most common method that Moses used to transfer these images to her paintings was to directly trace them with pencil over carbon paper onto the pristine white surface of her prepared Masonite board, though larger compositional studies on onion skin tracing paper with multiple figures, which she would transfer whole cloth to her painting surface, do exist. Rather than traditional pasted paper collage, as she used on the base of her tilt-top table, this technique might be better called "uncollage," a term invented by the artist and curator Todd Bartel to describe the combining of multiple borrowed image sources into a cohesive painted whole without leaving any trace of their disparate origins.[27]

This technique of compiling multiple unrelated clippings into distinct new images echoes the practice of another of America's best-known self-taught artists of the mid-twentieth century, Joseph Cornell. Though Cornell ran in progressive cultural circles and is typically understood to be an integral part of America's artistic avant-garde from the mid-1930s until his death in 1972, like Moses he came to his practice completely independent of any academic training. In a way, the introduction of surrealism to America, largely through the Julien Levy Gallery in New York, where Cornell first exhibited his work, provided a framework to understand Cornell's assemblages of found objects and images as "fine" art. Though best known for his boxed constructions, collage formed a critical aspect of Cornell's artistic practice from the early 1930s through the mid-1940s. Like Moses, he was astoundingly inventive in his use of found sources, often repurposing a favored image again and again, sometimes decades apart. Cornell kept his source materials filed in his basement studio in some 150 loosely categorized, highly personal dossiers, which he described as "a diary journal repository laboratory, picture gallery, museum, sanctuary, observatory, key . . . the core of a labyrinth, a clearinghouse for dreams and visions . . . childhood regained."[28] This poetic description beautifully echoes Moses's less-structured system. Diana Korzenik recalls Moses sharing her "art secrets" with her when she visited the artist as a young girl, pulling out a large painted trunk filled with clippings that she would riffle through to find inspiration.[29] Typical of Cornell's collages is a design he created for front and back covers of an issue of the avant-garde arts magazine *View* in 1943 (fig. 16). Serving as the opening salvo for a special thematic issue of the magazine, whose overarching theme was "Americana Fantastica," Cornell's collage, like Moses's paintings, draws on familiar tropes of resonant, stereotypical American imagery. In his case they tend to be more iconic, specifically identifiable subjects, such as Niagara Falls, Native Americans in feather headdresses, the Empire State Building and King Kong, and their juxtapositions are intended to be provocative and create both visual and psychological tension as well as a great deal of humor. Occasionally Moses also created the humorously surreal image, such as *Horseshoeing* (plate 40), with its speeding train and horses headed full-tilt toward a group of stationary figures only a few feet away, or *Halloween* (plate 23), with its bedsheet ghosts and hooded figures wreaking havoc everywhere, including the rooftops. Cornell allowed his source material to speak for itself, pasting his cutouts directly, typically onto a larger found landscape image, without further alteration beyond their recontextualization. Moses dramatically altered and abstracted the source material in her borrowings, transferring only their bare outlines to her prepared Masonite board, which she then painted over in loosely applied strokes of bright, largely unmodulated color, obliterating any sense of illustrative detail while maintaining the original source's associative quality. The real magic in Moses's paintings is the fact that she is able to pull together such disparate images into cohesive, reassuring wholes, as though they were always meant to be together, as though they were her own memories.

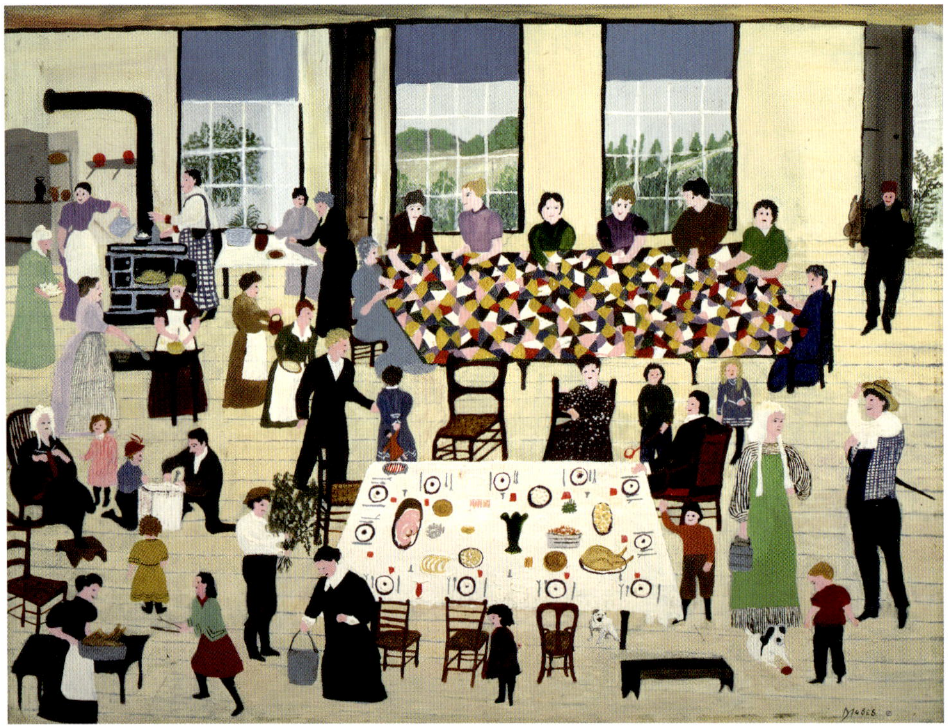

FIG. 17
Anna Mary Robertson ("Grandma") Moses. *The Quilting Bee*, 1950. Oil on pressed board, 20 × 24 in. Private Collection, courtesy of Galerie St. Etienne, New York

POSTMODERN POSTSCRIPT

Moses's life spanned the entire history of modern art. She was a toddler when Édouard Manet painted *Le Déjeuner sur l'herbe* (1862–63) and died the year before Andy Warhol's breakthrough exhibition of Campbell's Soup can paintings ushered in postmodernism. Yet, despite the parallels between Moses's work and some of the key figures of modernism, in many ways her art is more in line with the basic tenets of postmodernism that came to define the art world in the decades immediately after her death, especially pop art of the 1960s and feminist art of the 1970s. Postmodernism saw a breaking down of perceived dichotomies, such as those between "high" or "fine" art and "low" or "popular" art, which, as we've already seen, was an inherent aspect of Moses's work. This period also saw the advent of a grassroots interest in artistic diversity, not just feminism, but identity politics more broadly and the championing of artists and visual cultures of all types, well beyond the white male hegemony of the New York–centric art world. In describing the artistic mind-set of the English predecessors of American pop in the late 1950s, Richard Hamilton the most famous among them, the art critic Lawrence Alloway noted, "We assumed an anthropological definition of culture in which all types of human activity were the object of aesthetic judgment and attention."[30] As unlikely a comparison as it may seem, Warhol, who was a major collector of folk art and served on the board of the American Folk Art Museum in New York, had a surprising amount in common with Moses. As a commercial illustrator in the 1950s, he was just as voracious as Moses in "stealing" and adapting

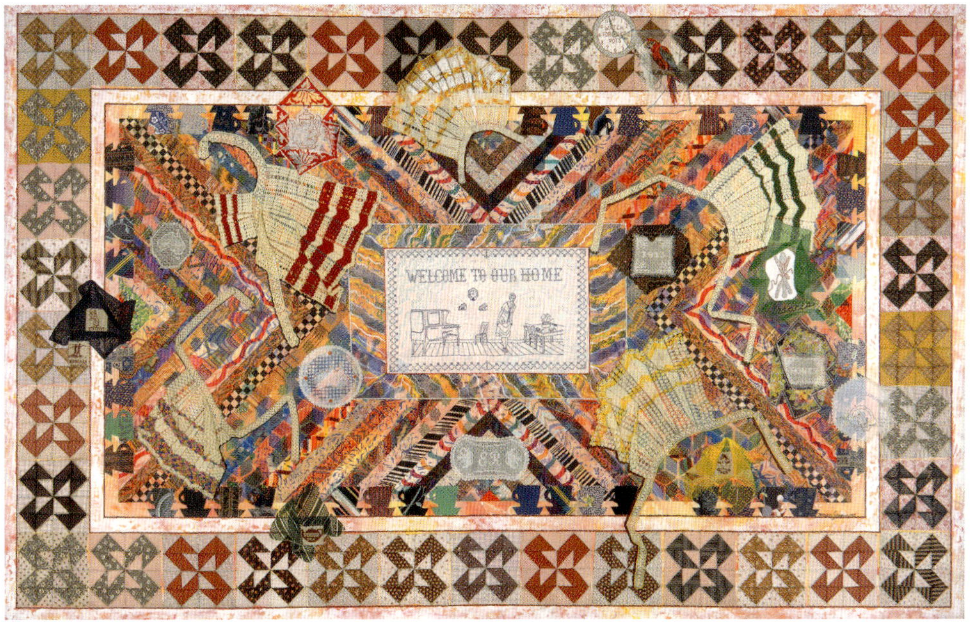

FIG. 18
Miriam Schapiro. *Wonderland*, 1983. Acrylic, fabric, and plastic beads on canvas, 90 × 144 ½ in. Gift of anonymous donor. Smithsonian American Art Museum, Washington, DC/Art Resource, NY

his imagery from popular printed sources. And given his penchant for celebrity, it is hard to imagine he wasn't drawn to Moses's work at the prestigious Carnegie International exhibitions in his hometown of Pittsburgh, where her work was shown every year from 1945 to 1950.[31] This is not to make a claim of direct influence; rather, I simply find it astounding how resonant Moses's practices were with larger trends in the art world, and how little it has been commented upon. In fact, it seems the only time critics ever cited Moses during the 1950s through the 1970s was in a negative light, as when the art critic Hilton Kramer used her in an attack on Jasper Johns's bold new work in 1959: "His hand-painted American flags, targets, numbers and so on, are a kind of Grandma Moses version of Dada. . . ." After referencing this review in his recent book-length study of the relationship between folk art and the origins of pop art in America, Thomas Crow wisely questions the surprisingly short-term memory of the New York art world in so quickly forgetting the folk/modern agenda that MoMA so vigorously promoted just a couple of decades earlier.[32]

The artists Miriam Schapiro and Melissa Meyer's 1978 article "Waste Not, Want Not: An Inquiry into What Women Saved and Assembled—Femmage," synthesizes many of the key elements of feminist art in the 1970s, including an interest in reviving materials, techniques, and processes historically associated with traditional women's art, especially textiles, quilting, and collage, and emphasizing the communal and collaborative aspects of art made by women. Moses was well versed in needlework of all types, as any female who grew up in rural America during the 1860s and '70s had to be, especially one who worked as a hired hand. In addition to making embroidered pictures, which played a significant role in the development of her iconic painting style, Moses also made pieced quilts and rag dolls. Her painting *The Quilting Bee* emphasizes the domestic, communal, female-dominated nature of this quintessential nineteenth-century tradition (fig. 17). Schapiro's fabric painting *Wonderland* is a perfect complement to Moses's painting; with its pieced border in a traditional quilt pattern and collage-like field of vintage textiles, centered by a kerchief embroidered with a scene of a woman in a kitchen beneath the text, "Welcome to Our Home," which invites the viewer, male or female, into the stereotypically feminine sphere (fig. 18). Given these parallels, it is surprising that Schapiro, and other feminist artists, critics, and theorists, didn't reference Moses directly. The lack of interest in Moses' work by first-generation feminists and postmodern insiders was likely due to two factors: First, Moses' collage-like technique of appropriation was largely unknown until Jane Kallir "outed" the artist in her 1982 book *Grandma Moses: The Artist Behind the Myth*. Secondly, Moses's adaptations of commerical imagery are devoid of conscious irony, a key element of post-modern practice. The women's studies professor Jean McMahon Humez, a rare exception, cast Moses as a "home spun feminist" who supported women's suffrage, insisted on economic self-sufficiency, and was able to find a balance between her family life and her artistic career.[33]

Moses's art didn't directly take part in the intellectual underpinnings of modernism or postmodernism, yet her work *is* modern, is postmodern, without trying to be. After the craze for "primitives" in the 1930s and '40s, the works of Moses and other non-mainstream artists were positioned outside the linear historical progression of modernism proper, not significant in their own right but as fodder and inspiration for mainstream, avant-garde artists. Postmodern theorists and practitioners such as Lippard and Schapiro began to rethink this classist, imbalanced approach in the 1970s, even if they rarely acknowledged Moses's work as a potentially significant exemplar of their ideas. In his catalog essay for the groundbreaking exhibition *Parallel Visions,* which looked at the relationship between so-called insider and outsider art in the twentieth century, the art historian Donald Preziosi posited an approach in which "modernism is expanded beyond the interlinked series of avant-gardist practices canonized by art history and museology," wherein "all manner of artistic practices become, in effect, part of the 'story' of modernism."[34] With this look at Moses's own artistic practice, in direct comparison to paragons of both modernism and postmodernism, I hope we can begin to understand her not as an anomalous self-taught, folk superhero but as a real contributor to the story of American art of the twentieth century. A disarmingly down-to-earth farm wife from rural upstate New York, Moses created visually sophisticated paintings that melded her memories of growing up in a preindustrial America with her more recent experiences in an increasingly modernized, homogenous America, saturated with printed images that often drew upon nostalgic tropes of a much romanticized golden age that was just beyond the direct experience of most viewers. Built on a foundation of selective memory—that of the artist as well as of the viewers of her work—and the associative power of popular imagery, her paintings have become iconic images in America's collective consciousness. They serve today, as much if not more so than they did during her life, as a paradigm for coming to terms with a conflicted present and building a better future. Moses's paintings have been providing viewers with an eternally longed for "promised land" ever since they made their way beyond the boundaries of Washington County, New York, nearly eighty years ago.

NOTES

1. Alfred H. Barr Jr., *Fantastic Art, Dada, Surrealism* (New York: Museum of Modern Art, 1936), 7.

2. Ibid., 179. Hand-drawn chart illustrating the development of modern art, c. 1936, Museum of Modern Art, New York, accessed Aug. 10, 2015, http://www.moma.org/learn/resources/archives/archives_highlights_02_1936.

3. Alfred H. Barr, Jr., *Masters of Popular Painting: Modern Primitives of Europe and America* (New York: Museum of Modern Art, 1938), 9.

4. Thomas Crow, *The Long March of Pop: Art, Music, and Design, 1930–1995* (New Haven, CT: Yale University Press, 2014), 7.

5. Diana Korzenik, "Portrait of the Artist as an American," *New England Quarterly* 85, no. 1 (Mar. 2012): 165.

6. Karal Ann Marling, *Designs on the Heart: The Homemade Art of Grandma Moses* (Cambridge, MA: Harvard University Press, 2006), 222–25. Marling provides an overview of the 1950 European tour of Moses's work.

7. Jane Kallir, "Rethinking Grandma Moses," in *Grandma Moses in the 21st Century* (New Haven, CT: Yale University Press in association with Art Services International, 2001), 24.

8. Lucy Lippard, "The Pink Glass Swan: Upward and Downward Mobility in the Art World," in *The Pink Glass Swan: Selected Essays on Feminist Art* (New York: New Press, 1995), 124, originally published in *Heresies* 1 (Jan. 1977).

9. Marling, *Designs on the Heart*, 225.

10. Ibid., 171.

11. Grandma Moses, *My Life's History*, ed. Otto Kallir (New York: Harper & Brothers, 1952), 49.

12. Ibid., 133.

13. "Art: Grandma's Imaginings," *Time* 52, no. 10 (1948).

14. Henry Geldzahler, "Interview with Helen Frankenthaler," *Artforum* 4, no. 2 (Oct. 1965): 37.

15. John Elderfield, "The Pleasure of Not Knowing," in *Painted on 21st Street: Helen Frankenthaler from 1950 to 1959* (New York: Gagosian Gallery, 2013), 9.

16. Oral history interview with Helen Frankenthaler conducted by Barbara Rose, Archives of American Art, Washington, DC, Aug. 1968, http://www.aaa.si.edu/collections/interviews/oral-history-interview-helen-frankenthaler-12171.

17. Geldzahler, "Interview with Helen Frankenthaler," 37–38.

18. Gene Baro, "The Achievement of Helen Frankenthaler," *Art International* 20 (Sept. 1967): 36.

19. Kallir, *Grandma Moses in the 21st Century*, 221.

20. "Two American Originals," *See It Now*, CBS, Dec. 12, 1955 (season 5, episode 3).

21. Elderfield, "Pleasure of Not Knowing," 32.

22. Ibid., 33.

23. James Hamilton, *Making Painting: Helen Frankenthaler and JMW Turner* (Margate, UK: Turner Contemporary, 2014), 22–23 and 42–43.

24. Françoise Gilot and Carlton Lake, *Life with Picasso* (New York: McGraw-Hill, 1964), 317. A more popular version of this saying is, "Good artists copy; great artists steal"; however, there is little evidence Picasso ever said these exact words. The most widely disseminated attribution of the statement to Picasso came from Apple founder Steve Jobs. Many other artists/writers have used similar expressions, most notably T. S. Eliot: "Immature poets imitate; mature poets steal."

25. Jane Kallir, *Grandma Moses: The Artist Behind the Myth* (New York: Clarkson N. Potter, 1982).

26. Marling, *Designs on the Heart*, 102.

27. Email correspondence between author and Todd Bartel, March 13, 2015. "Do Joseph: Attempts at a Unified Theory," Thompson Gallery, The Cambridge School of Weston, Weston, MA, accessed Nov. 17, 2015, http://www.csw.org/page/News-Detail-Thompson-Gallery-Exhibitions-Detail?pk=632967&fromId=196842.

28. Charles Simic, *Dime-Store Alchemy: The Art of Joseph Cornell* (New York: New York Review of Books, 1992), 37.

29. Korzenik, "Portrait of the Artist as an American," 161.

30. Crow, *Long March of Pop*, vii–viii. Alloway taught at Bennington College in the 1950s.

31. Email correspondence July 28, 2015, and conversation, August 4, 2015, with Blake Gopnik. I'd like to extend my thanks to Blake Gopnik for sharing some of his yet-to-be-published biography of Warhol with me and noting the fact that Warhol would have undoubtedly seen Moses's work at the Carnegie Annuals during the second half of the 1940s.

32. Crow, 34 and 36.

33. Jean McMahon Humez, "The Life and Art of Anna Mary Robertson Moses," *Woman's Art Journal* 1, no. 2 (Autumn 1980–Winter 1981): 7–12.

34. Donald Preziosi, "Art History, Museology, and the Staging of Modernity," in *Parallel Visions: Modern Artists and Outsider Art*, ed. Maurice Tuchman and Carol S. Eliel (Princeton, NJ: Princeton University Press in association with Los Angeles County Museum of Art, 1992), 304.

PLATE 1

Anna Mary Robertson ("Grandma") Moses

CATCHIN' THE TURKEY

1955. Oil on pressed wood, 12 × 16 in.

Bennington Museum, Museum purchase, Bennington, Vermont, 2007.41

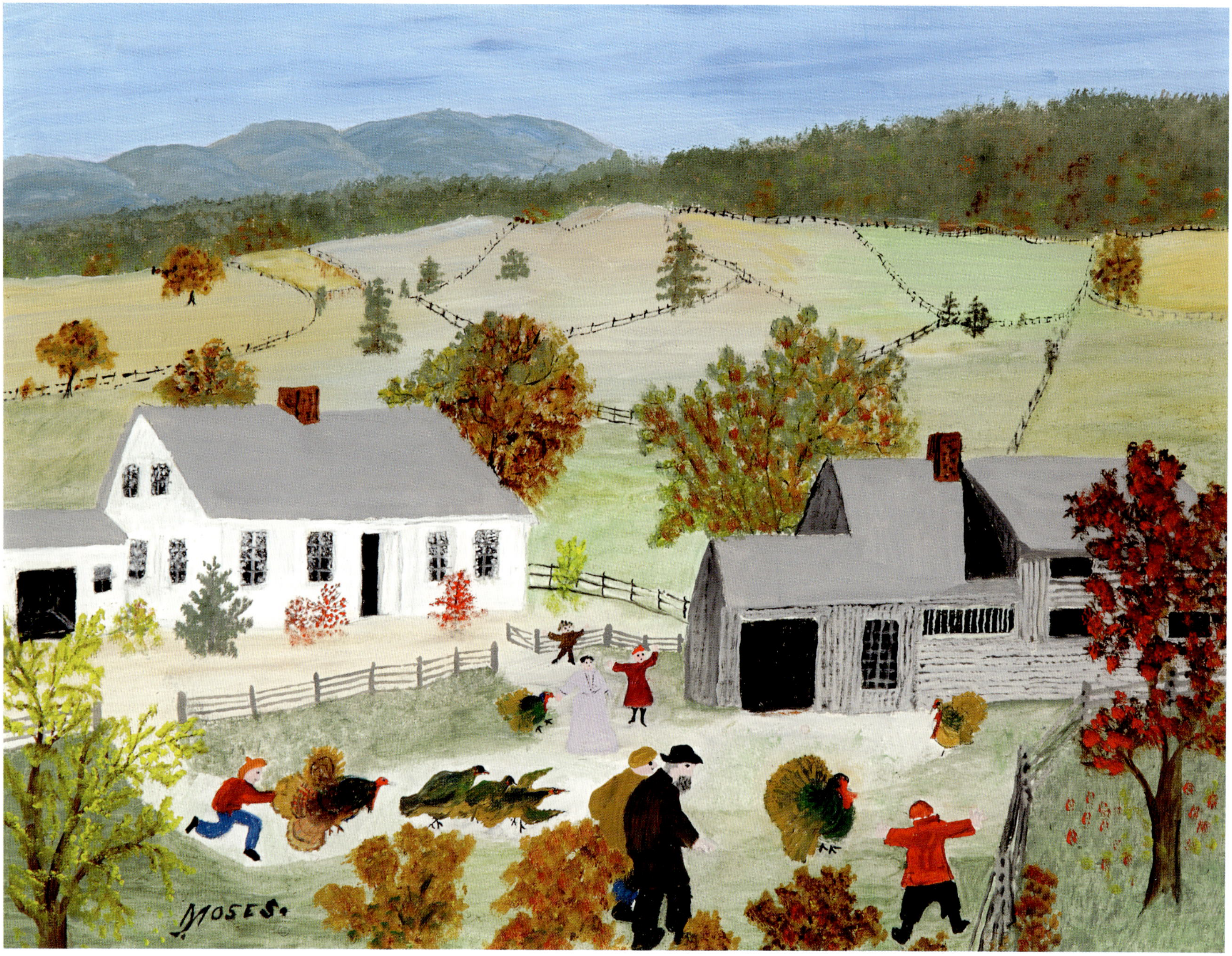

PLATE 2

Anna Mary Robertson ("Grandma") Moses

THE OLD HOUSE AT THE BEND OF THE ROAD

c. 1940. Oil on cloth, 10 3/4 × 12 1/2 in.

Bennington Museum, Gift of Sylvia Partridge, Bennington, Vermont, 1995.13

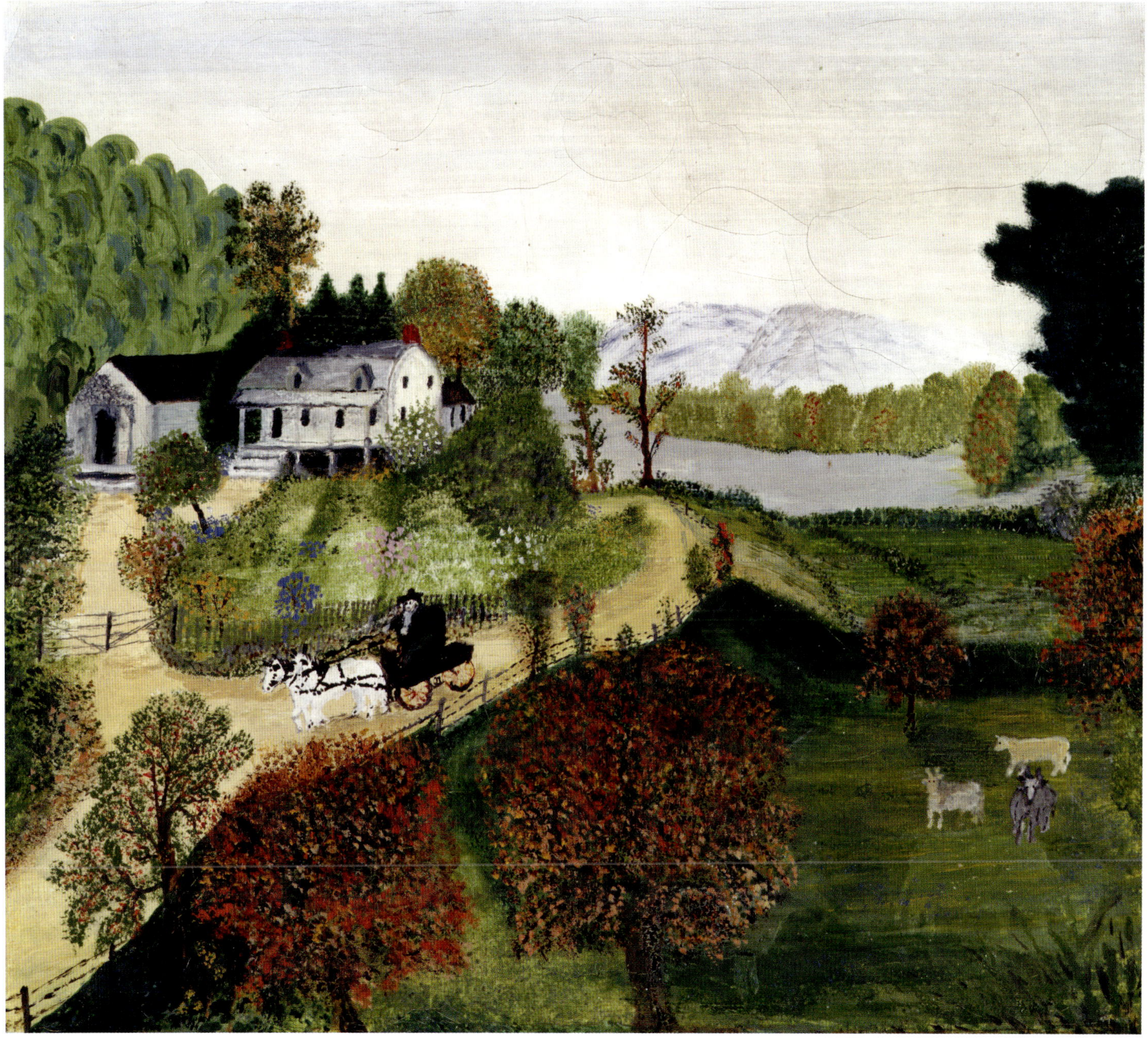

PLATE 3

Anna Mary Robertson ("Grandma") Moses

THANKS GIVEN DAY

1943. Oil on pressed wood, 9 1/4 × 11 1/4 in.

Collection of the Cleveland E. Dodge, Jr. 2005 Trust

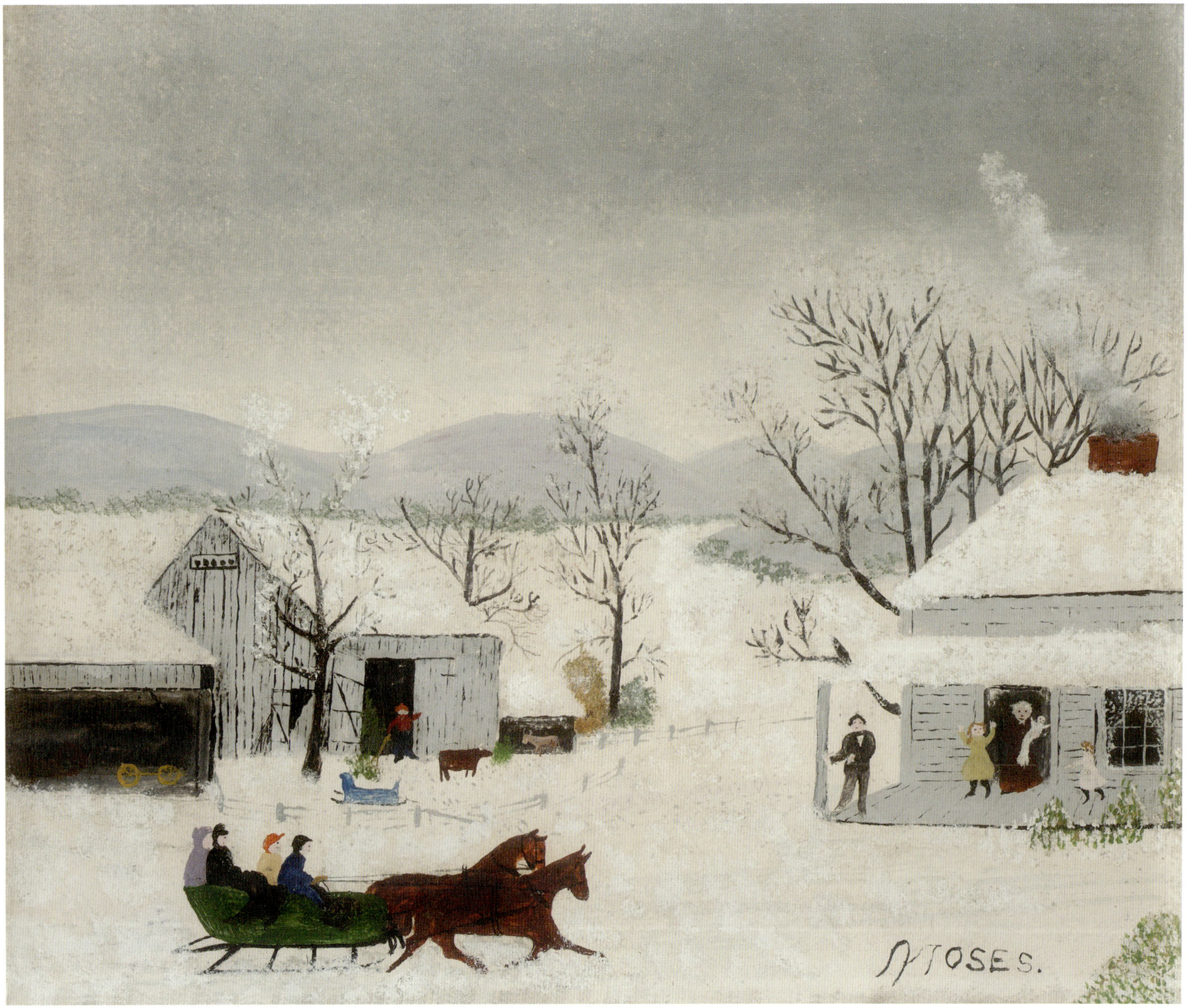

PLATE 4
Anna Mary Robertson ("Grandma") Moses
CAMBRIDGE VALLEY
1942. Oil on pressed wood, 23 1/2 × 27 in.
Private Collection, courtesy of Galerie St. Etienne, New York

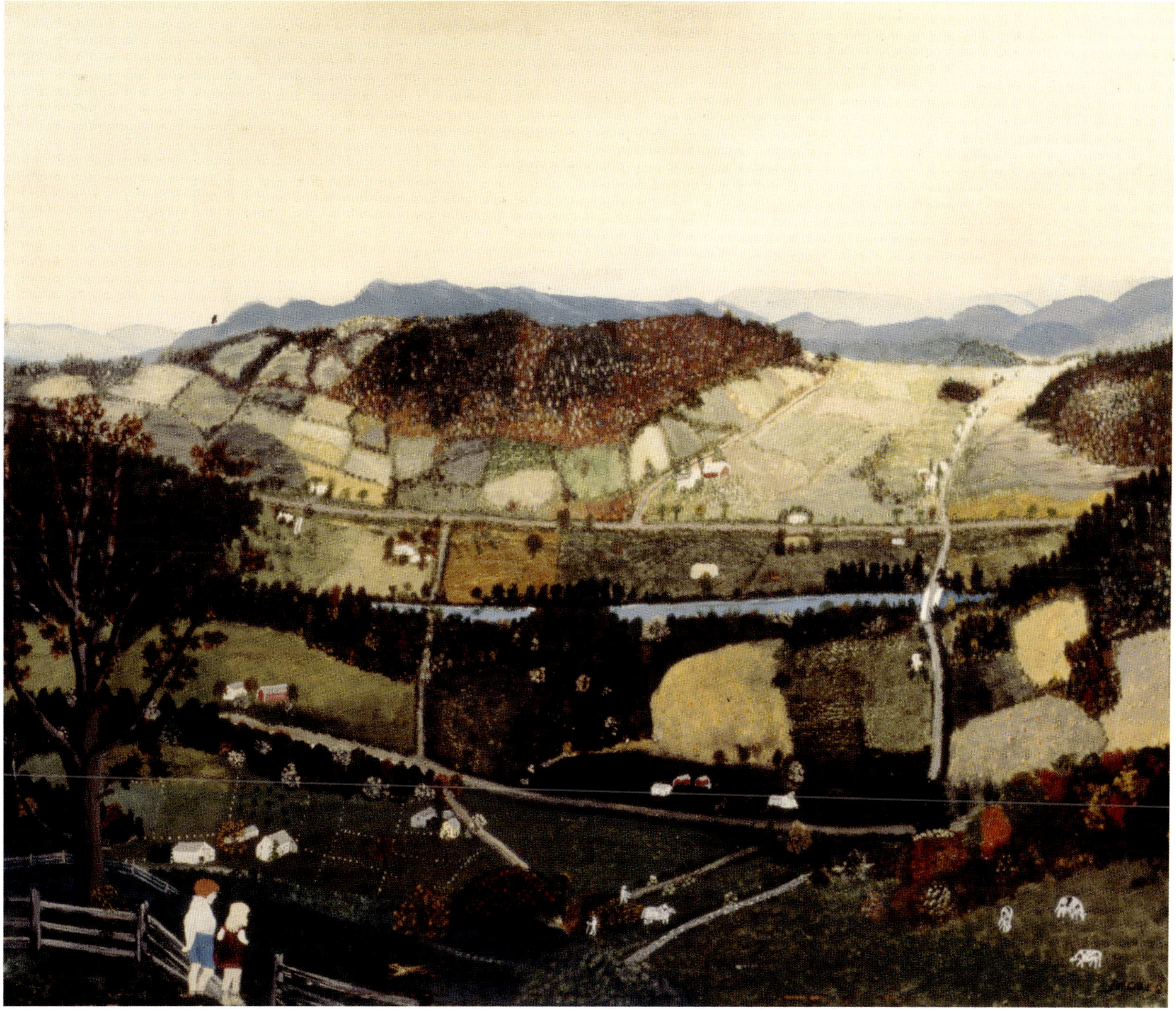

PLATE 5

Anna Mary Robertson ("Grandma") Moses

VILLAGE OF HOOSICK FALLS

1943. Oil on pressed wood, 18 × 24 in.

Bennington Museum, Museum purchase, Bennington, Vermont, 1998.1

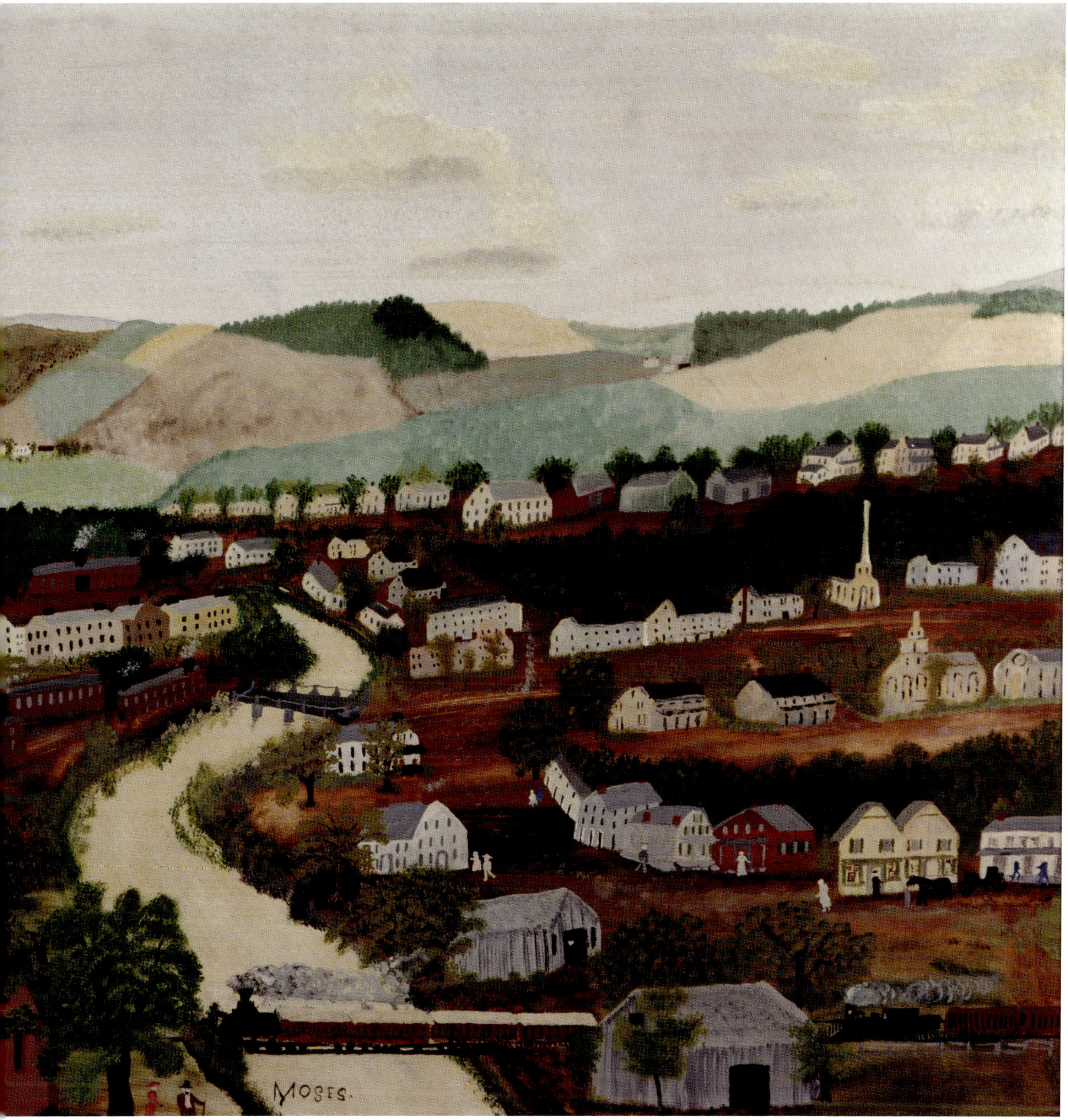
MOSES.

PLATE 6

Anna Mary Robertson ("Grandma") Moses

ON THE ROAD TO GREENWICH

1940. Oil on cardboard, 14 × 22 in.

Private Collection, courtesy of Galerie St. Etienne, New York

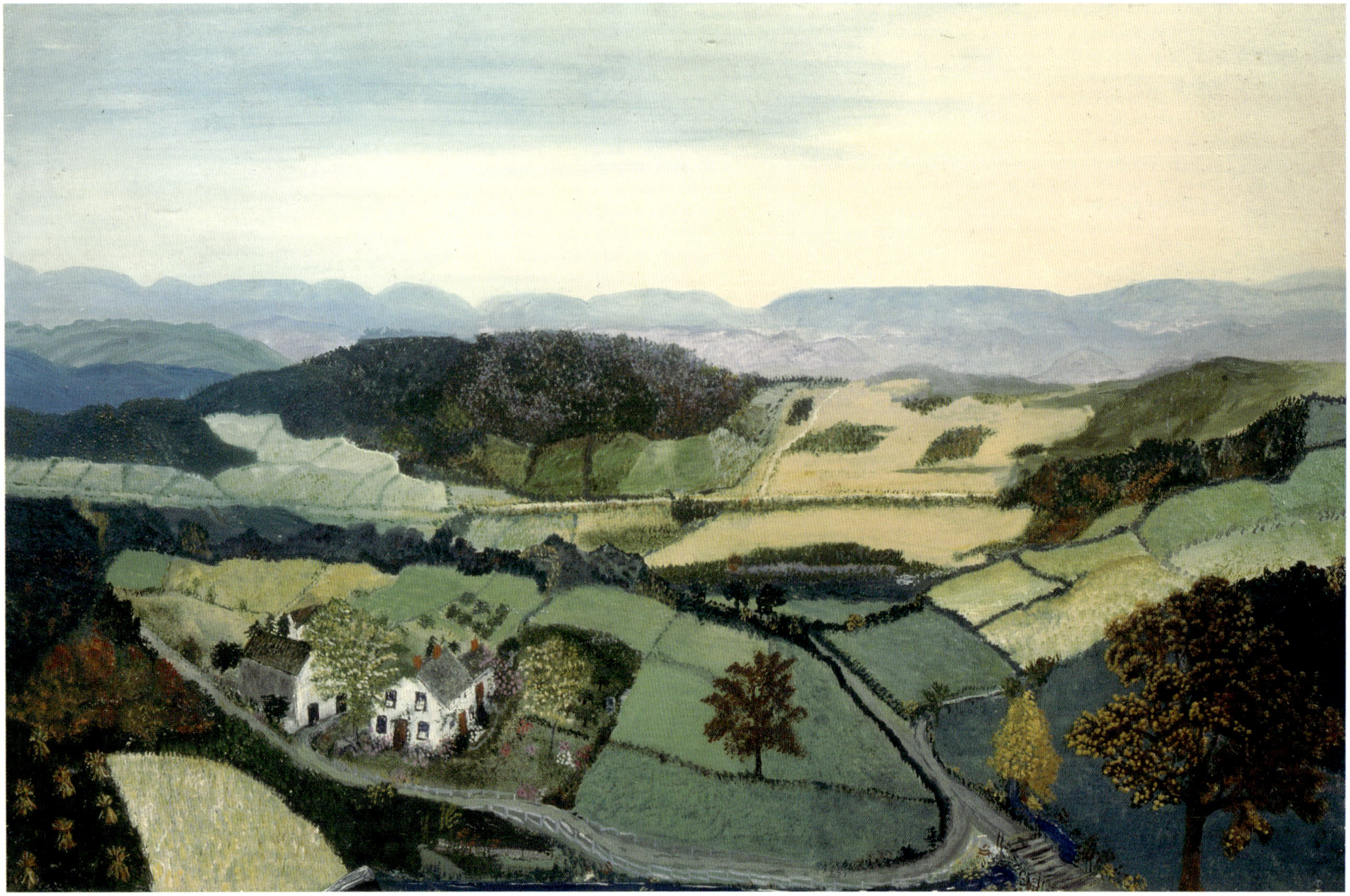

PLATE 7
Anna Mary Robertson ("Grandma") Moses
SUGARING OFF
1943. Oil on pressed board, 23 × 27 in.
Private Collection, courtesy of Galerie St. Etienne, New York

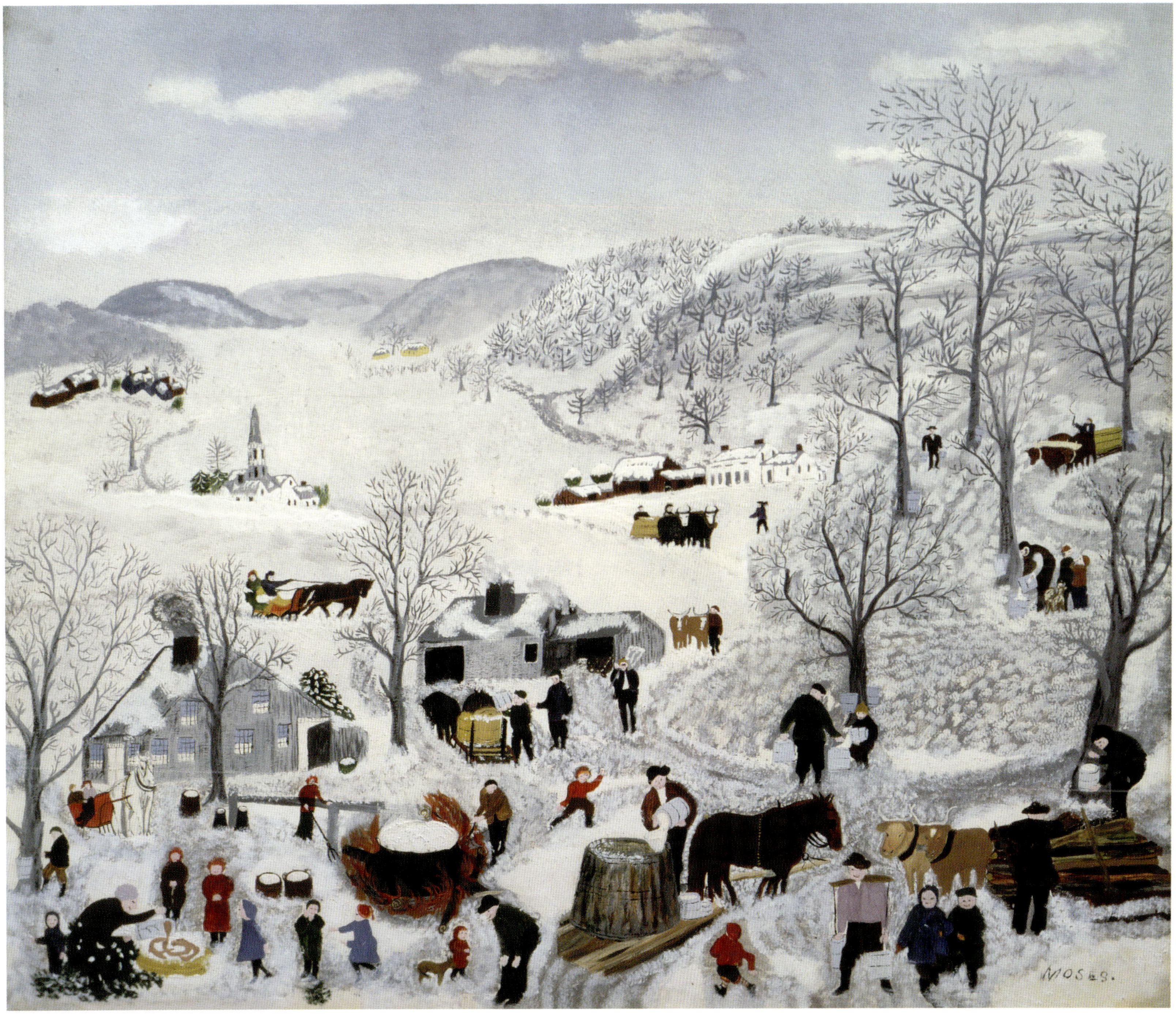

PLATE 8

Anna Mary Robertson ("Grandma") Moses

CHECKERED HOUSE

1959. Oil on pressed wood, 12 × 16 1/4 in.

Bennington Museum, Gift of Arthur R. Armstrong, Bennington, Vermont, 1986.130.1

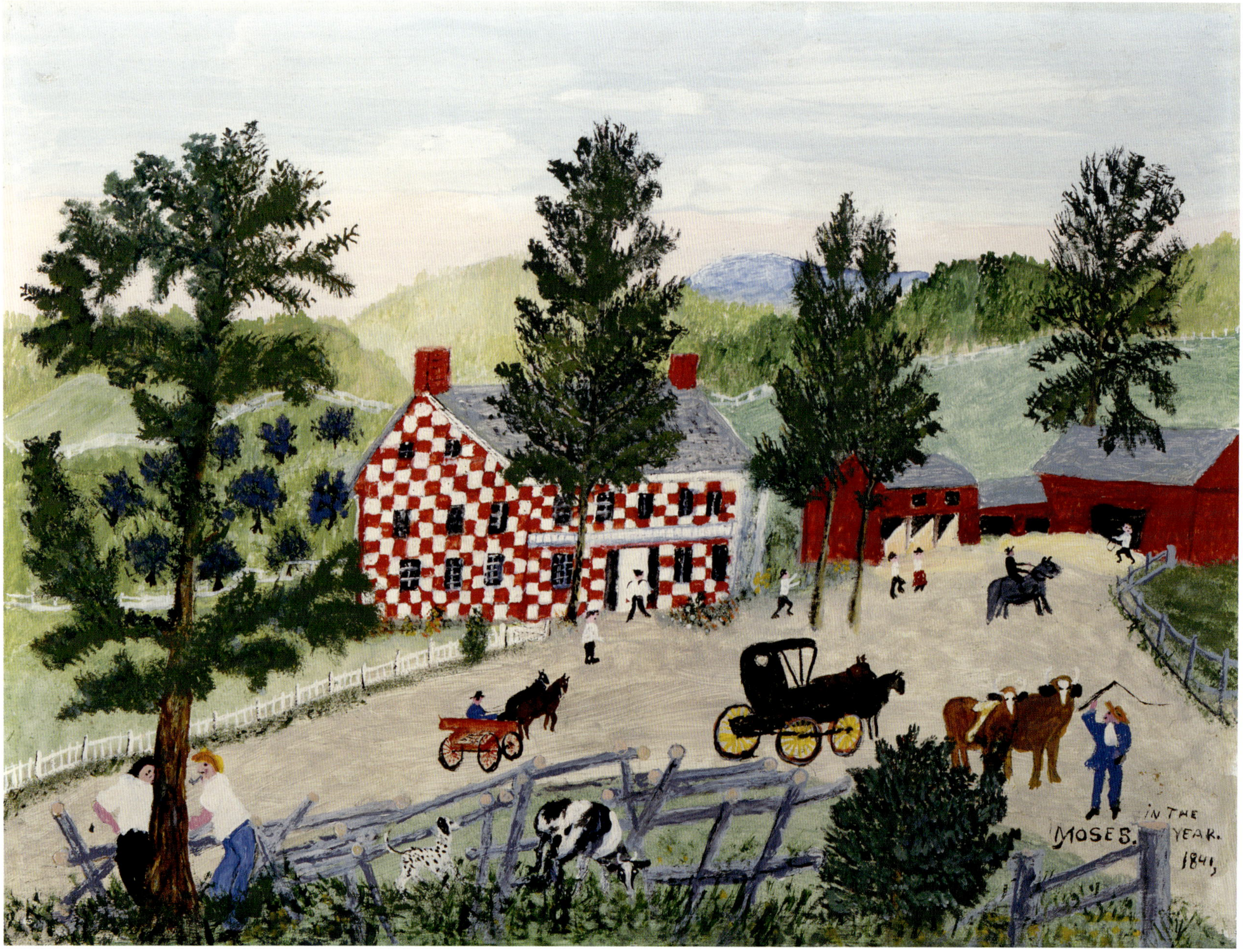

PLATE 9

Anna Mary Robertson ("Grandma") Moses

TAKING IN LAUNDRY

1951. Oil on pressed wood, 17 × 21¾ in.

Kallir Family Foundation, New York

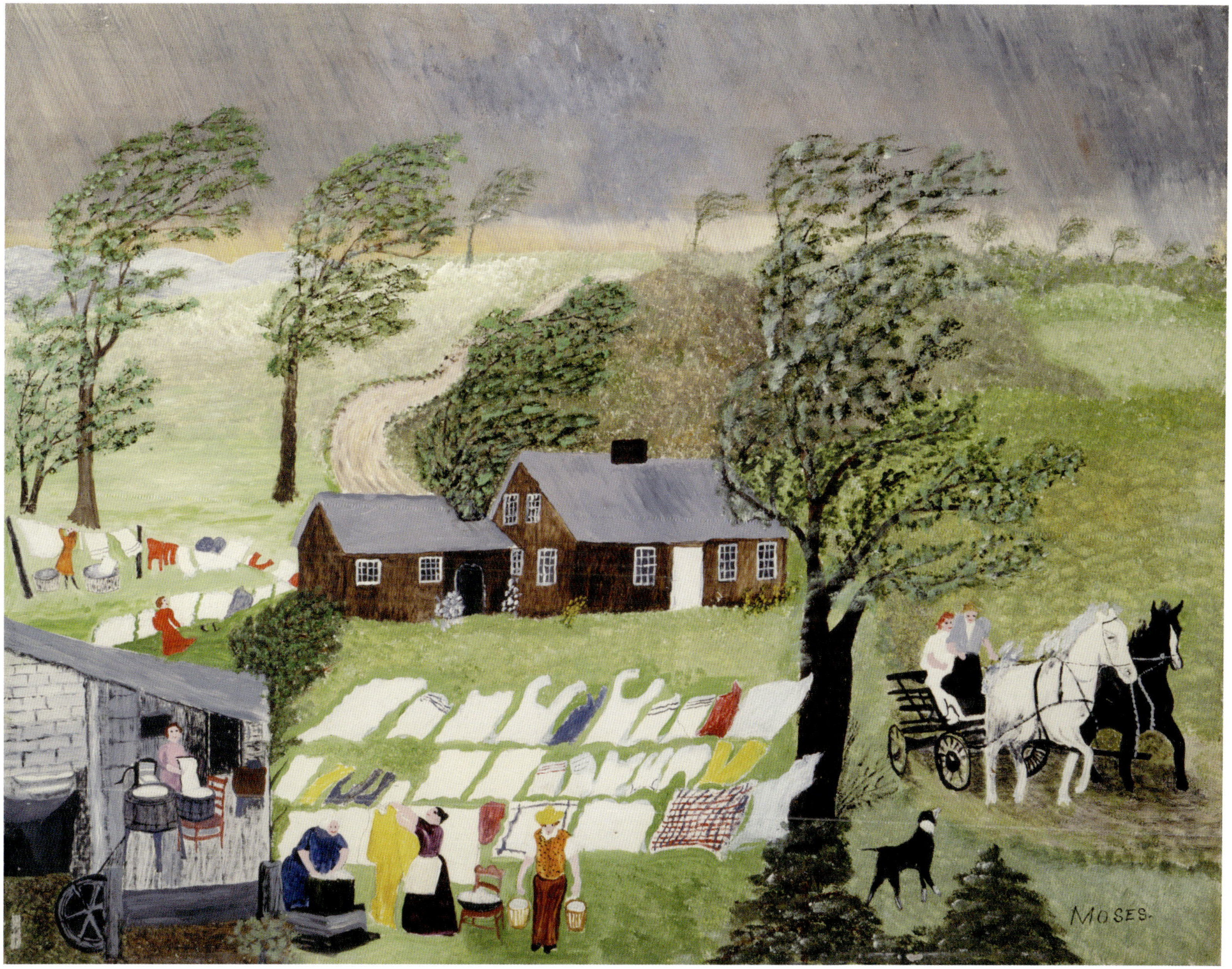

PLATE 10

Anna Mary Robertson ("Grandma") Moses

OVER THE RIVER TO GRANDMOTHER'S HOUSE

1944. Oil on pressed wood, 20 × 36 in.

Collection of Carol Wakefield and Sharon Curry

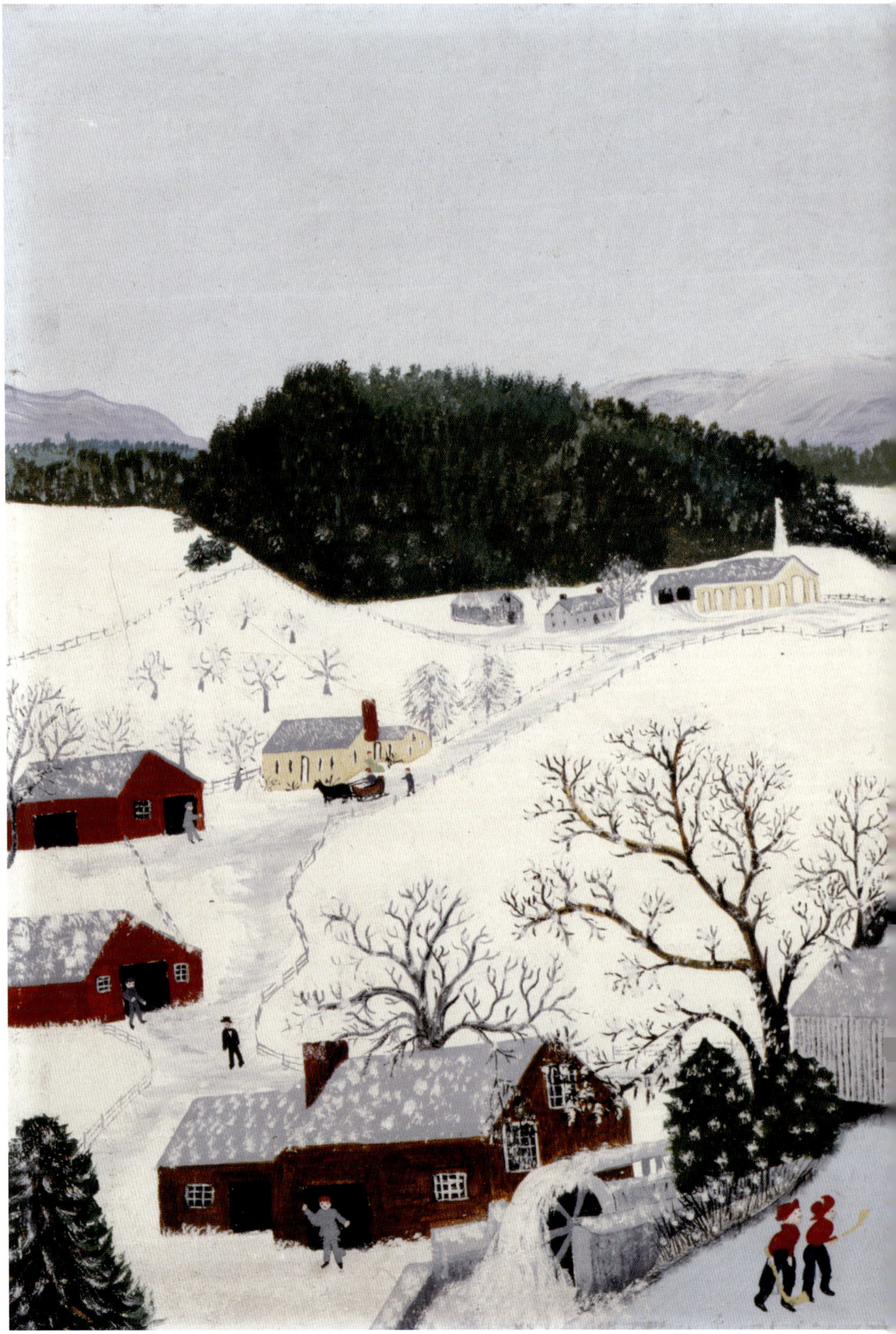

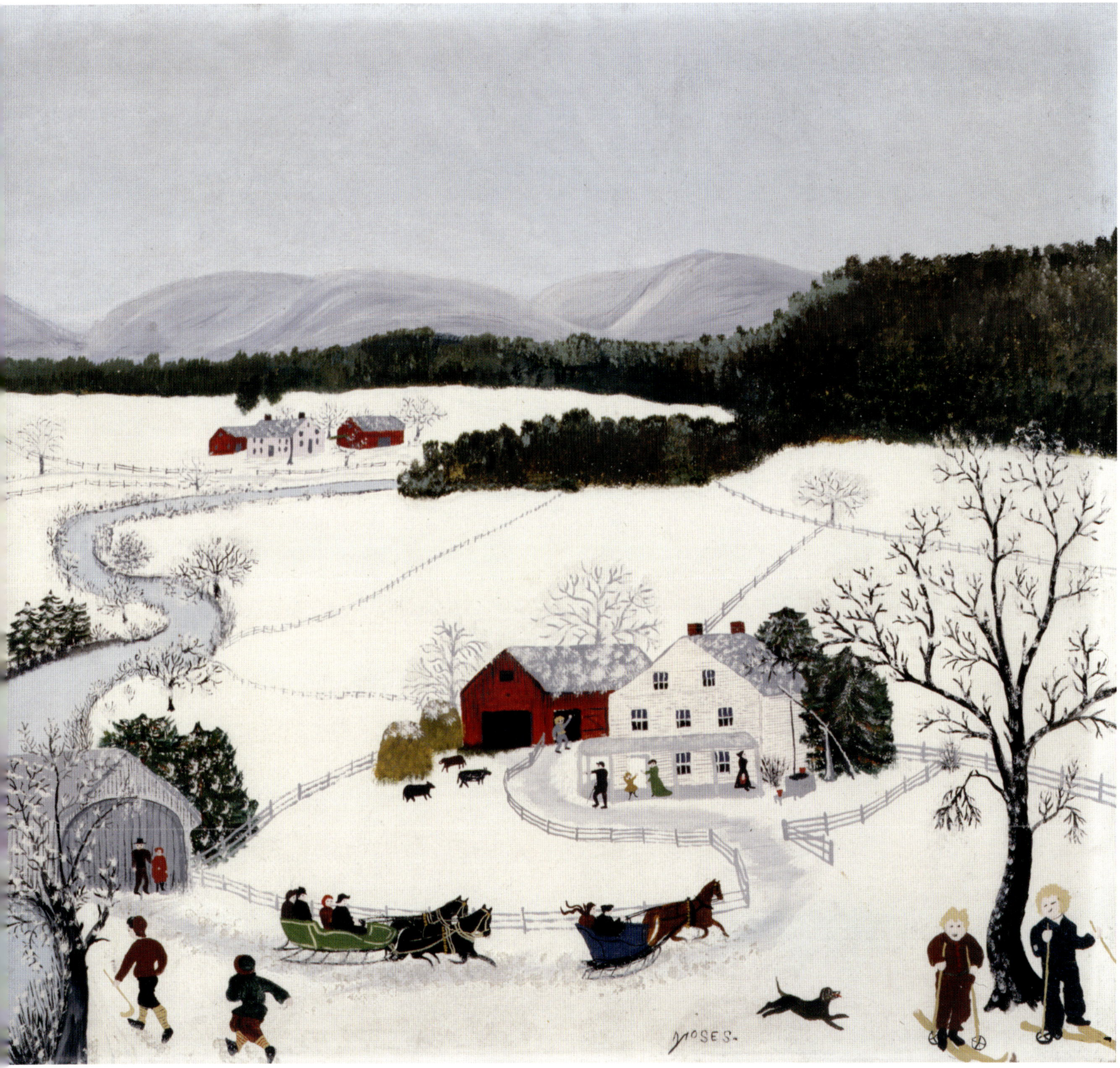
MOSES.

PLATE 11

Anna Mary Robertson ("Grandma") Moses

THE BURNING OF TROY

1939. Oil on pressed wood, 9 × 11¼ in.

Private Collection, courtesy of Galerie St. Etienne, New York

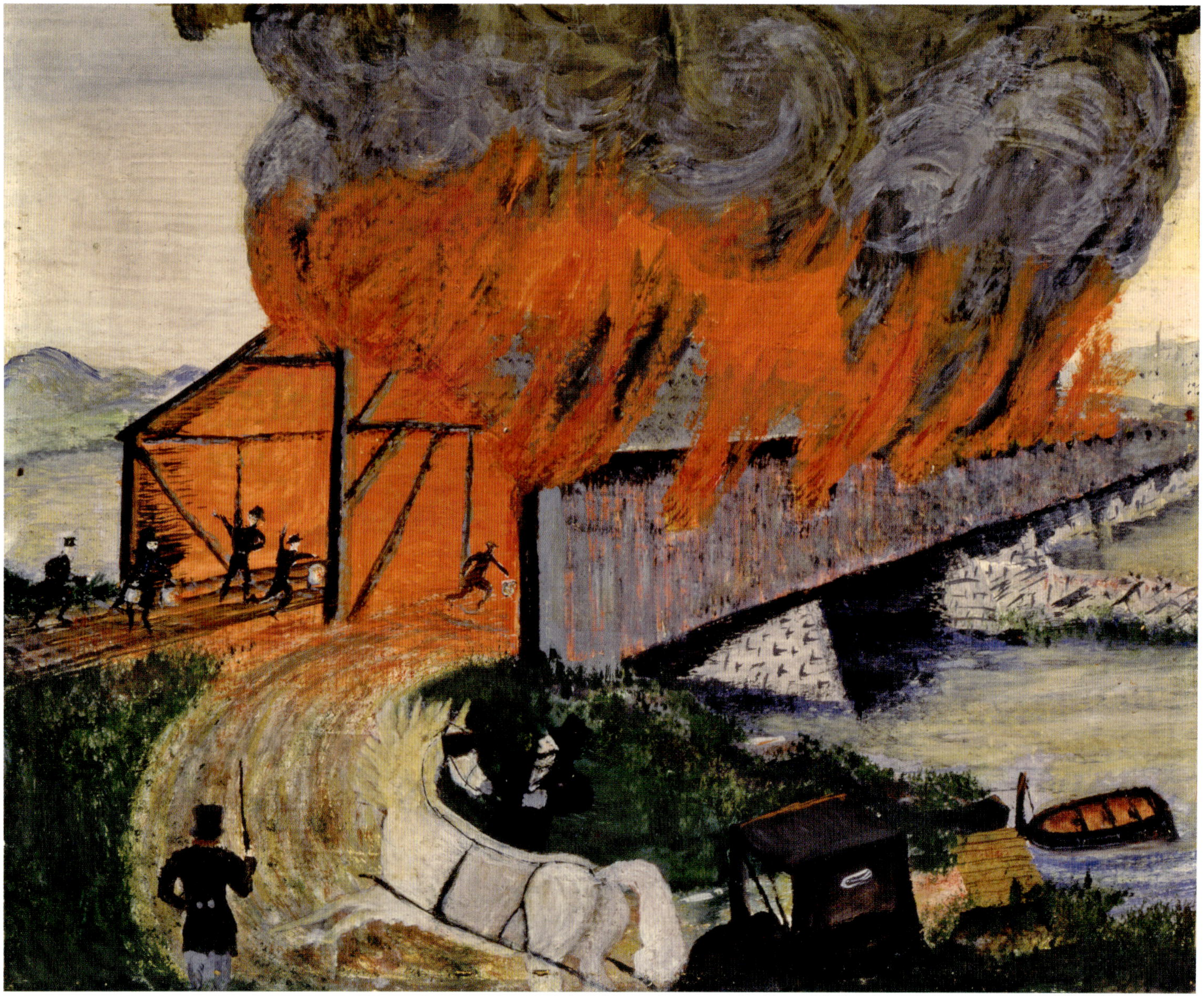

PLATE 12

Anna Mary Robertson ("Grandma") Moses

IN HARVEST TIME

1945. Oil on pressed board, 18 × 28 in.

Kallir Family Foundation, New York

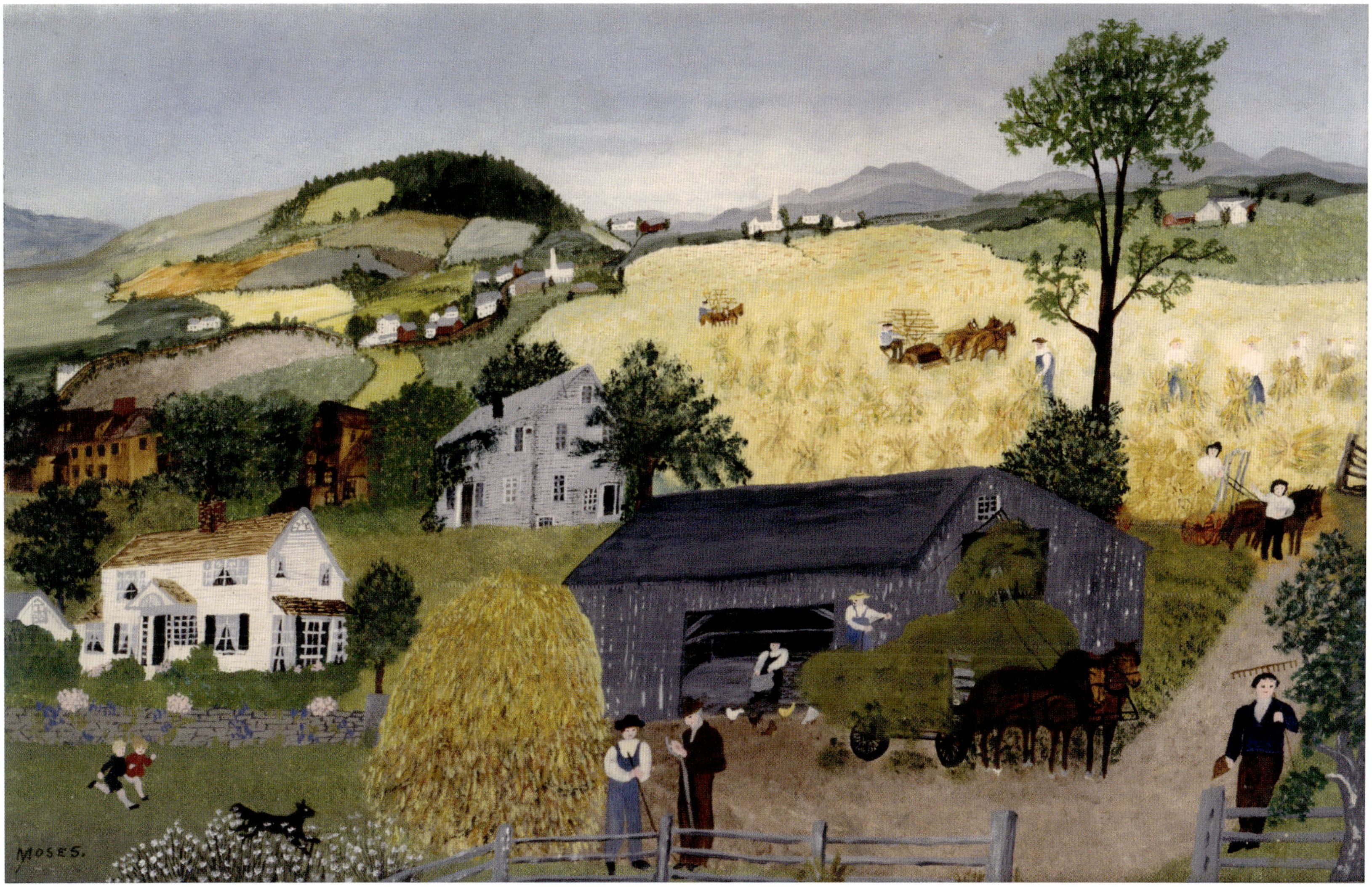

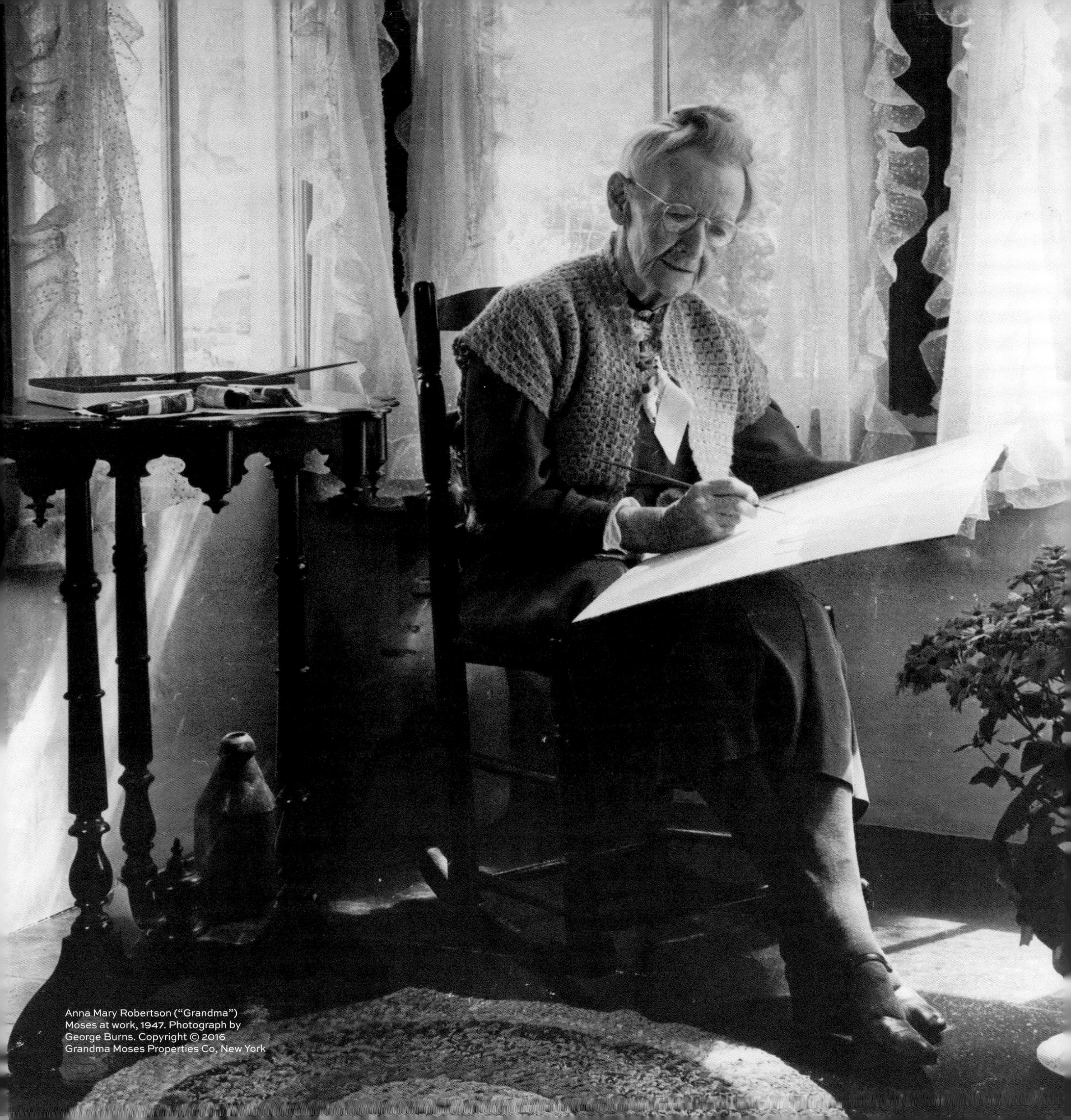

Anna Mary Robertson ("Grandma") Moses at work, 1947. Photograph by George Burns. Copyright © 2016 Grandma Moses Properties Co, New York

ANNA MARY ROBERTSON MOSES: RETHINKING SELF-TAUGHT

DIANA KORZENIK

OF THE MANY GOOD THINGS my parents provided for me, one has been particularly consequential: a visit to Grandma Moses in 1948 when I was seven and a half. This meeting took place soon after the artist had celebrated her eighty-eighth birthday, when *Life* magazine had declared, this "little old lady is one of the best-known and best-paid painters in America. . . . Admirers make pilgrimages to see her."[1] In New York City my art-attentive parents picked up the cue. They contacted the artist and asked if we might visit her. Her assent brought us to her cozy white house in Eagle Bridge, New York, close to the Vermont border. Bright-eyed Mrs. Moses welcomed us to her home, showed us her paintings, and told us about her art secrets, resting securely in her painted wooden trunk. Lifting its cover, she revealed a mountain of little paper men, women, children, horses, dogs, and turkeys. From among these forms—found, invented, or cut from stiff greeting cards—she selected shapes that she then traced, reversed, and used to inform her paintings. When my father told the artist, "Diana is going to be a painter," Mrs. Moses turned to me and offered, "If you make a picture for me, I will give you one of mine." I left with one of her small paintings—a white house in a snowy yard adorned with sparkles—thanking her and promising to send her a picture of my own (fig. 19).

In the course of days, I see Anna Mary Robertson Moses's artistic development and use of devices as far more typical of American painters than has been generally believed. Moses devised works that interested her—based on painted, printed, and photographic images she saw around her, images other people were making in her presence, and images she knew had been commercially

FIG. 19
Anna Mary Robertson ("Grandma") Moses. *Untitled*, c. 1948. Oil on pressed wood. 5 1/4 × 7 1/2 in. Bennington Museum, Gift of Diana Korzenik, Bennington, Vermont, 2015.12.1

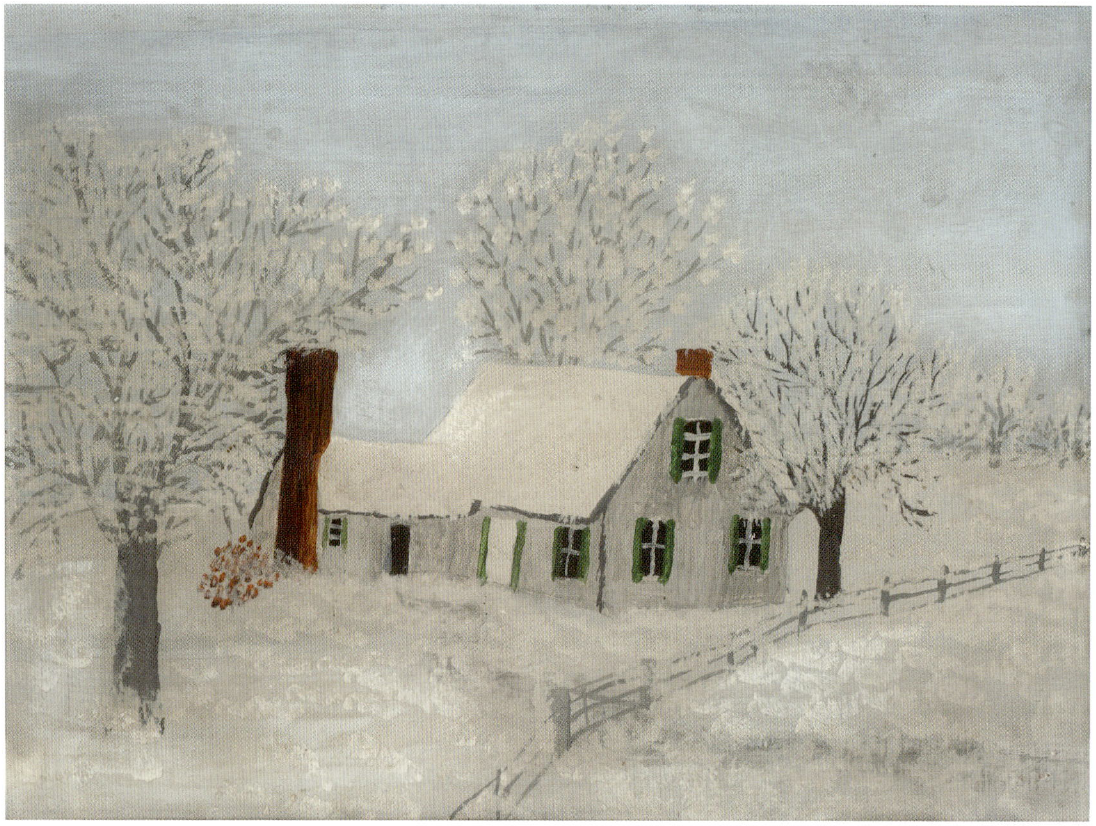

produced. Throughout her life, Moses, in all she was doing, was paying attention, feeding her inborn appetites, trying out and critiquing what she saw, in a process of evolving her art.

It is time we shed such condescending words as "naive" and "primitive" applied to her and her work. These labels only eased the way for the *New York Times* art critic Stuart Preston to separate "women painters like Grandma Moses" from serious "real painters" like Jackson Pollock.[2] Moses reminded us that these words did more harm: they offended her family, who sensed "naive" and "primitive" implied they were illiterate. In time, pigeonholing Anna Mary Robertson Moses as "Grandma" and "primitive" became a double-edged sword. Such labels served to create a broadly appealing market for her art, and related merchandise—reproductions of her paintings on Hallmark cards, curtains, and upholstery fabric, and even a Grandma Moses–inspired "Primitive Red" lipstick inspired by the painting *The Old Checkered House* (plate 37)—but they obscured her strengths and her kinship with artists of her time.

In her autobiography, *My Life's History*, Moses wrote, "I had always liked to paint, but only little pictures for Christmas gifts and the like."[3] Gifting her art was part of her art-making process, in the spirit of the writer Lewis Hyde's *The Gift*, in which he documents how the ancient practice of gifting—the movement of objects—preceded the marketing of objects of value.[4] No wonder Moses spontaneously offered me that painting as a gift. Her attitude toward her art underwent a significant change when her husband, Thomas, then close to death, suddenly seemed to see her art for the first time and to be awed by it. One night, drawn to works his wife had been painting all along, he asked, "Who did that painting? That is really good." Thereafter, he kept looking; he kept seeing. "He just couldn't keep away," Mrs. Moses reported. "When I started a painting he was right there watching, and liked it so much."[5]

Moses's artwork did not emerge from herself alone. Her passion for and astuteness in picture making sprouted, took root, and grew in the rich soil of her nation's rising artistic ambitions. Prior to her birth, art advocates—"art crusaders," as the art historian Peter Marzio called them—were publishing books urging Americans to attend to the beauty of the nation's landscape, to draw and paint and cultivate an American art form.[6] Though no evidence suggests that Moses painted in response to this effort, a sampling of widely distributed nineteenth-century books and magazine articles reveals the fervor for landscape art. American art crusaders challenged their countrymen and women—accustomed to adorning their parlors with European prints and, if affluent, paintings—to cease that practice. *The American Magazine of Useful and Entertaining Knowledge* challenged Americans in 1834 to look around them, to make their art from American scenery, asserting "with confidence" that "there is not in the world, a country more fertile in subjects for the fancy of the novelist, the imagination of the poet, or the pencil of the artist, than the United States. . . . Should not one glimpse at a correct description and well-executed engraving of his own Monadnock, or White Mountains, afford him more pleasure and swell his bosom with a higher and holier feeling of pride, than the sketches and engravings of other places that are annually imported to our shores?"[7]

The artist and writer William Dunlap published his two-volume *The History of the Rise and Progress of the Arts of Design in the United States* in that same year to inspire Americans to take up art making. By profiling the lives of painters, living and nonliving alike, Dunlap intended to make evident that "there was an intuitive desire in the individual to express by lines the images of things."[8] For example, he described Benjamin West's childhood creations of crude images of flowers and birds made "of charcoal and chalk, mixed with the juice of berries . . . with such colors laid on with the hair of a cat drawn through a goose quill" and Washington Allston's inventive childhood constructions formed of twigs and mud.[9] He also wrote of his own childhood joy, recalling a kind gentleman who invited him to search his book closet for such volumes as caught his fancy. The old man looked on, taking delight in "watching the growth of mental faculties. . . . I received his

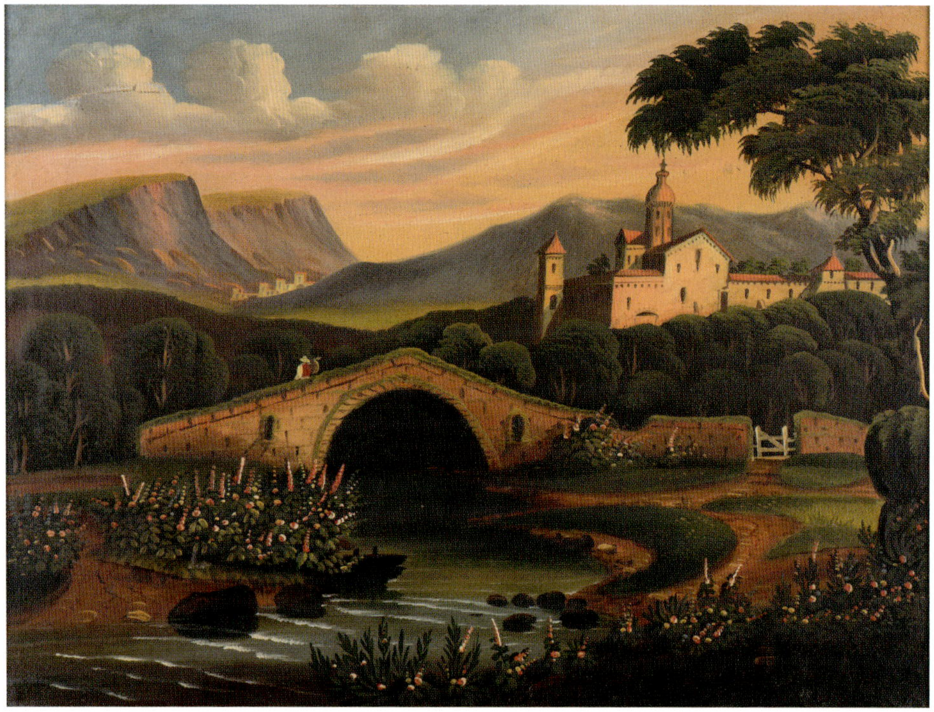

FIG. 20
Thomas Chambers. *Italian Scene with Bridge*, 1840–60. Oil on canvas, 23 1/2 × 29 3/4 in. Collection of Shelburne Museum, Shelburne, Vermont, 1959-265.12

explanations of the pictures . . . hours that expanded my intellect and laid the foundation of my love for books and pictures."[10] Dunlap's premise—one that I share—is that along all American artists' winding paths toward their cherished vocations, each sought out and found early on some materials that stimulated them and instructors who inspired and nurtured them; they were anything but self-taught!

Shortly after the publication of Dunlap's book, another art advocate, British-born American painter Thomas Cole, then thirty-three, addressed a prestigious New York audience. He chided them to appreciate that the aesthetic capacity is innate and that, with education, each individual's response to beauty may take shape. After faulting Americans' tendency to demean their own American landscape as "less fashionable" than that of Europe, Cole told Americans to praise wild and uncultivated American scenery (fig. 43). Likewise, two Thomas Chambers paintings from 1840–60 show how the artist would alternate between European and American subject matter (figs. 20 and 21). As if anticipating Grandma Moses's art, Cole spoke of how artists have choices within the arena of painting American landscape: "The cultivated (land) must not be forgotten." Of paintings that encompass "our homes," he said, "its quieter spirit steals tenderly into our bosoms mingled with a thousand domestic affections and heart-touching associations human hands have wrought, and human deeds hallowed all around."[11] When Cole's lecture was published in *American Monthly Magazine* the following year, his words traveled far beyond New York City, inspiring American readers to see, admire, and make art depicting the land of their own country.

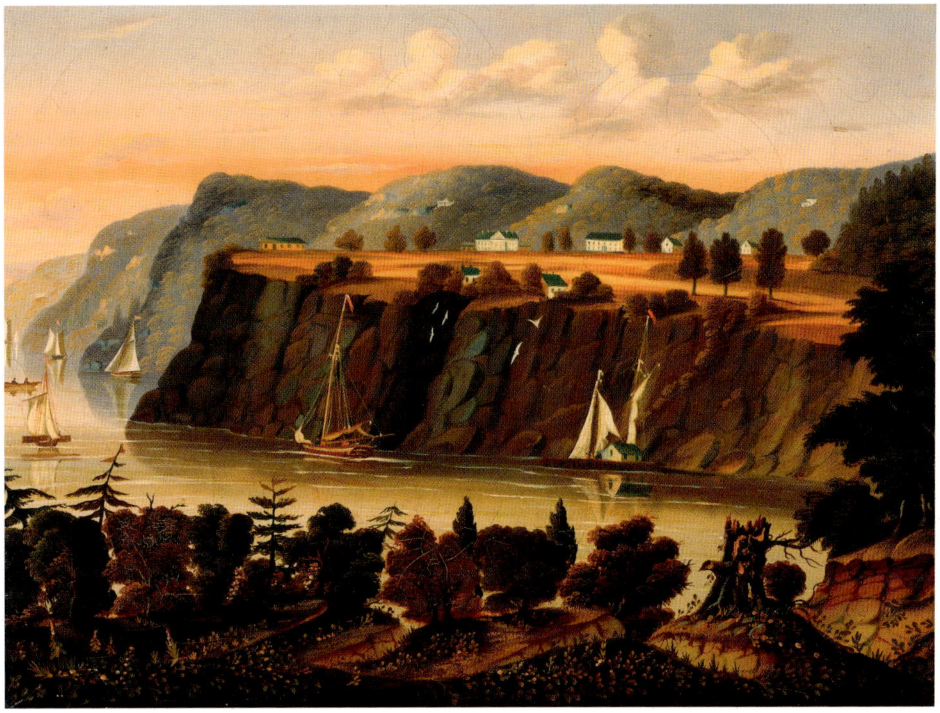

FIG. 21
Thomas Chambers. *View of West Point*, 1840–60. Oil on canvas, 28 3/8 x 36 1/2 in. Collection of Shelburne Museum, Shelburne, Vermont, 1957-690.26

• • •

Anna Mary Robertson Moses, born into "American scenery"—specifically on a farm in Washington County, New York—considered her development as anything but self-taught. She credited her abundant talents to her four ancestral lines: "From the Kings I got art, from the Robertsons inventive faculty, from the Shanahans thrift, the Devereaux generosity."[12] In identifying the source of her artistic gifts, she may have been thinking of her father's ancestor Hezekiah King. Having enlisted in the Sixteenth Albany County Militia in New York, he served at the Battle of Ticonderoga, which he memorialized by incising a parade of tiny *X*'s, akin to needlework sampler stitches, along the arc of his powder horn. This family heirloom was in Moses's possession until she was ninety-three, when she donated it to the museum at Fort Ticonderoga (fig. 22). Through another line—that of the Robertsons—her gray-bearded father, Russell King Robertson (1820–1909), whom she described as "a farmer, and inventor, a dreamer and a believer in beauty and refinement," bestowed on his daughter the inventiveness that opened her eyes to endless possibilities and readied her hands for countless clever and useful creations.[13] The thrift Moses inherited from her mother, Margaret Shanahan Robertson (1840–1909), was another form of ingenuity useful to the housewife and teacher. Margaret's thrift inspired her daughter to paint on any available surface, such as window glass or a thresher cover. And as for the generosity that descended through the Devereaux line and its applicability to

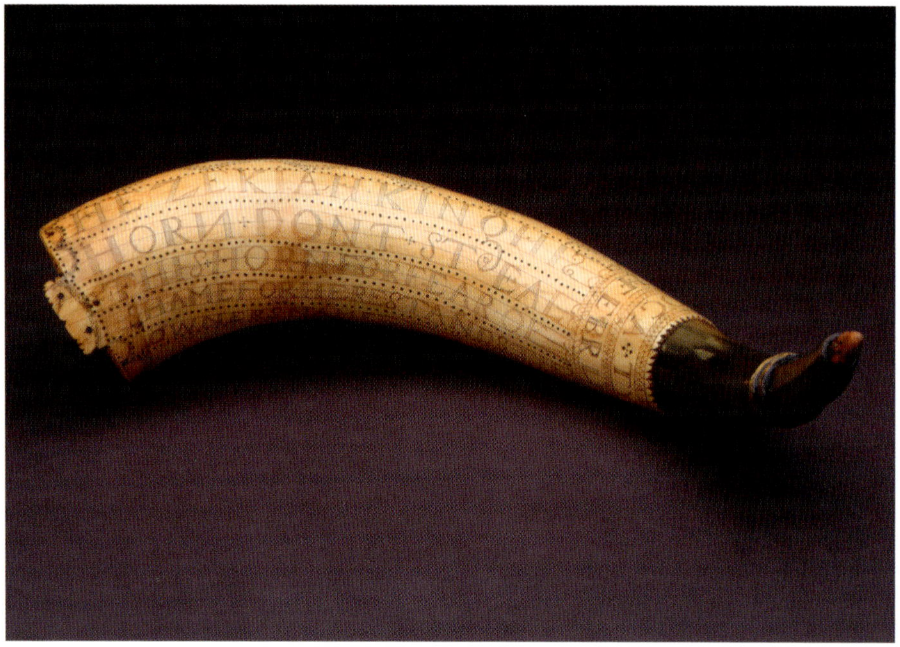

FIG. 22
Powder Horn of Hezekiah King, February 24, 1777. Horn, wood, 13 ½ in. long. Fort Ticonderoga Museum, Ticonderoga, New York

art making, we need only recall the philosopher Simone Weil's comment, "Attention is the rarest and purest form of generosity."[14]

Moses was fond of crediting her father, who owned his own flax mill and painted landscapes, as her first teacher and for influencing and nurturing her proficiencies.[15] Women artists before the nineteenth century were commonly trained by their fathers or other male relatives.[16] So it was in the Robertson home. Moses recalled, "When I was quite small . . . my father would get me and my brother white paper by the sheet, it was used for newspapers. . . . It was a penny a sheet and it lasted longer than candy." All the children drew. "My oldest brother liked to draw steam engines, the next brother went in for animals."[17] She remembered her sister Sarah drawing on a blank page at the end of their great-uncle's 1833 Henry Wilkins medical book. There Sarah drew what "was supposed to be my parents' home, Oak Hill. She had a great hand at drawing with a pencil, it was a natural gift for her," a talent she used to bribe her younger brother into obedience. She would say to the boy, "Come on Hugh, if I draw a picture, will you go to bed?" Her sister Celestia also painted. "She took lessons when she was about 16 or 18, she was a beautiful painter, but she never did much of it," Anna noted, with a tinge of disappointment. Moses liked to tell interviewers about a dream her father once had: "I was along about 9 years old when my father said one morning at the breakfast table, 'Anna Mary, I had a dream about you last night.' 'What did you dream, pa?' 'I was in a great, big hall and it was full of people. And you came walking toward me on the shoulders of men.' As of now, I have often thought of that since."

Russell Robertson did more than just encourage his children's art making and supply them with art materials, however; he surrounded them with his own art. He once asked his wife, "How would you like me to paint the walls? And mother said she didn't care just so they were clean." Young Anna Mary would watch him paint: "He commenced in one corner of the room and painted a scene he had seen the spring before up at Lake George. It was so pretty, mother told him to do some more . . . so he painted different scenes all around the room. That was a lasting wall paper." The artist recalled how, as a child, she painted on pieces of slate and windowpanes. "Then I had some pretty pictures . . . some brilliant sunsets, and father would say, 'Oh, not so bad.'" Even as a child, "the redder I got my skies with my father's own paint, the prettier they were."

• • •

In all her gracious acknowledgments of her artistic influences, nowhere did the artist make explicit that she had been raised in a time and in a culture that had been determined to produce American artists, and that she had grown up in a brave new world of images. In fact Moses was heir to three remarkable visual/graphic innovations: widespread participation in free, government-supported art education; access to and manipulation of inexpensive tintype photography; and the proliferation of dazzling full-color chromolithographic prints that aspiring artists could learn from and copy.

When Moses was ten, the nearby state of Massachusetts launched free public art education for children and adults with the passing of the Massachusetts Drawing Act of 1870, requiring that drawing be taught in all public schools throughout the commonwealth and mandating free instruction in industrial or mechanical drawing be offered in evening schools to those adults—defined as older than fifteen—in cities and towns with populations exceeding ten thousand.[18] Famed British art educator Walter Smith, recruited to implement the Massachusetts law in Boston, observed: "There is an unworked mine of untold wealth among us in the art education of women . . . . It seems to me that an infinite amount of good would be done by opening up the whole field of art instruction and art workmanship to the gentler sex. We shall double the agency and area of art culture, and provide employment for a large number of excellent persons who suffer the lack of it now."[19]

The best venue for showcasing the artwork of Smith's Boston students was the Centennial International Exhibition of 1876, in Philadelphia, the nation's response to Europe's competitive trade fairs. The millions of tourists who converged in the city's Fairmount Park would have seen,

FIG. 23 AND FIG. 24
Walter Smith. *American Drawing Cards—First Series*, 1873. Published by James R. Osgood and Co. Ink on paper; seven cards, instructions, and printed envelope: 3 ⅛ × 5 ½ in. each. Diana Korzenik Collection of Art Education Ephemera, Henry E. Huntington Library, San Marino, California

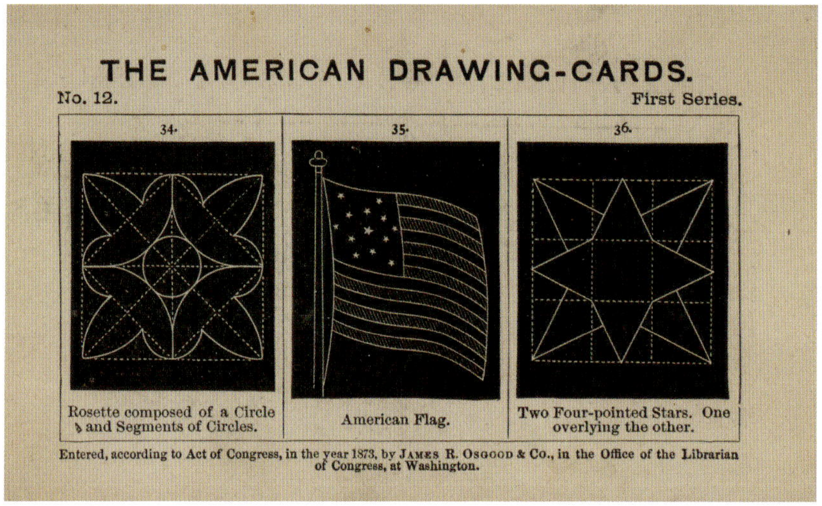

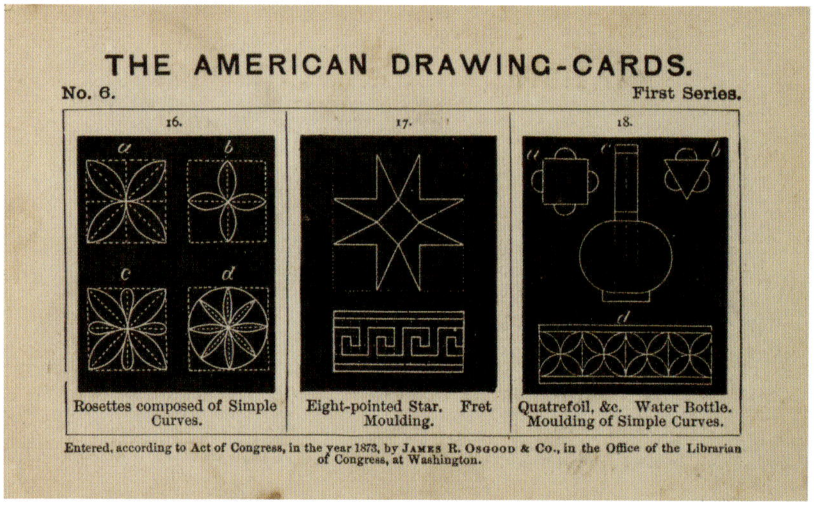

among many other wonders, artwork of a new class of maker: talented artists of the working class, including war widows and single women, who had received artistic training for a wide range of industrial employments. The impressive results of the Massachusetts program drew the attention of government and business leaders, who soon strove to elevate the quality of art teaching in their own states. The Robertsons did not go to Fairmount Park, however. That week they satisfied their curiosity at the local agricultural fairgrounds between Albany and Troy, New York, where for three days they walked through displays of flowers, poultry, and cast iron cookstoves.

Although the style of Robertson family artworks bore no resemblance to the techniques that Smith taught, Moses's meticulously controlled handwriting and her sentiments, read at the finale of her formal schooling, would have pleased him. She said: "Industry is a homely virtue yet worthy of all praise,"

> Look around and see what has been done by the busy hand of nature . . . see her with industrious fingers . . . weaving flowers, flowers and grasses . . . and trees and shrubs to ornament every part of the earth. Will you not adorn [your home] by your industry as nature adorns the fields and the forest. Let man be happy adorning his home. . . .[20]

Moses maintained this ethos for the rest of her life.

The introduction of tintype photography enabled a new, inexpensive means of self-documentation. Moses's first visit to a studio photographer was in 1864; her portrait shows the artist as a tiny four-year-old girl standing in front of a large backdrop painted with a landscape of the sort her father might have painted (fig. 27). Such backdrops were used in the studio to emulate outdoor settings, such as a forest or the seaside (figs. 25 and 26). Also among the photographer's tools was the newel post and the standing rod with an adjustable clamp, used to hold a subject's head perfectly still during the long exposure time required to capture a clear likeness; Moses remembers such a clamp in use for her portrait.[21] Eleven years later, the artist, a womanly fifteen years old, was photographed wearing a high-waisted silk dress, its skirt hemmed with fine pleats, and holding a fancy, flowered hat in her lap (see page 79). The next known photographic portrait was a head shot taken around the time of her September 20, 1887, marriage to Thomas Moses (1862–1927). During the years the Moseses farmed in Virginia's Shenendoah Valley, they continued to have their lives recorded in photographs. One image shows the artist crouched behind a studio photographer's velvet-upholstered armchair on which her two youngest children, Hugh and Anna, are seated. Many years later, in 1957, Moses would revisit the grouping of mother and children in *Mother* (fig. 28). The group portrait bears an uncanny resemblance to the overpainting technique commonly used half a century earlier, when painters applied oil paint onto the tintype to make it resemble a painting, as seen in two examples shown here (figs. 29 and 30). Moses's thick application of paint, which simplifies and flattens the forms, omitting extraneous detail, serves to highlight the emotionally expressive moment in which the mother is almost eclipsed by her two active, adoring children.

Chromolithography is a means of printing multiple colors from separate slabs of limestone. In America, following the Civil War, this new technology enabled artists to print colored images.

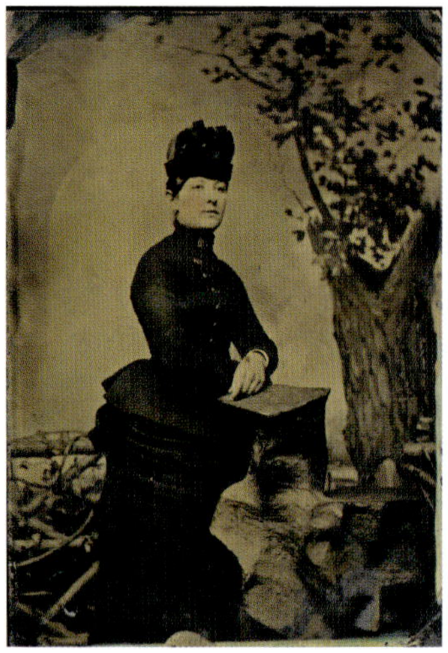

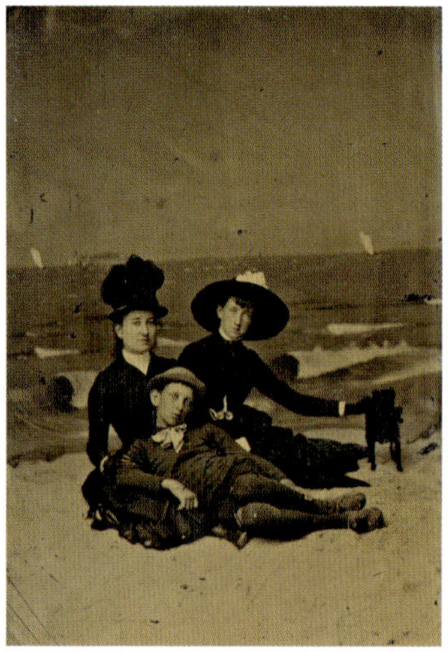

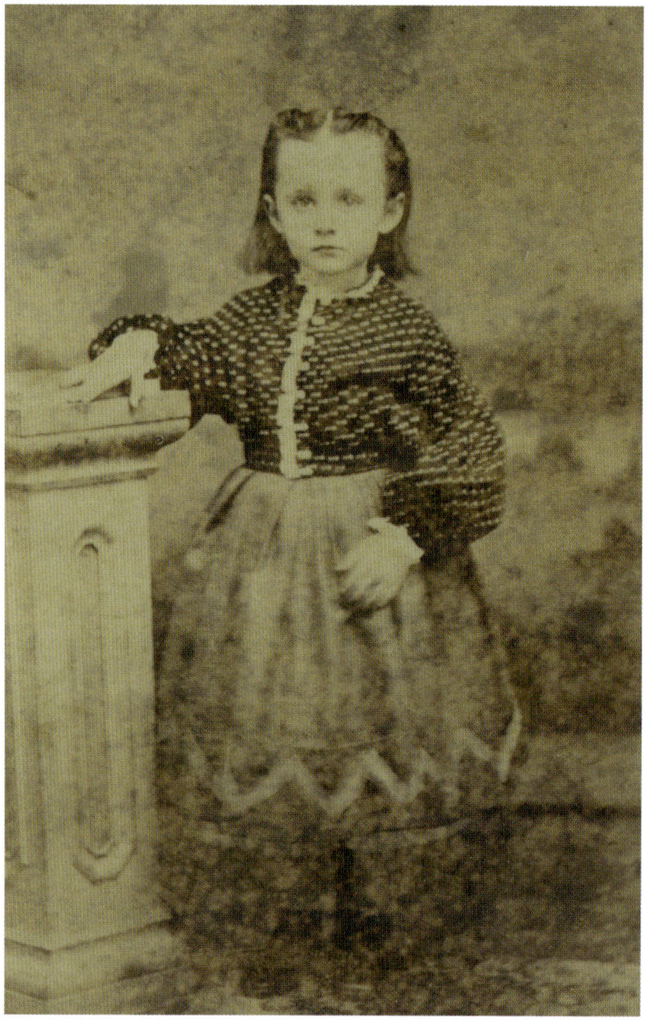

FIG. 25 (TOP LEFT)
Unidentified photographer. *Untitled (Woman next to tree)*. Photograph, tintype, 6 3/4 × 4 13/16 in. Historic New England, Diana Korzenik Collection, Boston, MA

FIG. 26 (BOTTOM LEFT)
Unidentified photographer. *Untitled (Group of three people at the seaside)*. Photograph, tintype, 5 × 3 1/4 in. Historic New England, Diana Korzenik Collection, Boston, MA

FIG. 27 (RIGHT)
Unidentified photographer. *Anna Mary Robertson ("Grandma") Moses, age 4*, c. 1865. Albumen print, 4 × 2 1/2 in. Bennington Museum, Bennington, Vermont, Museum purchase, 2004.604

Dazzling advertising, book illustrations, children's art making kits, and prints intended for home decor were suddenly made widely available to the middle-class consumer. Manufacturers of products ranging from supermarket staples to sewing machines saw the opportunity to invest their wares with added social value by producing small, eye-catching how-to-draw booklets for children, with illustrations of their products for coloring and tracing (fig. 31). One such booklet may even have inspired a young Andy Warhol: *The Heinz Kindergarten Book,* a series published in his hometown of Pittsburgh when he was a child that included graphic line drawings of bottles of tomato ketchup and cans of baked beans.[22]

Moses recollected how, as a child, she delighted in making paper dolls, dressing them in corsets and tissue-paper flounces.[23] Paper dolls were often assembled into scrapbook dollhouses, each page of which was designated as a specific room of a house (figs. 32 and 33). When opened, a "floor" would fold out, creating a three-dimensional scene in which to position the dolls and paper furnishings.

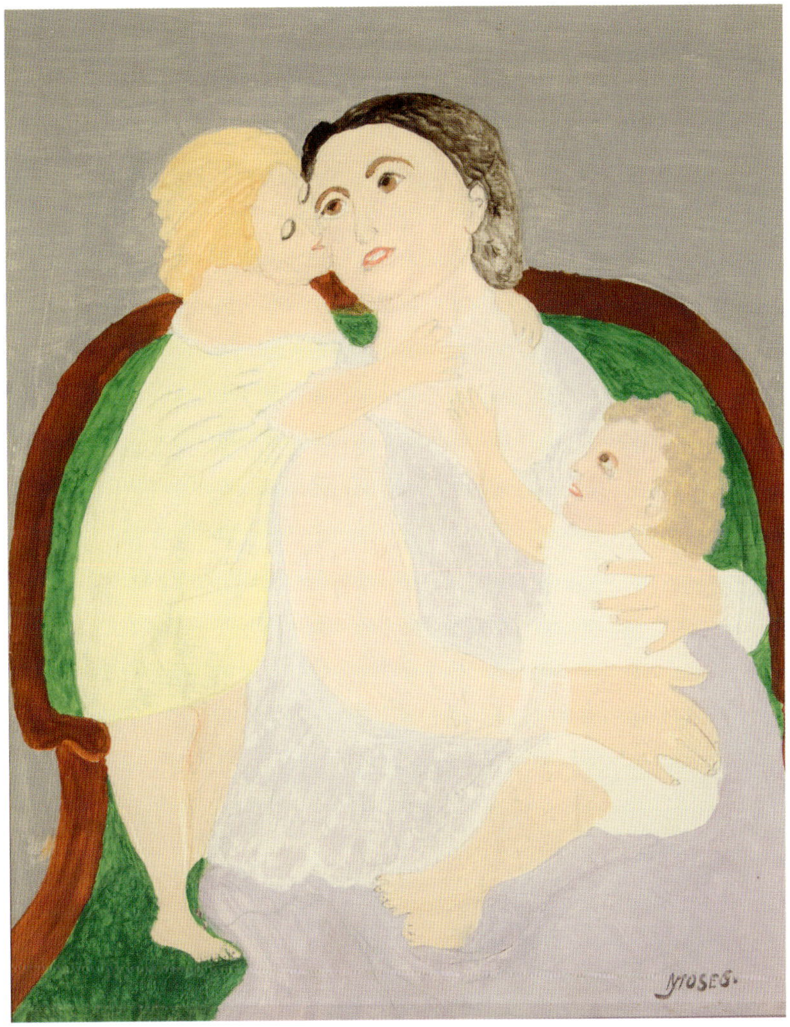

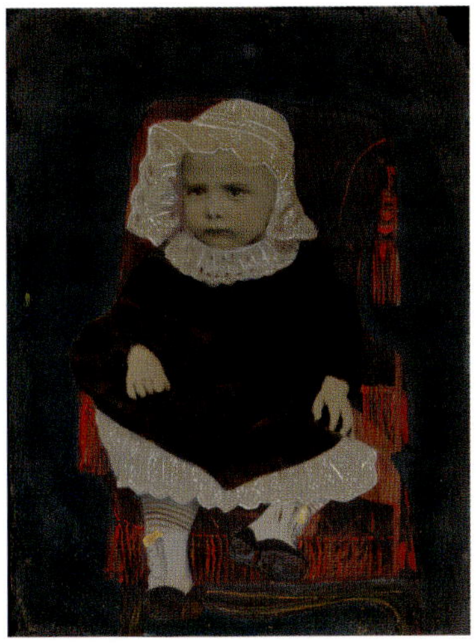

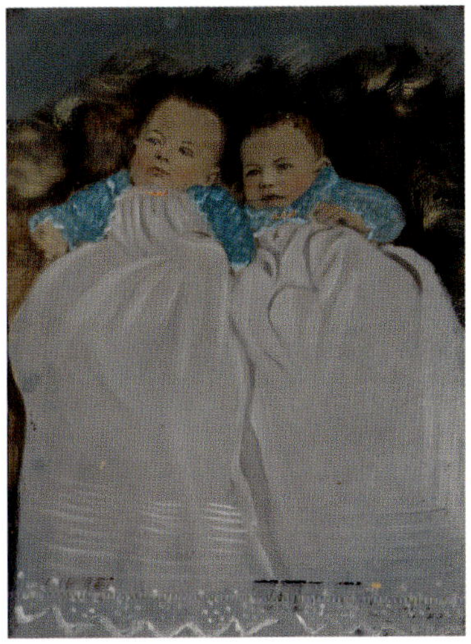

FIG. 28 (LEFT)
Anna Mary Robertson ("Grandma") Moses. *Mother*, 1957. Oil on pressed wood, 16 × 12 in. Private Collection

FIG. 29 (TOP RIGHT)
Unidentified photographer. *Untitled (Baby with striped socks)*. Photograph, tintype, 8 3/8 × 6 3/8 in. Historic New England, Diana Korzenik Collection, Boston, MA

FIG. 30 (BOTTOM RIGHT)
Unidentified photographer. *Untitled (Twin babies)*. Photograph, tintype, 9 × 6 7/8 in. Historic New England, Diana Korzenik Collection, Boston, MA

One commercially produced chromolithographed example is *The House That Glue Built* (1905), by Clara Andrews Williams and George Alfred Williams: thick, stiff pages depicting seven rooms of a house and illustrations of dolls, furniture, and accessories for cutting out and pasting in (fig. 34). Moses's rare, fascinating paintings of interiors, such as *A Tramp on Christmas Day*, seem akin to the rooms of such dollhouse scrapbooks, though no evidence survives that she had a scrapbook dollhouse of her own. Moses's "art secrets," the miniature cutouts she stowed in a trunk, may have been inspired by yet another art product commercially marketed to children. *Drawing and Painting Exercises After Models for Children* resembles a small book but actually is a shallow box containing a variety of art materials: a set of blank drawing papers, a tiny palette with paints, and a set of die-cut lithographed figures—men, women, children, farm animals—to be used as tracing stencils (fig. 35).

But the boldest of Moses's encounters with commercial chromolithography was in 1925, when she painted directly on top of a print, *In the Berkshires*, a reproduction of a painting by Andrew

FIG. 31
The Singer Drawing Book for Young Artists, c. 1900. Published by Singer Sewing Machine Co. Ink on paper; eight-page booklet with tracing paper inserts. Diana Korzenik Collection of Art Education Ephemera, Henry E. Huntington Library, San Marino, California

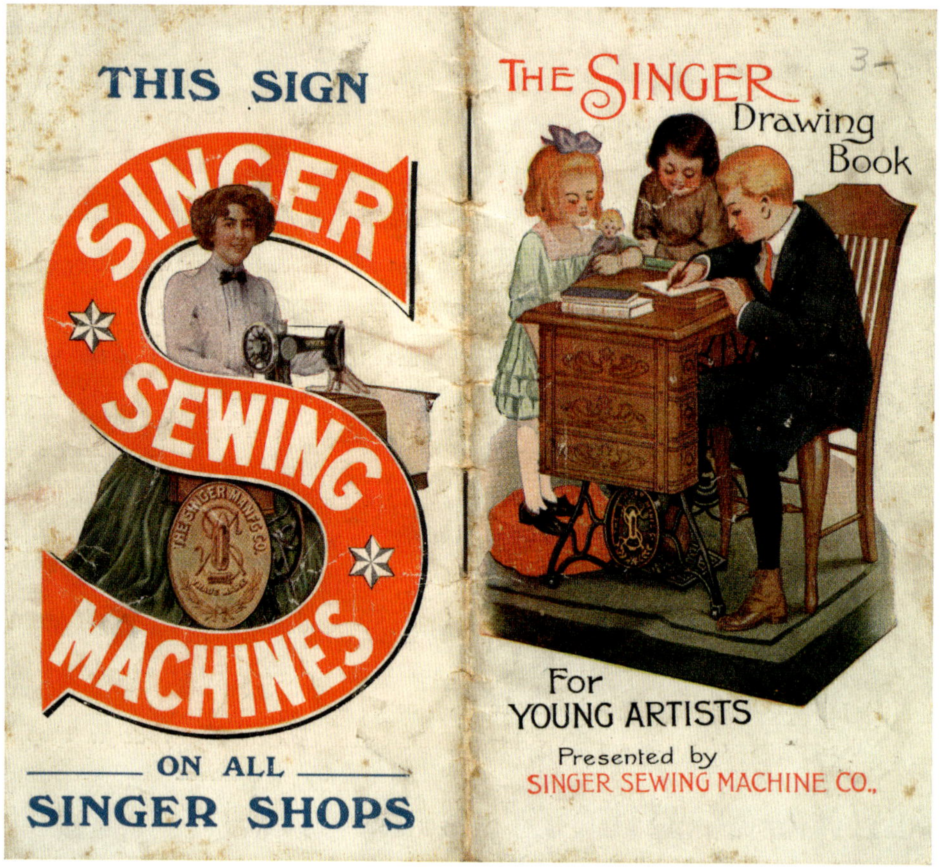

Melrose (1836–1901) published by the London firm Raphael Tuck & Sons for the American market. Moses overpainted the unusually delicate, pale "chromo," the nickname for these popular colored prints, with her preferred intense colors, juxtaposing strong dark browns and brilliant whites and reworking Melrose's scene, imposing on it the stamp of her own aesthetic.

• • •

This examination of Moses's sources, and the redefinition of "self-taught," ends when, in 1938, Moses's son Hugh and his wife, Dorothy, brought his mother's work to Thomas's drug store in Hoosick, New York, where New York City art collector Louis Caldor, touring the region, saw Moses's pieces and was captivated, believing he had found a self-taught American folk artist. My aim has been to free the term "self-taught" from the 1930s romantic and political associations. Now it seems dated and simplistic. In the context of Moses's life and art, we need to redefine the term to suggest how highly selective and experimental she was in examining, extracting, and using everything in

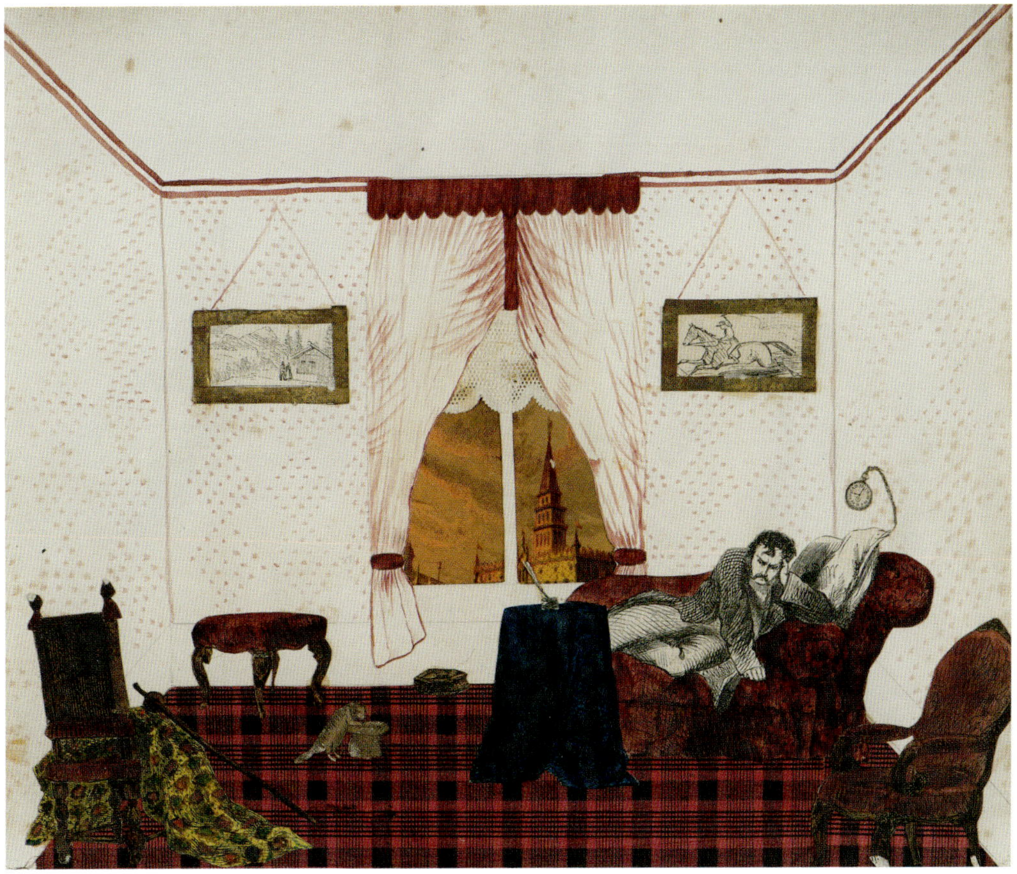

FIG. 32 (TOP)
Sarah Georgiana Winn. *Victorian Room Settings and Paper Dolls Scrapbook*, c. 1859. Paper, ink, and paint, 10 5/8 × 8 5/8 × 1 5/8 in. Collection of Shelburne Museum, Shelburne, Vermont, Gift of Susanna Adams, 1998-84.11. Photography by Andy Duback

FIG. 33 (BOTTOM LEFT)
Sarah Georgiana Winn. *Victorian Room Settings and Paper Dolls Scrapbook*, c. 1859. Paper, ink, and paint, 10 5/8 × 8 5/8 × 1 5/8 in. Collection of Shelburne Museum, gift of Susanna Adams, Shelburne, Vermont, 1998-84.11. Photography by Andy Duback

FIG. 34 (BOTTOM RIGHT)
Clara Andrews Williams & George Alfred Williams. *The House That Glue Built: Nursery*, 1905. Paper and ink on cardboard, 12 × 14 1/2 × 1/2 in. Private Collection. Photography by Andy Duback

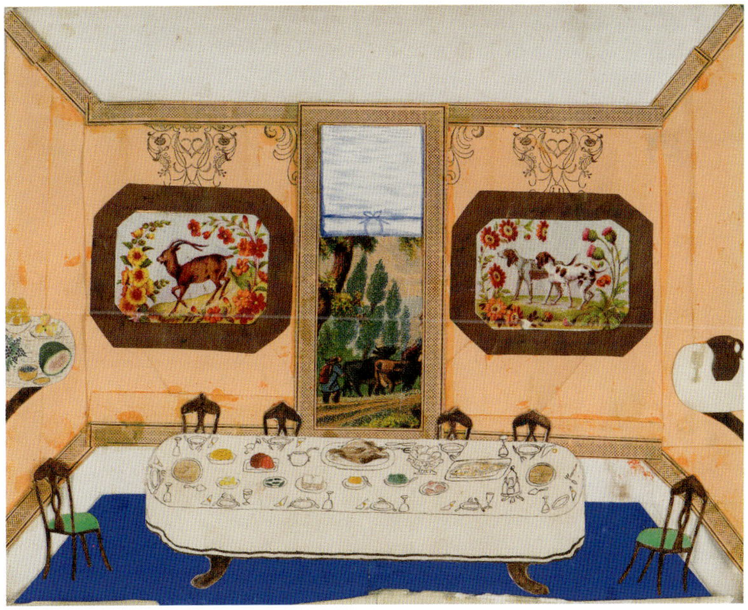

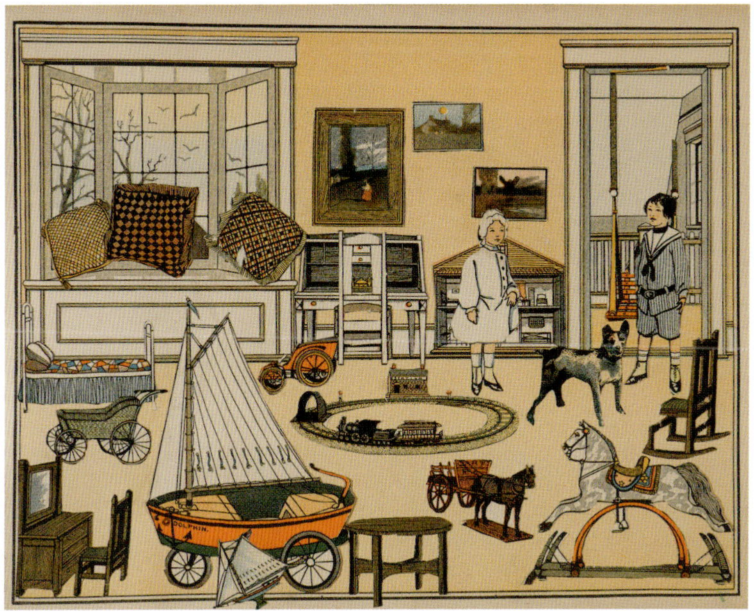

FIG. 35
Drawing and Painting Exercises After Models for Children, c. 1885. Published by W. & S. B. Wood and paperboard box; ink on paper, 4 3/4 × 6 3/8 in. Diana Korzenik Collection of Art Education Ephemera, Henry E. Huntington Library, San Marino, California

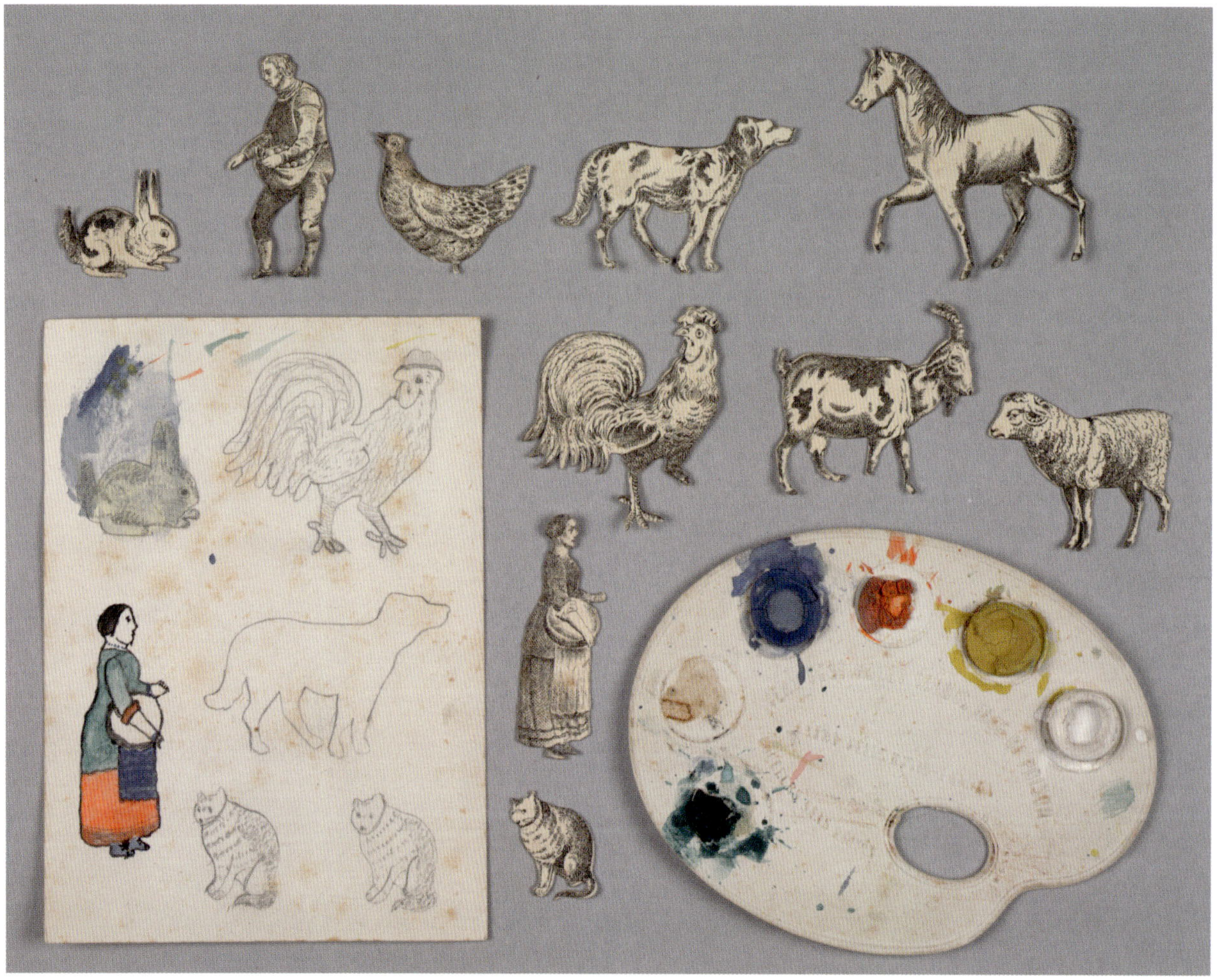

sight. Given Moses's appetite for her era's myriad personal and material art influences, all she saw, all she selected, all she absorbed became grist for her "inventive faculty." Having tried everything, worked at many things, learned from everyone, this sprightly, eclectic painter blazed her own path, giving us, in the twenty-first century, the opportunity to savor how with few-haired paintbrushes, she could move mountains and populate valleys.

NOTES

1. Bruce Bliven Jr., "Grandma Moses Has a Birthday," *Life* 25, no. 17 (Oct. 25, 1948): 76–78.

2. Stuart Preston. "Portrait of the Artist as an American," *New York Times Magazine* (April 27, 1958): 34–37.

3. *Grandma Moses, My Life's History*, ed. Otto Kallir (New York: Harper & Brothers, 1952), 125.

4. Lewis Hyde, *The Gift: Imagination and the Erotic Life of Property* (New York: Vintage Books, 1983).

5. Moses, *My Life's History*, 125.

6. Peter C. Marzio, *The Art Crusade: An Analysis of American Drawing Manuals, 1820–1860* (Washington, D.C.: Smithsonian Institution Press, 1976).

7. *American Magazine of Useful and Entertaining Knowledge 1*, no. 1 (Sept. 1834), 1.

8. William Dunlap, *The History of the Rise and Progress of the Arts of Design in the United States*, 2 vols. (New York, 1834).

9. Ibid., 1:38.

10. Ibid., 1:245.

11. Thomas Cole, "American Scenery," *American Monthly Magazine* (Jan. 1836): 3.

12. Moses, *My Life's History*, 10.

13. Ibid.

14. Although this quotation is often repeated and attributed to Simone Weil, scholars are not able to find the original score. Simone Weil, *Gravity and Grace* (Lincoln, NE: University of Nebraska Press, 1952).

15. Moses, *My Life's History*, 17–18.

16. Ann Sutherland Harris and Linda Nochlin, *Women Artists: 1550–1950* (New York: Alfred A. Knopf in association with Los Angeles County Museum of Art, 1977); and *Angela Rosenthal, Angelica Kauffman: Art and Sensibility* (New Haven, CT: Yale University Press, 2006).

17. This and subsequent quotes regarding artistic life within the Moses family can be found in Moses, *My Life's History*, 26–27, 128, 134, and 138.

18. Diana Korzenik and Rudolf Arnheim, *Drawn to Art: A Nineteenth-Century Dream* (Lebanaon, NH: University Press–New England, 1985).

19. Walter Smith, *Art Education Scholastic and Industrial* (Boston: James R. Osgood, 1872).

20. Anna Mary Robertson Moses, "Let Home Be Made Happy," reprinted in Otto Kallir, *Grandma Moses* (New York: Harry N. Abrams, 1974), 69.

21. Moses, *My Life's History*, 16.

22. Jim Linderman, "Heinz Brands a (Young) Warhol," Paraphilia Magazine, Oct. 3, 2013, http://www.paraphiliamagazine.com/periodical/heinz-brands-a-young-warhol/.

23. Moses, *My Life's History*, 22.

PLATE 13

Anna Mary Robertson ("Grandma") Moses

A TRAMP ON CHRISTMAS DAY

1946. Oil on academy board, 15 ⅜ × 19 ⅜ in.

Collection of Shelburne Museum, Museum purchase, Shelburne, Vermont, 1961-210.2

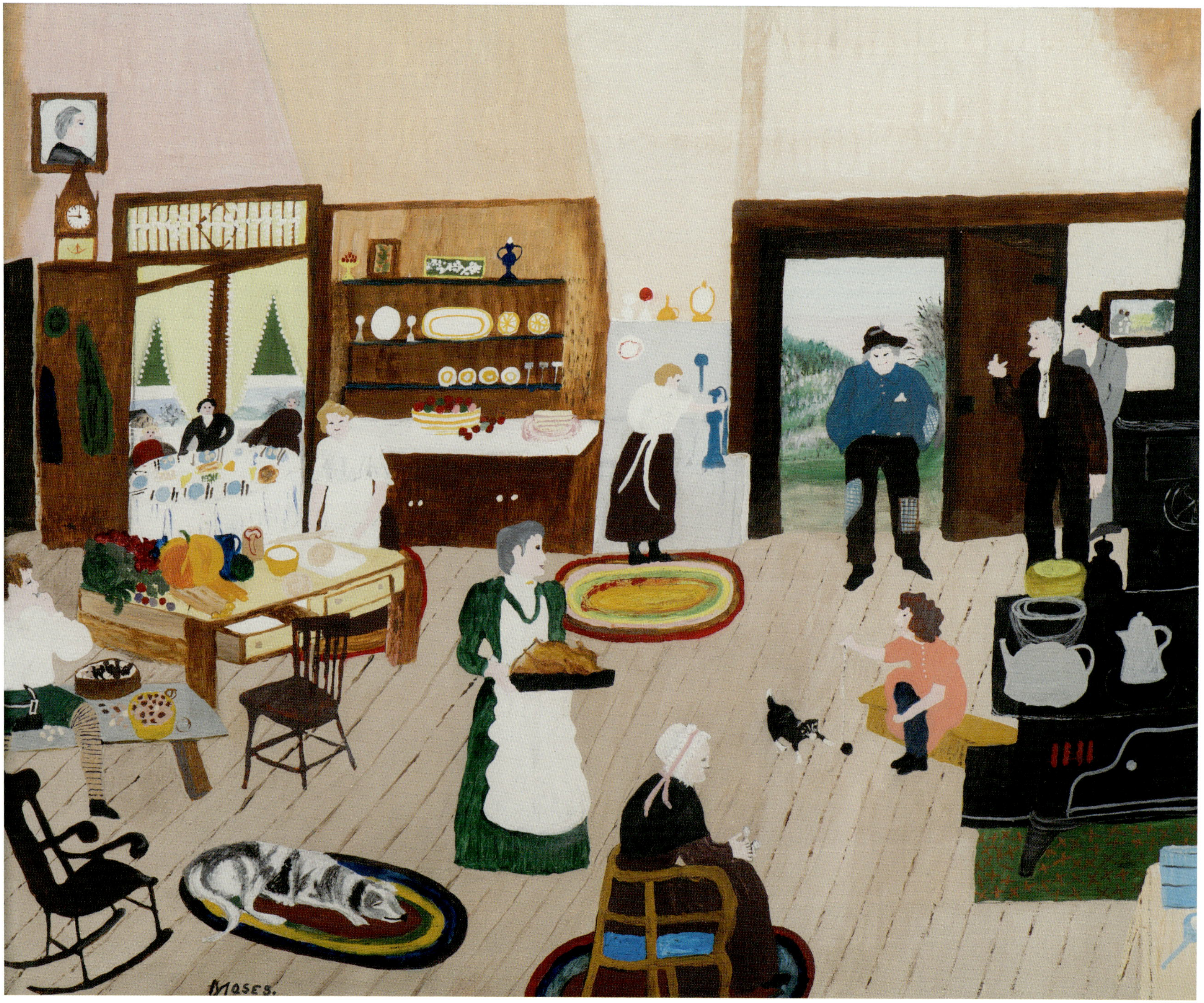

PLATE 14
Anna Mary Robertson ("Grandma") Moses
AT THE WELL
1950. Oil on pressed wood, 19 ½ × 23 ½ in.
Bennington Museum, Museum purchase, Bennington, Vermont, 2001.1

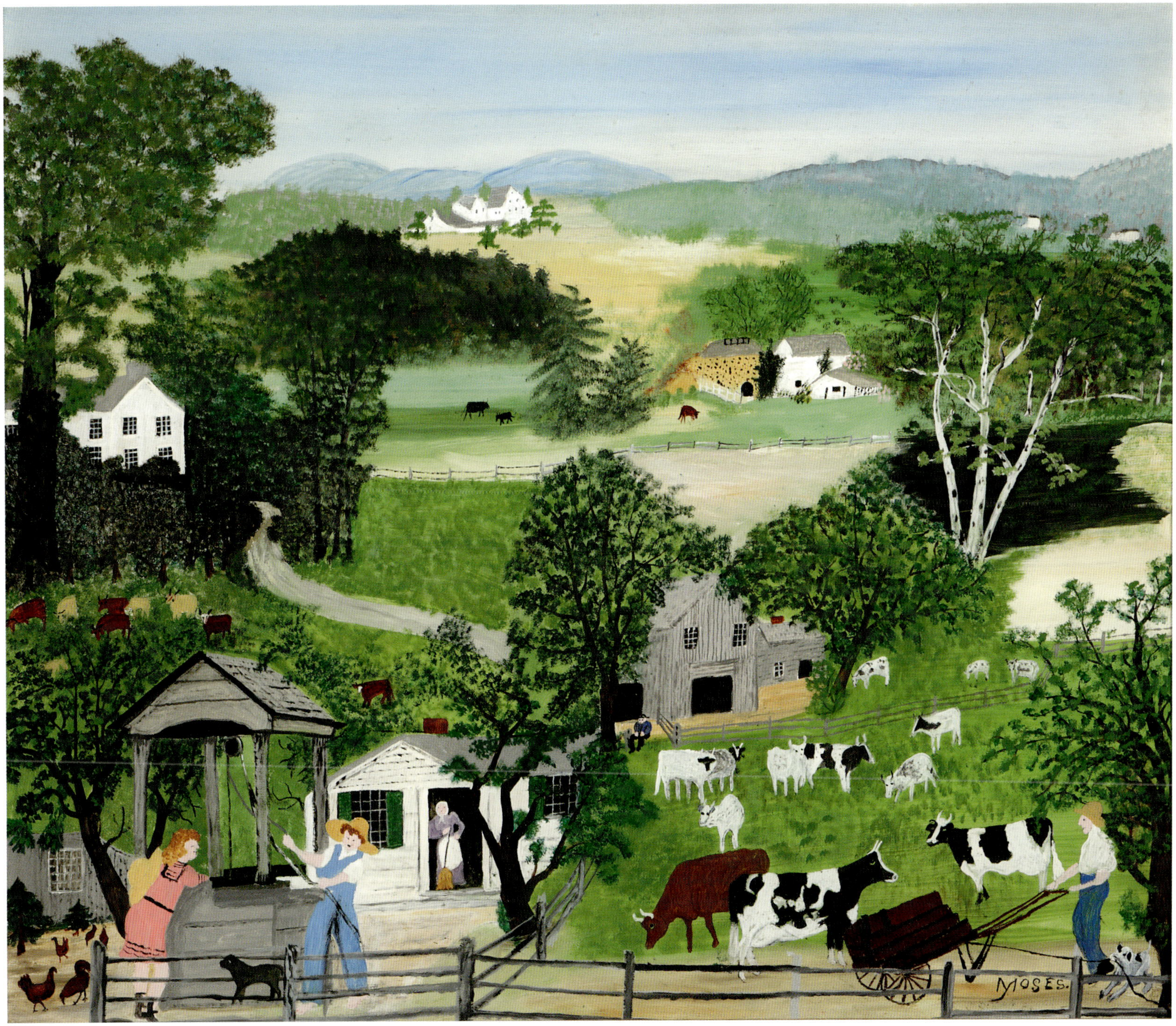

PLATE 15

Anna Mary Robertson ("Grandma") Moses

OLD TIMES

1957. Oil on pressed wood, 16 × 24 in

Private Collection, courtesy of Galerie St. Etienne, New York

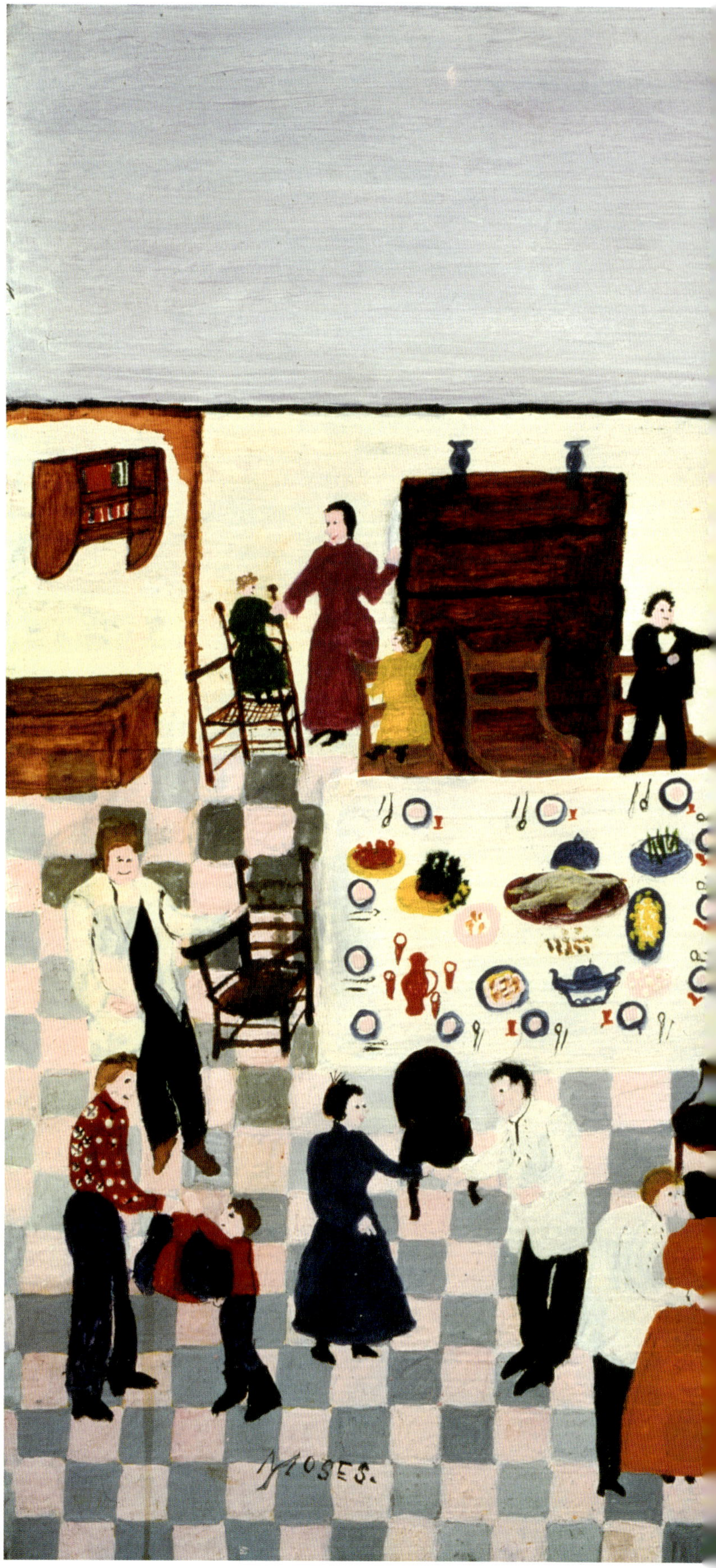

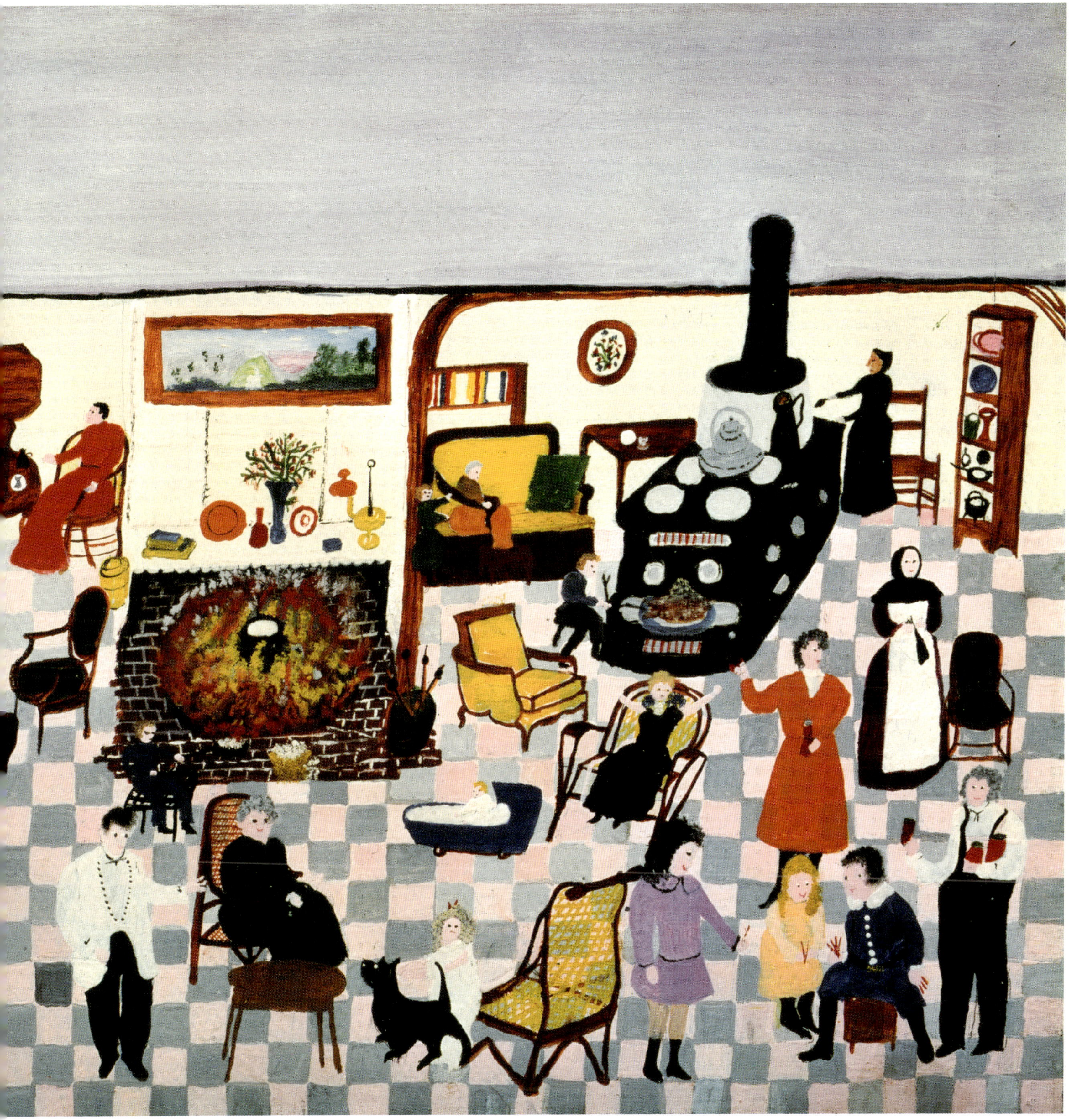

PLATE 16

Anna Mary Robertson ("Grandma") Moses

THE SALMON PLACE

1947. Oil on pressed wood, 10 × 12 $^{1}/_{8}$ in.

Bennington Museum, Gift of Mr. Harvey D. Carter, Sr., Bennington, Vermont, 1976.313

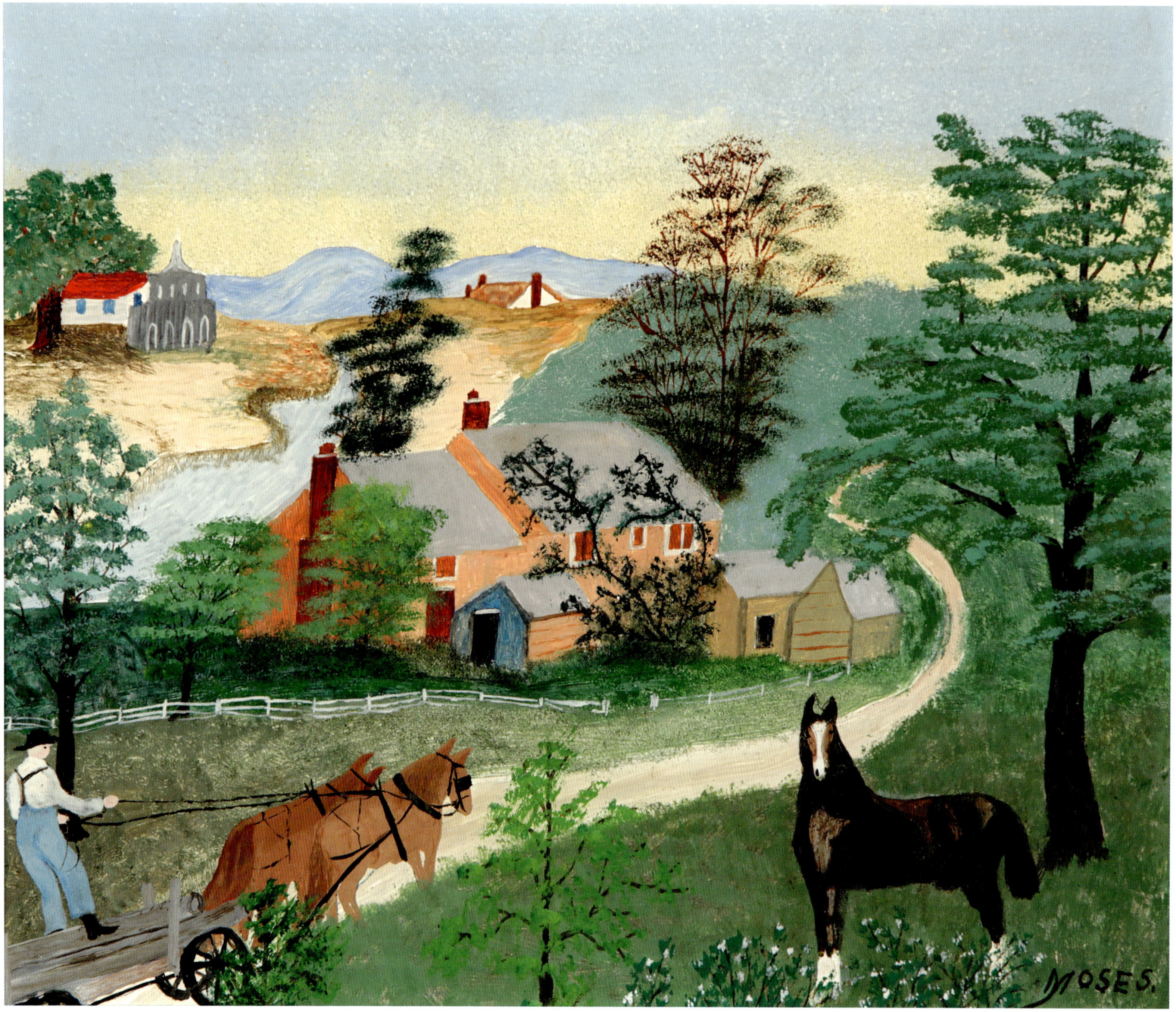

PLATE 17

Anna Mary Robertson ("Grandma") Moses

THE MAILMAN HAS GONE

1949. Oil on Masonite, 16 ⅜ × 21 in.

Collection of Shelburne Museum, Museum purchase, Shelburne, Vermont, 1961-210.4

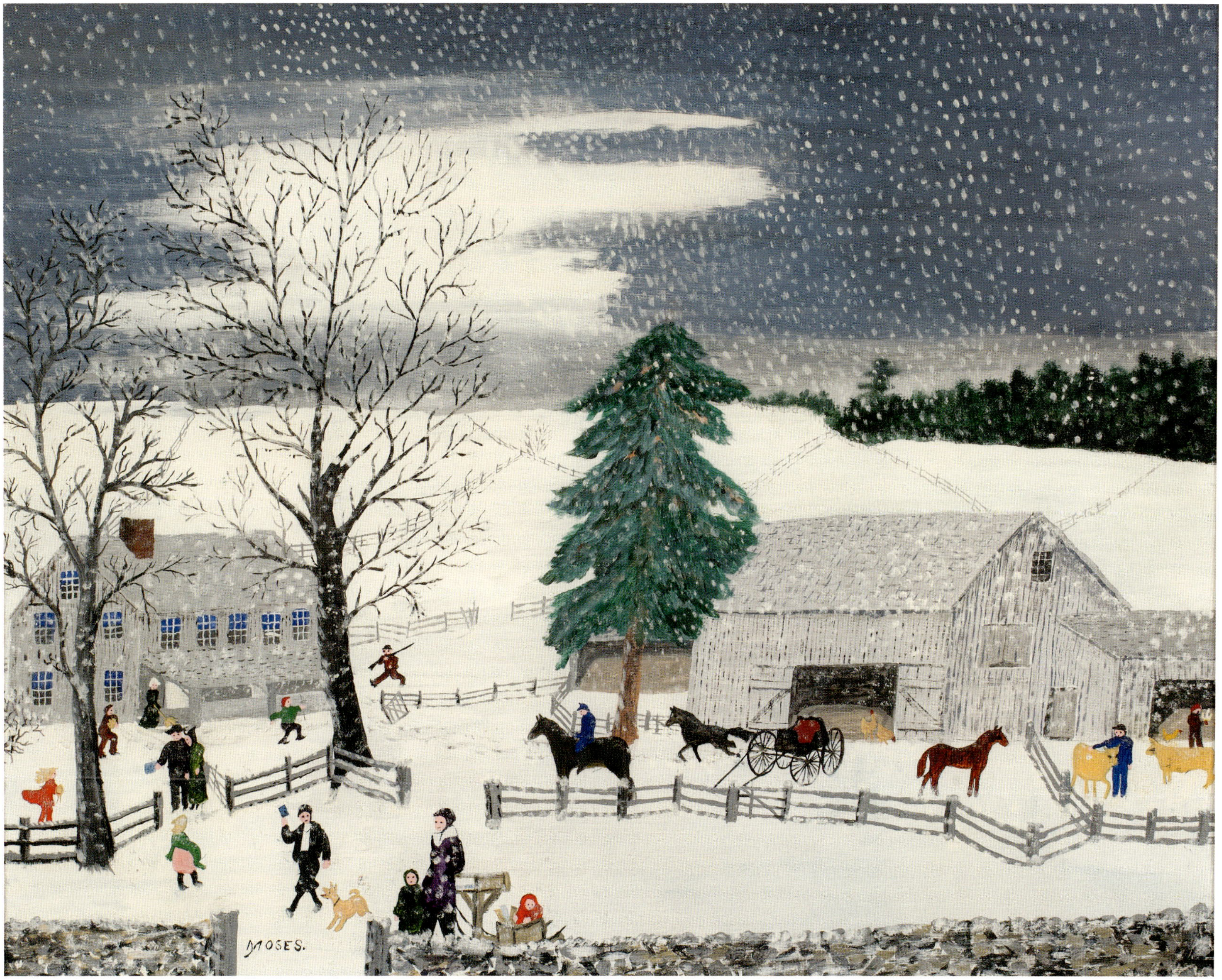

PLATE 18

Anna Mary Robertson ("Grandma") Moses

A COUNTRY WEDDING

1951. Oil on pressed wood, 16 ½ × 21 ½ in.

Bennington Museum, Museum purchase, Bennington, Vermont, 1998.79

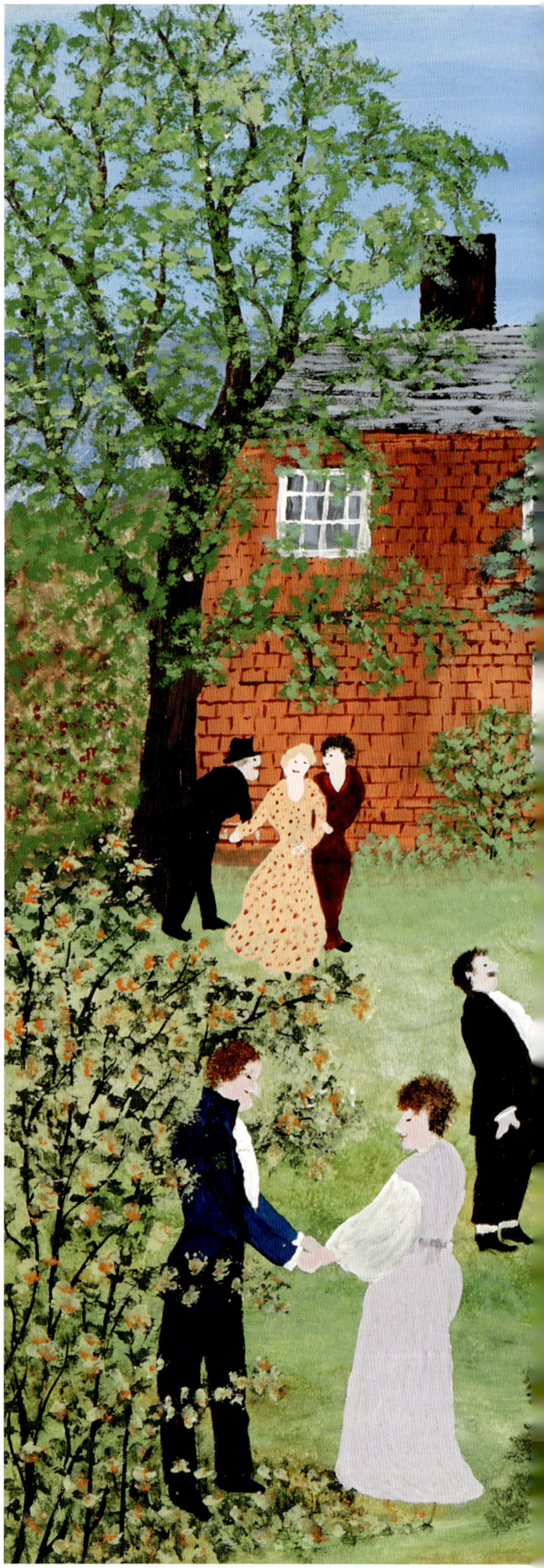

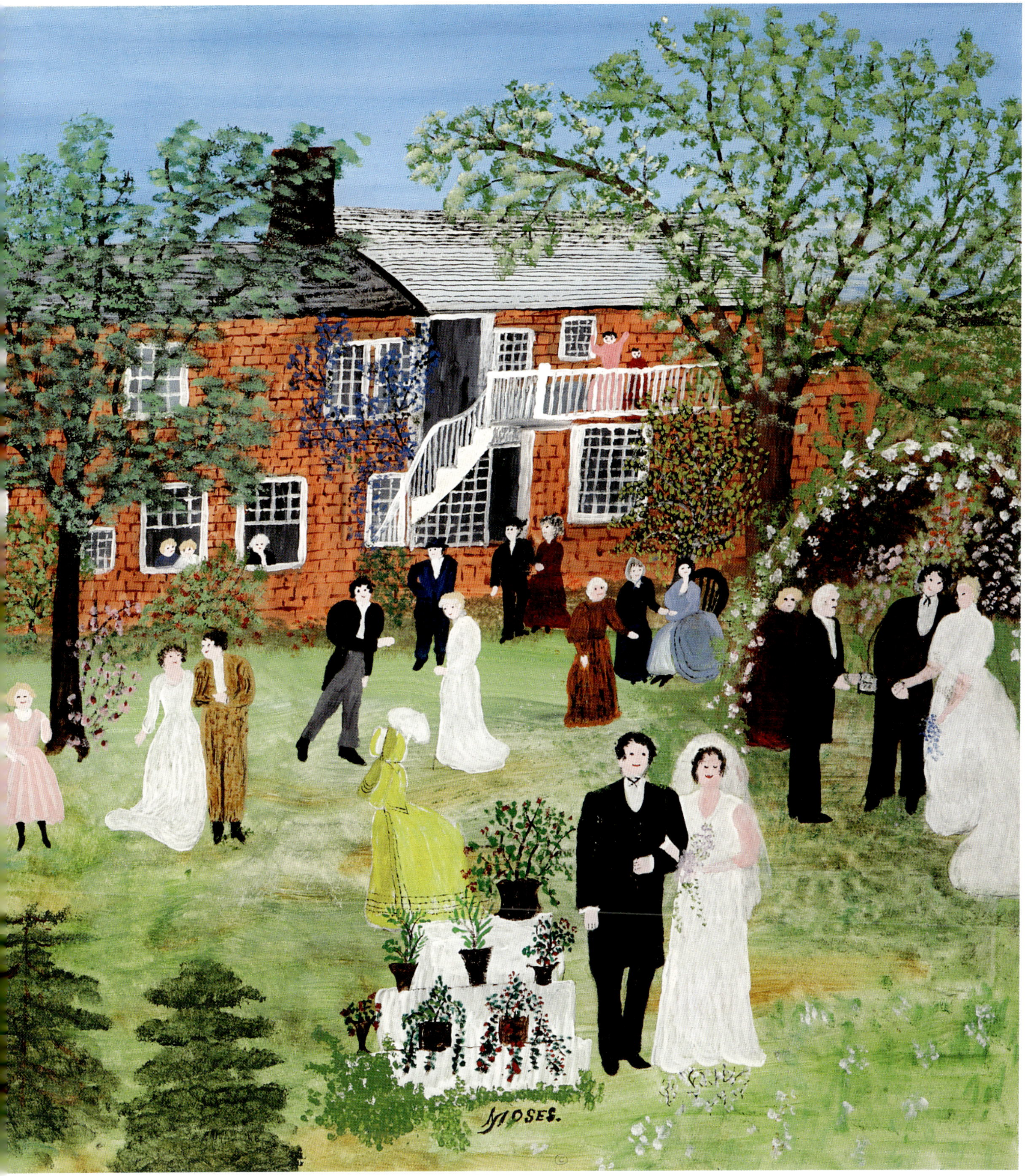
MOSES.

PLATE 19

Anna Mary Robertson ("Grandma") Moses

HAYING

1956. Oil on pressed wood, 11 ⅝ × 15 ½ in.

Collection of Shelburne Museum, Gift of Mr. and Mrs. Peter F. Carleton in Memory of Mrs. P. H. B. Frelinghuysen, Shelburne, Vermont, 1965-59.2

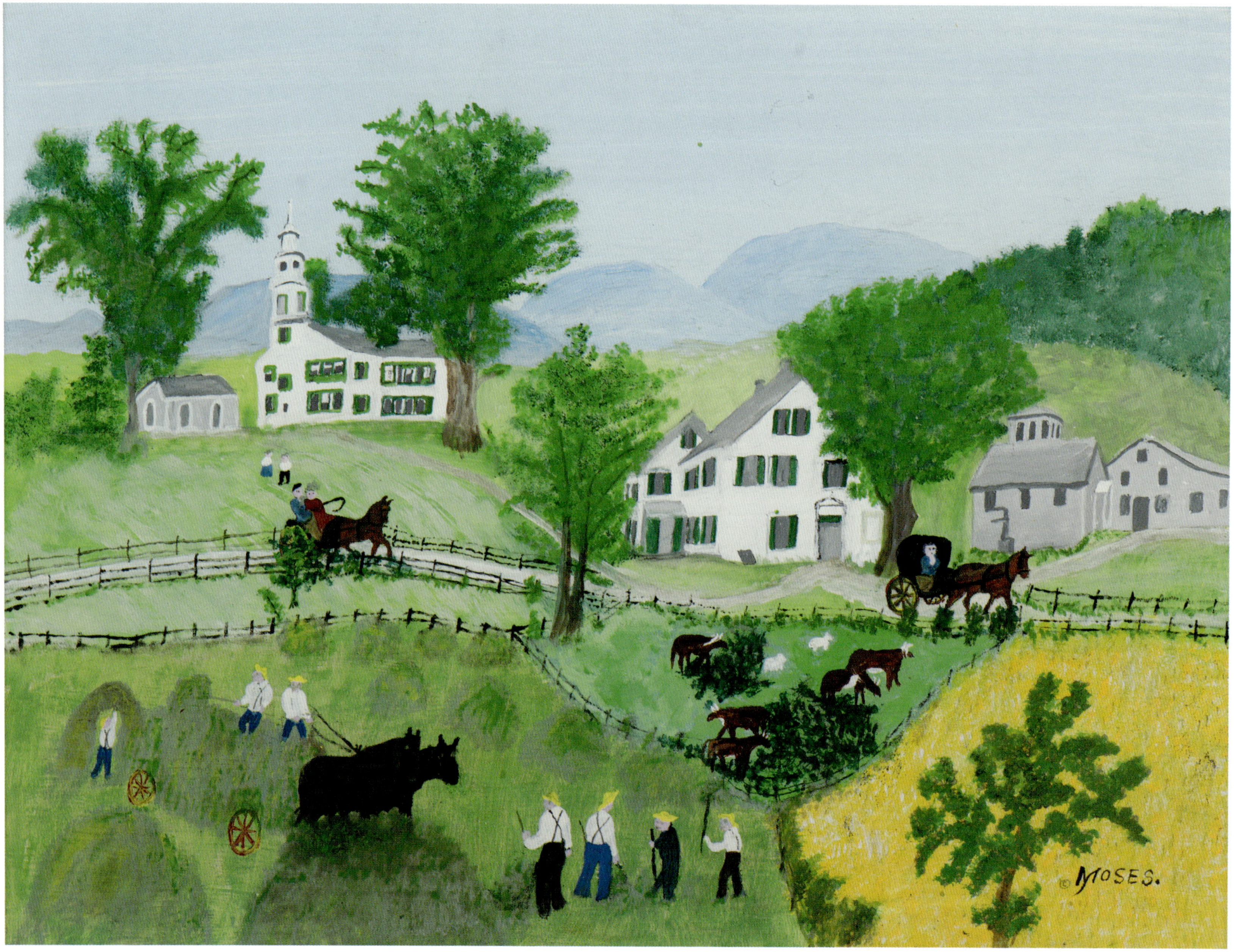

PLATE 20

Anna Mary Robertson ("Grandma") Moses

WHITE CREEK

1952. Oil on pressed wood, 17 × 21 ¼ in.

Collection of Linda Hailstone and Bruce McCart

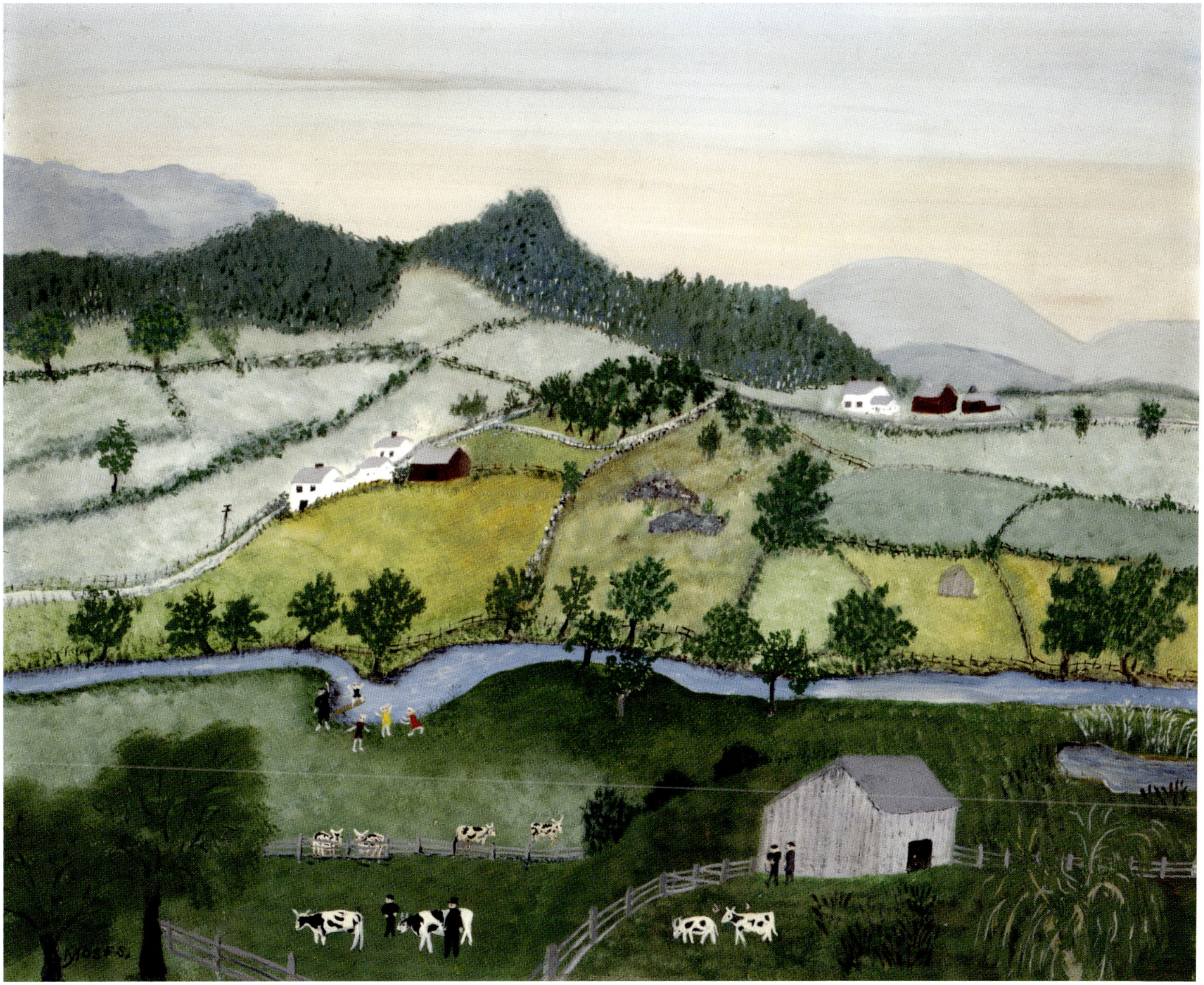

PLATE 21

Anna Mary Robertson ("Grandma") Moses

AFTER THE WEDDING

1942. Oil on pressed wood, 17 ⅝ × 29 ¹¹⁄₁₆ in.
Collection of Shelburne Museum, Gift of Mr. and Mrs. Peter F. Carleton in Memory of Mrs. P. H. B. Frelinghuysen, Shelburne, Vermont, 1965-59.1

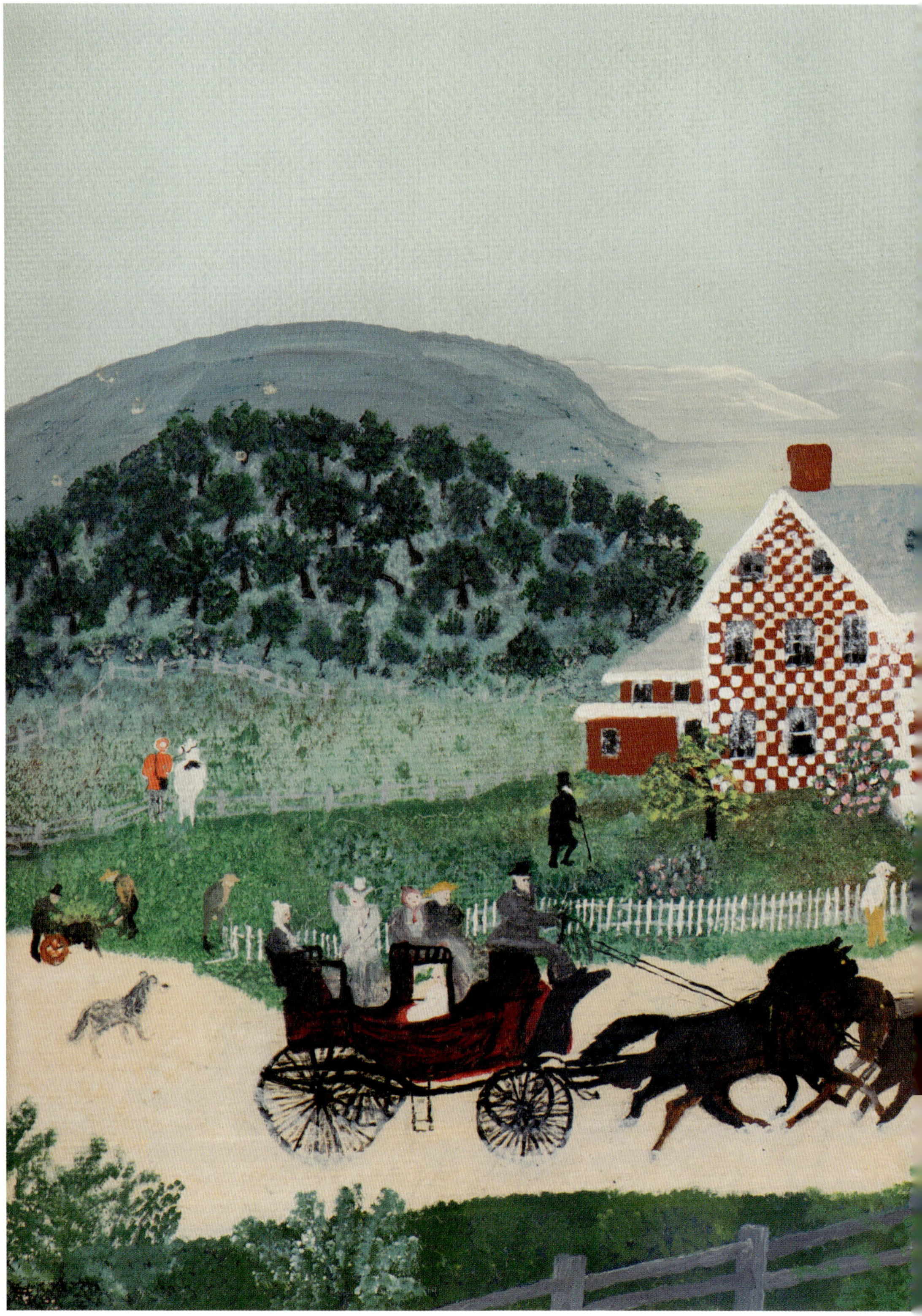

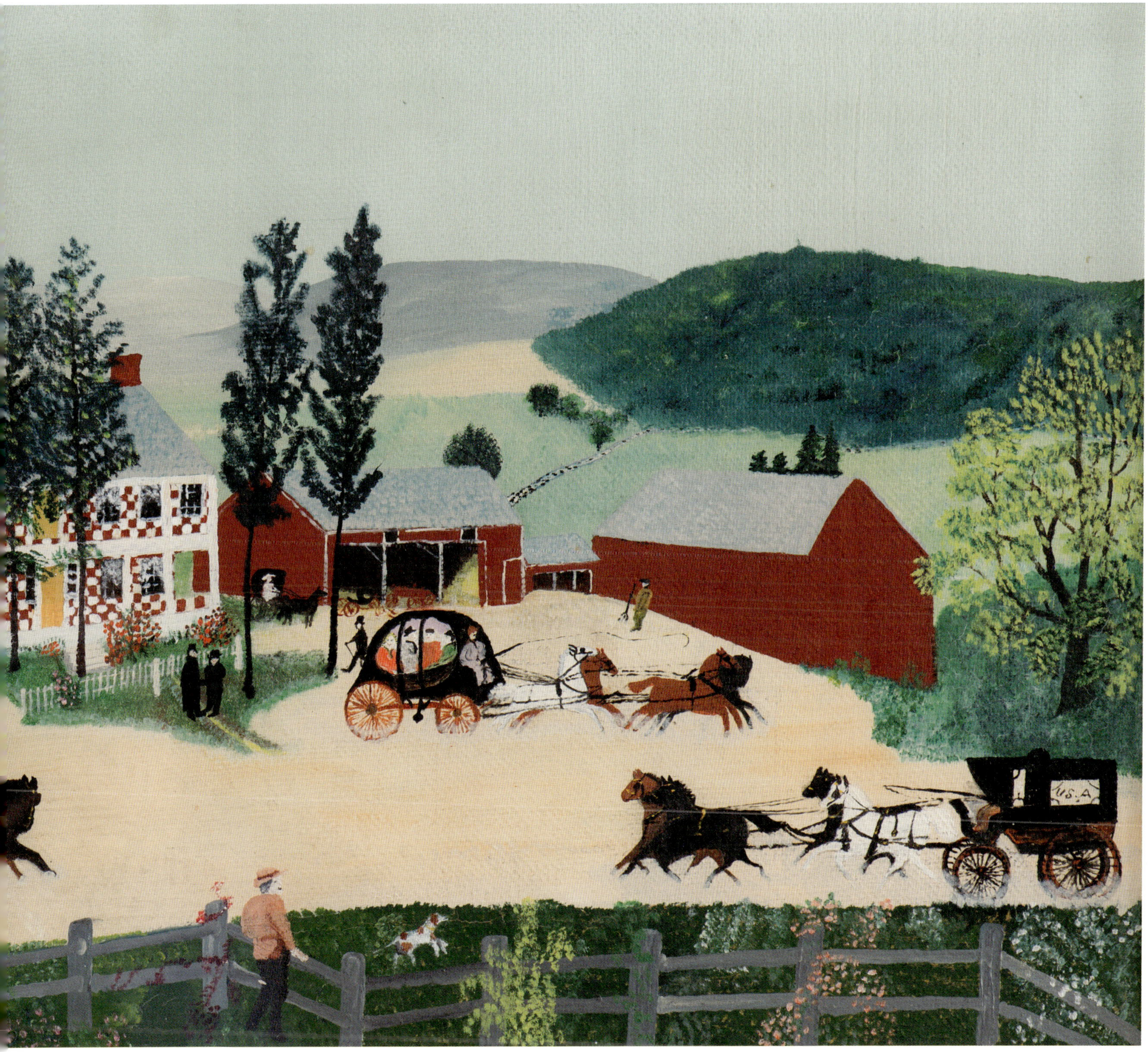

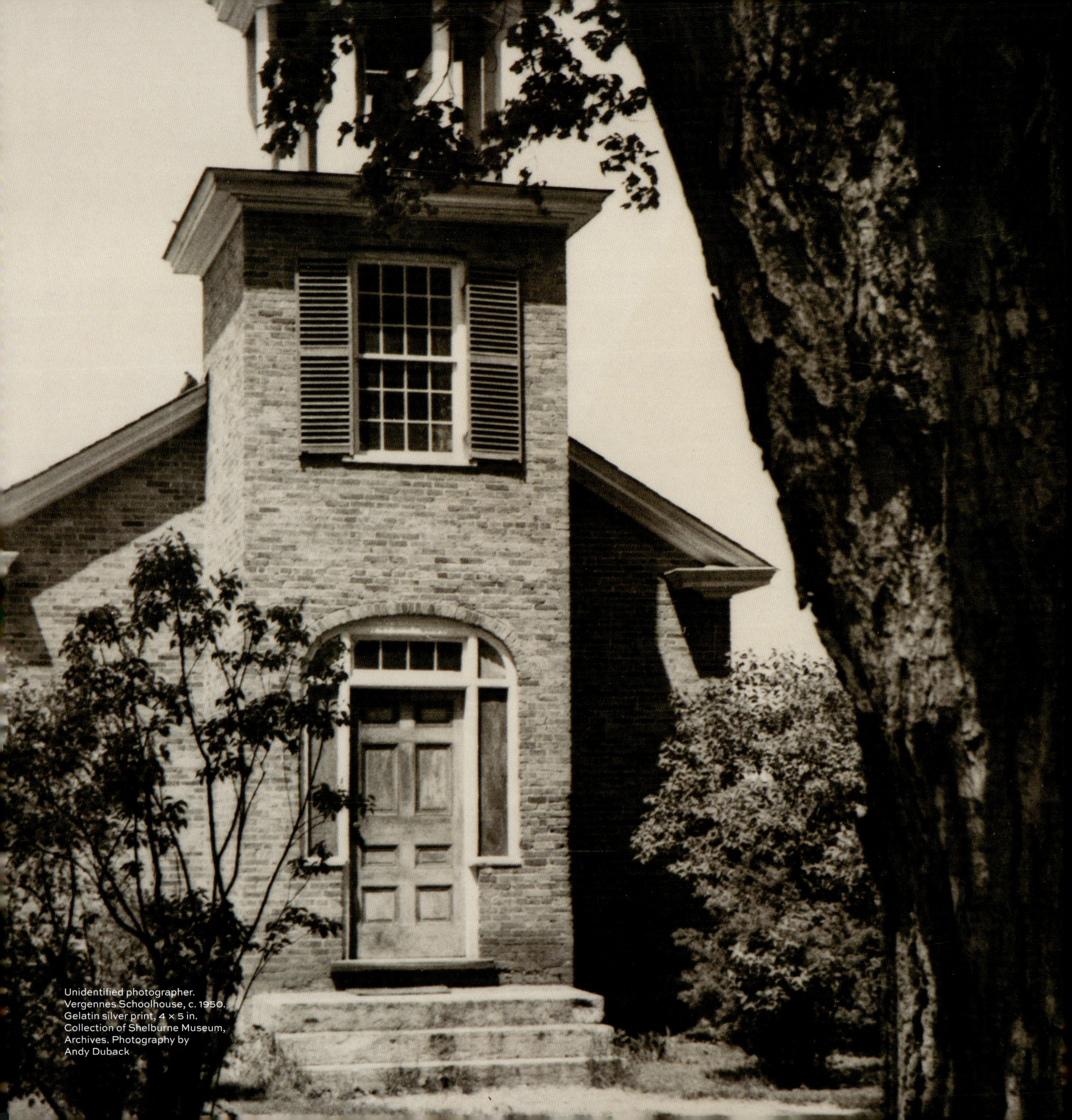

Unidentified photographer.
Vergennes Schoolhouse, c. 1950.
Gelatin silver print, 4 × 5 in.
Collection of Shelburne Museum,
Archives. Photography by
Andy Duback

THE GIFTED CHILD: SHIRLEY JACKSON AND GRANDMA MOSES

ALEXANDER NEMEROV

THE TWO DO NOT SEEM TO GO TOGETHER. The author of "The Lottery" and the painter of joyous farm and village scenes gave us, to say the least, different views of American life. Getting stoned to death and romping around the pasture fields beneath the ever-loving blue skies make for divergent dreams. The two women may stare across the page in a staged confrontation (figs. 36 and 37), but even this proximity states their separation: Shirley Jackson eyeing Grandma Moses as if askance, Moses looking cheerily, undaunted, into the eyes of her opposite. Bifocals they both have—other than that, there's nothing in common.

Look at the response to their work in the year 1948, when they both made the national news. Jackson received bags of mail, most of it hate mail, once "The Lottery" was published in the June 26, 1948, issue of *The New Yorker*. "Was the sole purpose just to give the reader a nasty impact?" one reader asked. Even Jackson's parents put it to her succinctly: "Dad and I did not care at all for your story in *The New Yorker*," her mother wrote. "Why don't you write something to cheer people up?"[1] Meanwhile, Grandma Moses—featured in a *Life* magazine story later that year—was one of the most revered painters in America, even more so after the publication of the article. Her philosophy helps explain: "What's the sense of making something to hang up on the wall," she said, "if it isn't pretty?"[2]

Pretty and nasty, and a gulf between. But Jackson and Moses were literally closer than you might think. They lived within ten miles of each other, Jackson in the town of North Bennington, Vermont, and Moses in Eagle Bridge, New York, just across the state line. Jackson, born more than

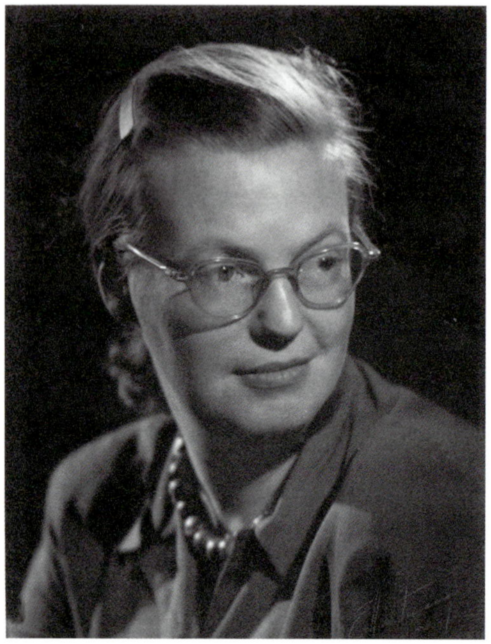

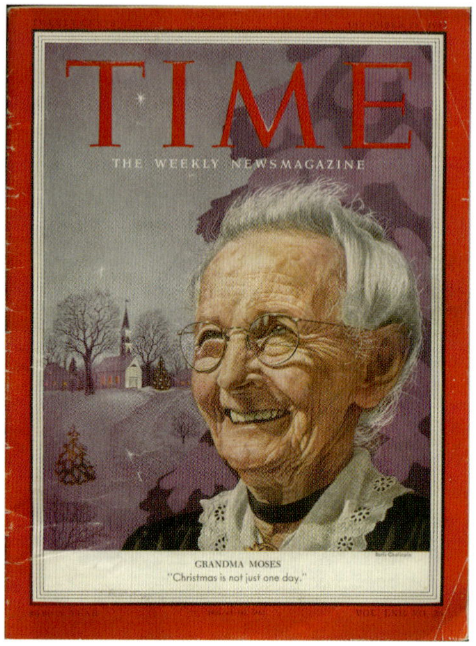

FIG. 36
Shirley Jackson, 1949. Photograph by Erich Hartmann, taken for Magnum. Courtesy of Shirley Jackson Estate

FIG. 37
December 28, 1953, cover of *Time* magazine, featuring Grandma Moses. Bennington Museum, Bequest of Margaret M. Carr, Bennington, Vermont, 1984.453.2

a half century after Moses, was nonetheless "curiously old-fashioned," in the words of her husband, the literary critic Stanley Edgar Hyman.[3] And in the year 1948, Jackson and Moses were both hard at work on their respective crafts, each imagining American village life.

Sometimes I even fancy that the opening sentences of "The Lottery" correspond to the bright aerial view of a Grandma Moses painting. "The morning of June 27th was clear and sunny, with the fresh warmth of a full-summer day; the flowers were blossoming profusely and the grass was richly green. The people of the village began to gather in the square, between the post office and the bank, around ten o'clock. . . ."[4]

Moses's 1945 painting of Bennington, Vermont—showing the town center just a few miles from North Bennington and Eagle Bridge—might almost be, if you squint your eyes, the setting for Jackson's impending disaster: the buildings, the people, the rituals of village life. And, as I keep fancying, I find it not hard to imagine a painting Grandma Moses never made—the main street, the town square, the appliquéd citizens painted in cheery array . . . all throwing rocks at one little scarecrow figure holding its hands up in double-V shapes of alarm.

Yes, I know, too personal—too much me, not enough history. Yet it is the personal that ultimately concerns me, because I am from Bennington, Vermont. I was born there in 1963, two years after Grandma Moses died at the age of 101 in nearby Hoosick Falls, New York, and two years almost to the day before Shirley Jackson died in a house not far from my family's, in North Bennington, where on the afternoon that she took a nap from which she did not wake up, dying at age forty-eight,

I may have been napping myself that very hour, three days before celebrating my second birthday. The question, you see, is personal for me, and it is not just about proximity but *inheritance*. What does it mean to come from the same place that produced Shirley Jackson and Grandma Moses? Is it at all sensible, or just plain superstitious, to think of these two figures poised respectively on my little shoulders?

And more broadly, the question for all of us is: What does it mean to inherit the past, to receive a cultural legacy, to acknowledge and own it even if we did not ask for it? We call a story like "The Lottery" and paintings like those of Grandma Moses "classic," meaning that they have outlived their time and continue to be relevant in ours, but what feeling—even a creepy, eerie feeling—is bound up with inheriting a past we did not request?

"The Lottery" speaks directly to these issues. Old Man Warner, one of the villagers, proudly announces that this is the "seventy-seventh year I been in the lottery." The tradition goes back far earlier. The black box holding the ballots dates to the time before Old Man Warner was born, and rumor has it that this black box was made of parts of a previous black box, a remnant of the time when the villagers, then fewer in number, used wood chips instead of paper to draw lots. It is plain enough: the townsfolk have inherited a practice they follow blindly.

Tradition of this kind in Jackson's story is closely linked to generations—to families. Legacies pass in the blood. In the opening sentences children gather in the town square, boys and girls freshly out of school that June. When it comes time to select lots, the head of each household draws for his family. In the case of Bill Hutchinson, unlucky enough to draw the paper with the black spot, the fateful slip then requires a separate lottery in which each member of Hutchinson's household—father, mother, and three children—must draw again. Tessie Hutchinson, Bill's wife, selects the unfortunate paper and is stoned to death. "It isn't fair, it isn't right," she insists.[5] What she means is, she did not really choose her fate; she went about it blind. Back somehow in the generations—gestating in the black box—is the ill-starred fortune that's been waiting for Tessie all along. She did not ask for it, but she was born for this day.

Jackson's conception of the story was similar. It came to her unbidden; she gave birth to it. As she described the genesis, she was pushing the stroller of her two-year-old daughter Joanne up a hill one morning, returning from a trip to the grocery store, when the idea appeared. She returned, put Joanne in her crib, and began working on the story, finishing it before her son Laurie came home from kindergarten for lunch. And what was this demon child she gave birth to that day? A horror story labeled the scariest one ever written, equal parts Hawthorne and the Holocaust, a kind of

FIG. 38
Peter Paul Rubens. *Deucalion and Pyrrha, Creators of Humanity after the First Flood (Ovid, Metamorphoses)*, 1636–37. Oil on panel, 10 3/8 × 16 3/8 in. Museo del Prado, Madrid. Erich Lessing / Art Resource, NY

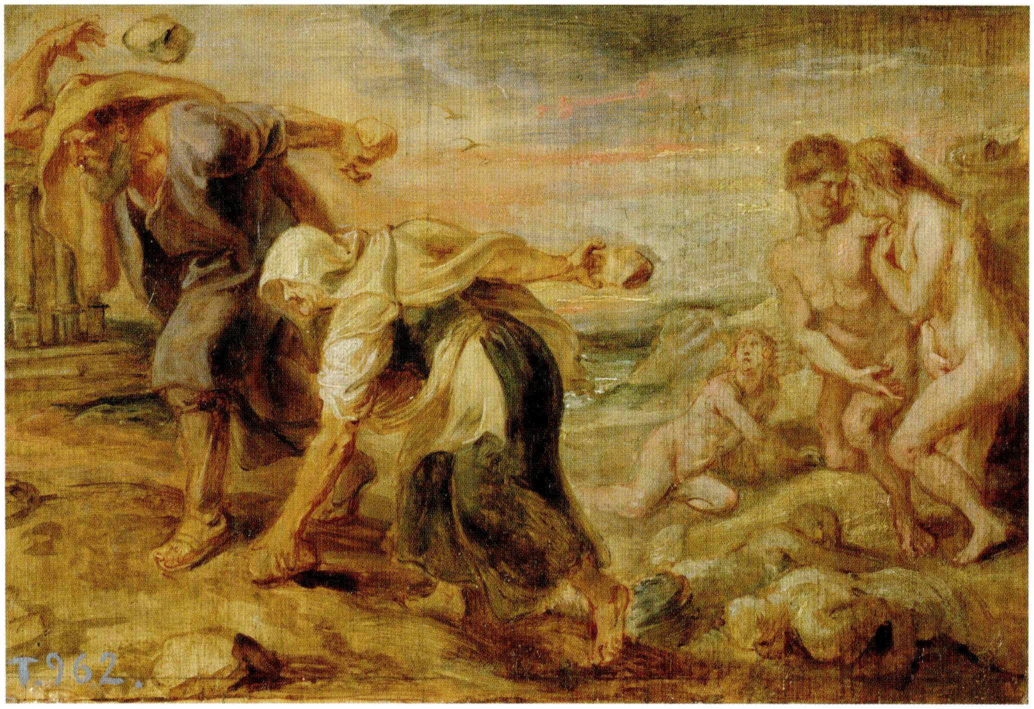

birthmark that would tattoo the writer as an object of envy, fascination, and hatred. The mail that came in bags to *The New Yorker*, hate-missiles of different kinds, resembled the stones of the story. Like Tessie Hutchinson, Jackson did not choose her fate.

The fact that "The Lottery" came from out of the blue—"on a bright June morning," Jackson recalled, "with blue skies and warm sun and no heavenly signs to warn me that my morning's work was anything but just another story"—makes the genesis of it all the more uncanny.[6] Colleagues of Hyman, Jackson's husband, believed that he had planted the idea and that "in return she had spilled out the story almost automatically," according to Jackson's biographer Judy Oppenheimer.[7] Hyman himself claimed later that his wife wrote the story while she was the "dummy" in a bridge game. "Wandering around aimlessly," with nothing else to do until the others finished the hand, she came back with "The Lottery."[8] In the folklore of the story's creation, Jackson is just a dummy—she writes almost "automatically"—as if the tale had been ripening, growing, inside her, and she were just the vessel. "Lottery in June, corn be heavy soon," a saying of Old Man Warner's reputed to be Hyman's one genuine contribution to the story, captures this sense of gestation.[9] Things grow inside us; it is a mystery. "She's written a real masterpiece," Hyman told a friend, "and I don't know where it came from."[10]

The curse of it is that the birth of such things is so linked to sterility and death. The stones are everywhere, from the ones the boys gather in the opening sentences, to the thud of the one that

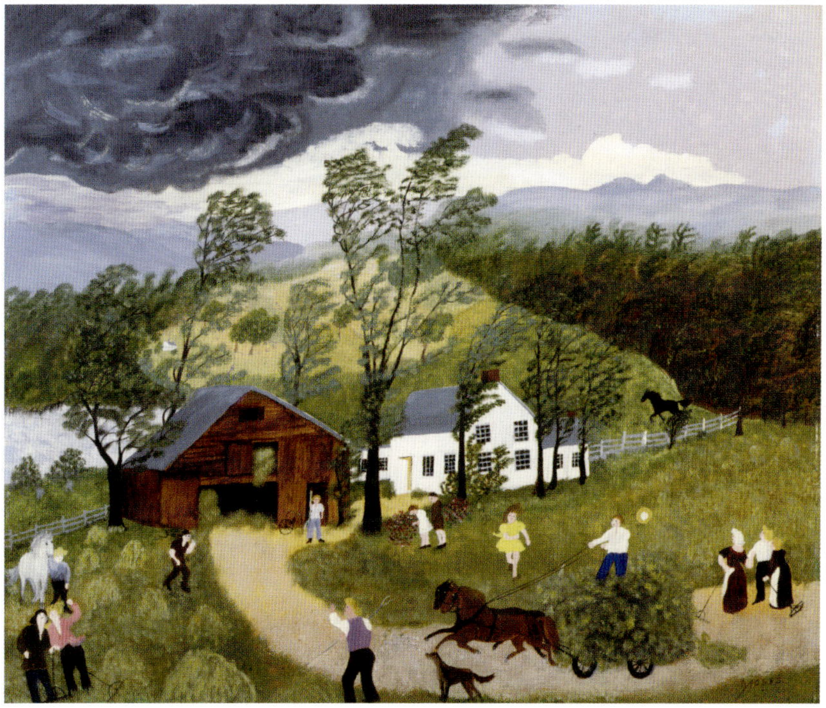

FIG. 39
Anna Mary Robertson ("Grandma") Moses. *Thunderstorm*, 1948. Oil on pressed wood, 20 3/4 x 24 3/4 in. Private Collection

hits Tessie Hutchinson on the side of her head at the end, to the handful of pebbles that the villagers thoughtfully give Tessie's toddler so that he, too, can take part. Deucalion and Pyrrha, in the tale told by Ovid, repopulate the barren earth by throwing stones over their shoulders—men emerging from Deucalion's stones, women from Pyrrha's, as in Peter Paul Rubens's rendition of the myth (fig. 38). But in "The Lottery," the stones are the sterility of the village, its deathly rite of renewal and regeneration—all those families, all those kids—linked to the taking, rather than giving, of life. We could call the conception of such a story Jackson's "inspiration," but that is putting too heavenly a word on so dark a thing. For the writer, the story is not a literary *creation*, a virgin birth, an Annunciation from the sky, but smooth and rounded like a tummy, an alien baby, a sinister black dot that has chosen her.

"Genealogy"—what better word is there for the art and life of Grandma Moses? Mother of ten children, five of whom survived into adulthood; grandmother to eleven grandchildren; great-grandmother to seventeen more, Anna Mary Robertson Moses came from the prodigious families of mid-nineteenth-century upstate New York—she had nine siblings herself. And her paintings often recall her childhood. *The Thunderstorm*, a Moses painting of 1948, recalls an episode that occurred when she was seven years old, a terrific summer storm in 1867 (fig. 39). Such pictures bridge eras as surely as if memories were genetic, waiting to be born again in the mind of someone who was herself born the year Lincoln was elected president and who remembered the black bunting draped in an adjacent village after his assassination.

Consider a remarkable photograph of "Grandma" Moses when she was fifteen (fig. 40). Looking for the similarity of features between the adolescent girl and the winsome grandmother, sure enough finding the grandmother in the girl, we marvel at the continuities in time. The genealogical relation of childhood to old age is as sure as the organic connection between Lincoln's era and Eisenhower's. Time itself appears genetic.

So does the making of art. Far from producing sterile portrayals of the olden days, fruitless nostalgic stones, Grandma Moses worked by a creative process of organic memory and sensation. It was in her blood. Her father was a painter; her sisters were painters; she taught her own children to paint. The grape juice and other dyes that as a girl she employed to make her pictures carried forth into the bright colors of her mature work. Just as the gulley of iron-rich soil unearthed by the thunderstorm flood of 1867 led her father to make paint from this earthy deposit—paint, she said, that in the 1950s she saw still coating many red barns in the vicinity of Eagle Bridge—so her paintings came from nature and passed indelibly through the generations. It was all in the family.

Which makes the gift Moses gave to seven-year-old Diana Korzenik in November 1948 seemingly such an unambiguously happy gesture. Korzenik had come to Eagle Bridge with her parents, who responded to that year's story in *Life* about the painter, and Moses had kindly offered to exchange one of her pictures for one of the young girl's. The painting Moses gave Korzenik, and which Korzenik has recently given to the Bennington Museum, is a picture of a farmhouse much like the painter's house in Eagle Bridge (fig. 19). Small, precious, child-sized, the painting shows a white house in the white snow, the snow glittering with sparkles that Moses added to the paint.

Here again is organic time, tradition passed down from one generation to the next. The gift goes to the little girl, who holds the legacy in her hands before bestowing it, gift into gift, to future generations at the museum. "What a strange thing is memory, and hope," said Moses in her 1951 autobiography. "One looks backward, the other forward. The one is of today, the other is the Tomorrow."[11] Meeting Korzenik now, I am in awe of a person who has met Grandma Moses, who was in turn a person with memories of Abraham Lincoln's time. Call it a lineage of history.

But there is a more unsettling way to think of it. Who is to say what unaccountable sleight of hand, what uncanny talent, has caused this picture to come into being? "Grandma Moses paints like a child," her art dealer Otto Kallir said in 1948, "but like one child in a million."[12] The maker of the picture was somehow chosen, among almost everyone who ever lived her span of years, to call up—to summon forth—vivid and mysterious memories and dreams of a long-ago time. If almost alone in her a certain past survives—incubated, warm and snug—this is a stranger generation than the stuff of family trees.

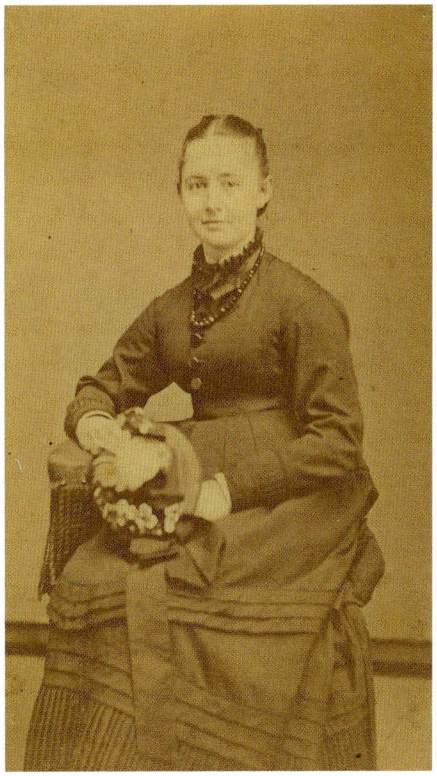

FIG. 40
Unidentified photographer. *Anna Mary Robertson ("Grandma") Moses, age 15*, 1875. Albumen print, 4 × 2½ in. Bennington Museum, Bennington, Vermont, 2011.272

The images came from nowhere, unaccountable, not least because they started appearing so suddenly, when Moses was in her seventies, when she took up painting in earnest nine years after her husband's death. She did so because it kept her busy and because it was easier on her rheumatic hands than making worsted pictures. But more than pragmatic activity was involved. There and then the painting tradition—the painting genealogy—not just of her father, not just of her younger sister Sarah, who died when she was only in her thirties, and who was apparently the much better artist, but of Grandma Moses herself, of who she was when she used to skip ahead of her brothers to pick up little birds back in the 1860s, this deep past—somehow appeared, bright and lush, intact, out of nowhere. Grandma Moses was the medium of herself.

No wonder the sparkles in the snow feel like a kind of magic dust thrown over the scene. The past gets conjured up in a snow-globe vision like Charles Foster Kane's in the movie *Citizen Kane* (1941), a poignant memory transmitted Rosebud-like through the ether. The child's-eye view, everything small, delicate, survives the child, survives even the woman who was the child, and becomes the home of another little girl into whose hands it is passed on. Having the aspect of a wrapped present—a precious pink-and-white package, neat and tied and gifted in the weeks before the holidays—the little painting comes on only one condition: that it never be opened. A box within a box, a nest of clapboards and eaves, chimneys and sparkling lace, it is a gift of remoteness, a scene

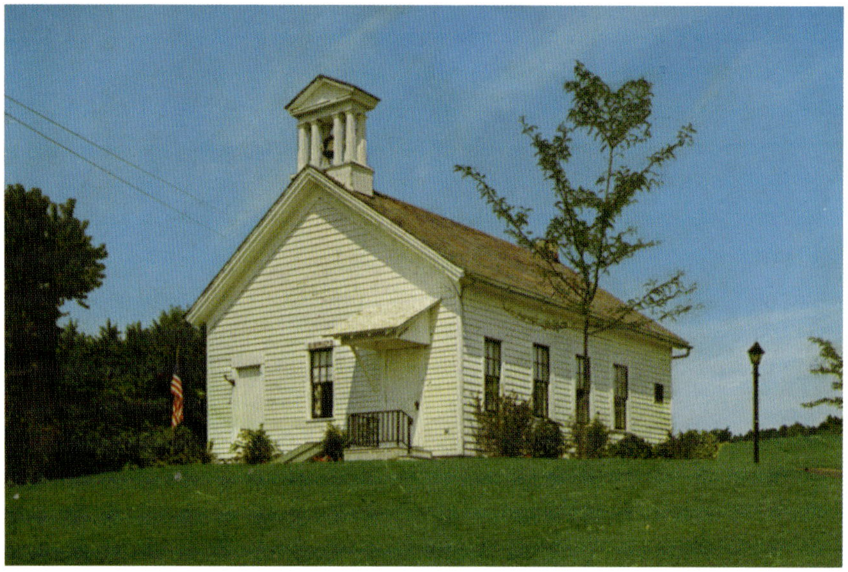

FIG. 41
Grandma Moses Schoolhouse after it was moved to Moses's farm, c. 1960. Printed color postcard. 3 1/2 × 5 1/2 in. Bennington Museum, Gift of Ruth M. Battles, Bennington, Vermont, 1992.137.2

from faraway and long ago, transported so stunningly into little hands that the last thing anyone would ever want to do is look too much into it. In magical terms, the painting is enchanted.

Meanwhile, the writer in North Bennington practiced her own sorcery. "Magic is the word that has been woven around the literary personality of Shirley Jackson," wrote the *New York Times*'s Harvey Breit in 1949, discussing the author's newfound fame.[13] Sure, it was a cliché, a marketing phenomenon: "There have been several odd witchcraft cases in the papers," Jackson wrote to her parents that year, "and it all mounts up into a general interest in magic and such" that her publishers were busy exploiting. And Jackson played along, regaling a clueless Associated Press writer that April with "stories about black magic and incantations and the practical application of witchcraft to everyday life."[14] But in truth Jackson was superstitious, a woman well known for wearing a necklace of small carved ivory skulls, keeping voodoo dolls of her enemies, and elaborately avoiding electrical sockets in her house for fear of the bad energies they might impart.

Literature was no less part of the wizardry. Where do stories come from? How are they summoned? For Jackson, they came out of nowhere, like the idea for "The Lottery," or like the human leg that mysteriously washes up on shore, unexplained, in another of her stories called "Pillar of Salt."[15] From a distance the leg looks like a mannequin's, but on closer inspection it proves to be, yes, an actual human leg. The visionary sees horrible things, evidence of catastrophe, not because she wants to—in fact, the gift of such sight, as for Lot's wife, is distinctly a petrifying burden—but because she cannot help it. "It was not something she would have wished on herself necessarily," Jackson's biographer Oppenheimer notes, "not an ability that made her life easier, certainly. It just *was*."[16]

To inherit gifts from magicians such as Jackson and Moses is then a curious thing. As long as we do not feel singled out by their magic, we remain impervious to its charms. We go to the school of the past, much as we might enter curiously into the old Vergennes Schoolhouse, the first building moved to the Shelburne Museum in 1946 (see page 72), right in the prime years of Jackson and Moses, or the schoolhouse moved to Bennington Museum in 1973 and used as a memorial gallery to the painter (fig. 41). We take it in and note it and go to the next place. No desk is ours. Every desk is ours. But when we feel chosen by some past tradition, singled out by it—chosen much as Mrs. Hutchinson was—not through any decision of our own but rather as a matter of fate, then it is another matter.

Then "The Lottery" goes from being a universal story—a story taught at school—to something chillingly specific, a tale that at its core targets a reader, some reader out there, for instance you or me. Then we feel called out to experience a physical sensation of the unjustness and cruelty of the world. Maybe that reader, in Jackson's case, is every reader she ever wanted to reach; such is the singling-out power of her story. But beneath that vast acclaim is the oddity of living within the shadow of its creation, of creating it (as she did), or of growing up in its midst (as I did), of being, somehow, *given* it. All of which makes it possible to cry, for someone who never asked for such a gift, to speak out just as Tessie Hutchinson did: "It isn't fair, it isn't right." But we must follow the rules and inherit our fate.

And of the little painting given to Diana Korzenik? It is sweet and heartfelt, the opposite of Mrs. Hutchinson's black spot. But it, too, comes from a deep past, an ancient tradition, and it, too, seeks out the person fated to own it. We think of the past as a dream of genealogies, of the wooden and brick and painted legacies of "our" history, but each object is made of a special separateness. And deep in the heart of each thing is the quiet of how it came to be, and perhaps the additional silence of how it came to choose us who have come to feel a special connection to it.

Superstition and history are not supposed to go together. One of our ways of assuring ourselves that there is no necromancy is to think of family histories, of creations that get passed along the generations, as natural as that. Definite objects with definite purposes adorn our days, swinging the past around to the present and back again in a farm field of sunny vistas and ritually returning seasons. But to be chosen for what we did not ask for—to be the recipient of the uncertain gift of the past, traditions hallowed and venerable, not to be avoided or shirked—is to live with a magic we will never understand.

NOTES

1. Shirley Jackson scrapbook, 1948, 1958, undated, Box 51, Library of Congress, Washington, DC, Manuscript Archives Department.

2. Anna Mary Robertson Moses, quoted in Bruce Bliven Jr., "Grandma Moses Has a Birthday," *Life* 25, no. 17 (Oct. 25, 1948): 76–78.

3. Stanley Edgar Hyman, ed., *The Magic of Shirley Jackson* (New York: Farrar, Straus and Giroux, 1965), vii–viii.

4. Shirley Jackson, "The Lottery," *The New Yorker* (June 26, 1948): 25.

5. Ibid., 25.

6. Hyman, *Magic of Shirley Jackson*, 36.

7. Judy Oppenheimer, *Private Demons: The Life of Shirley Jackson* (New York: Putnam, 1988), 130.

8. Jackson, "The Lottery," 25.

9. Ibid., 25.

10. Stanley Edgar Hyman, to the poet Ben Belitt.

11. Grandma Moses, *My Life's History*, ed. Otto Kallir (New York: Harper & Brothers, 1952), 3.

12. Otto Kallir, quoted in Bliven, "Grandma Moses Has a Birthday," 78.

13. Harvey Breit, "Talk with Miss Jackson," *New York Times Book Review*, June 26, 1949, 15.

14. Ibid., 15.

15. Shirley Jackson, "Pillar of Salt," *Mademoiselle* (Oct. 1948).

16. Oppenheimer, *Private Demons*, 18.

PLATE 22

Anna Mary Robertson ("Grandma") Moses

BENNINGTON

1953. Oil on pressed wood, 18 × 24 in.

Bennington Museum, Museum purchase, Bennington, Vermont, 1986.347

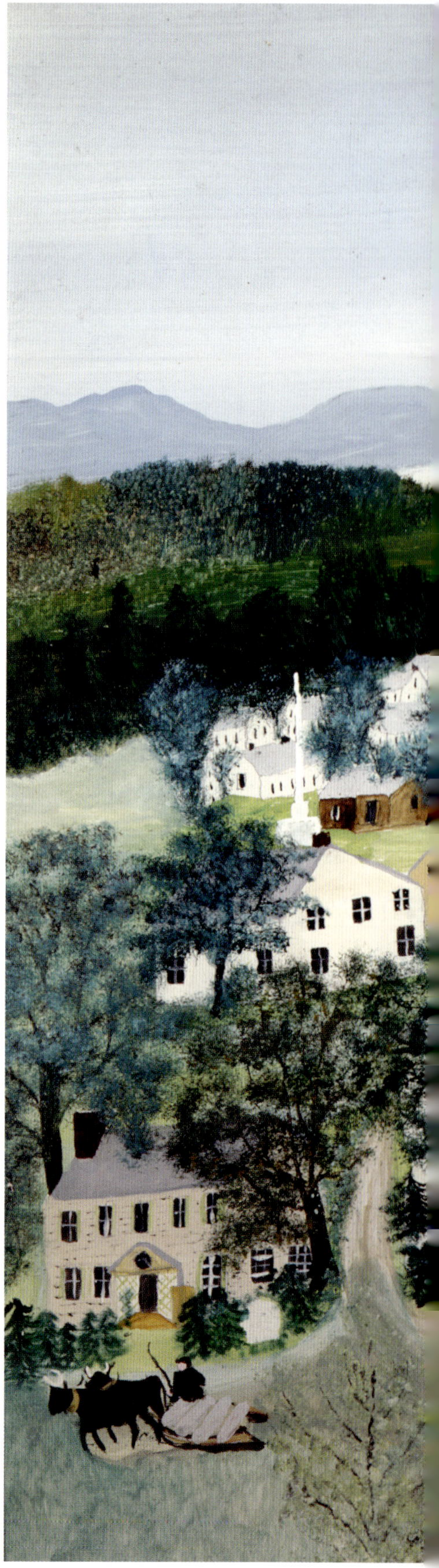

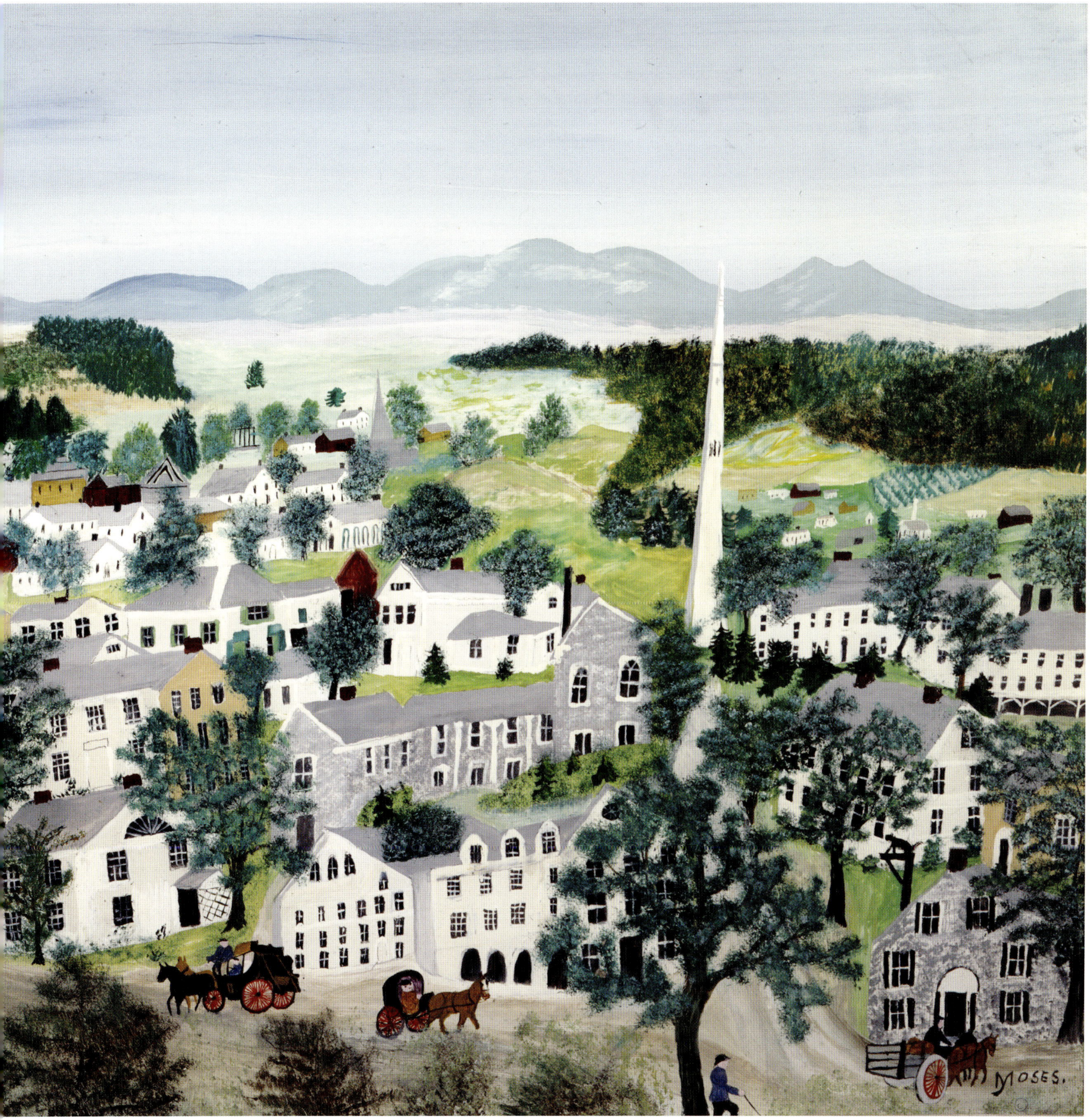
MOSES.

PLATE 23

Anna Mary Robertson ("Grandma") Moses

HALLOWEEN

1956. Oil on pressed wood, 14 × 24 in.

Bennington Museum, Museum purchase, Bennington, Vermont, 1999.71

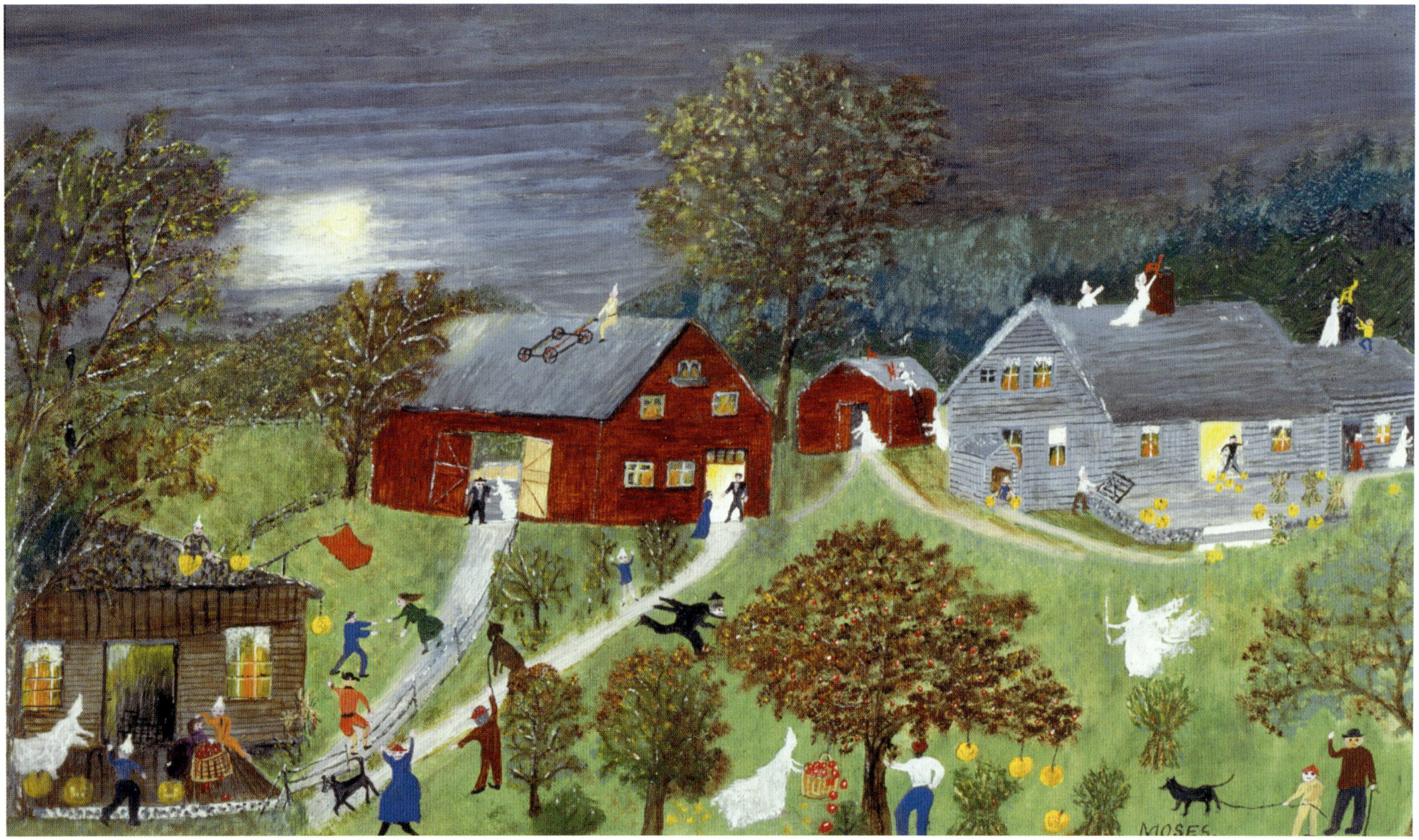

PLATE 24

Anna Mary Robertson ("Grandma") Moses

HOOSICK HILLS

1956. Oil on pressed wood, 16 × 24 in.

Cheney Library Collection, Hoosick Falls, New York

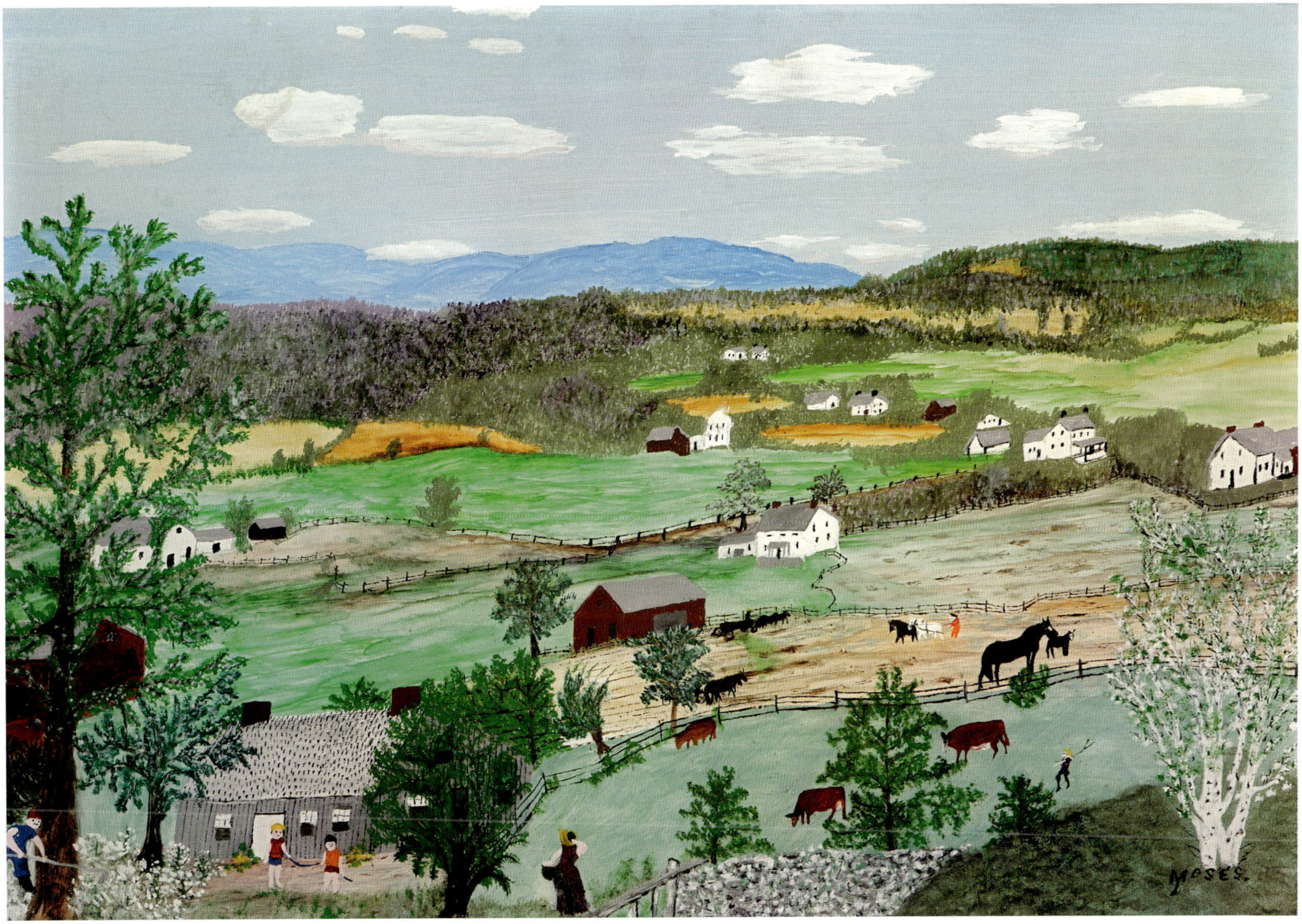

PLATE 25

Anna Mary Robertson ("Grandma") Moses

THE BATTLE OF BENNINGTON

1953. Oil on pressed wood, 18 × 30 in.

Bennington Museum, Gift of Carol and Arnold Haynes, Bennington, Vermont, 2014.40

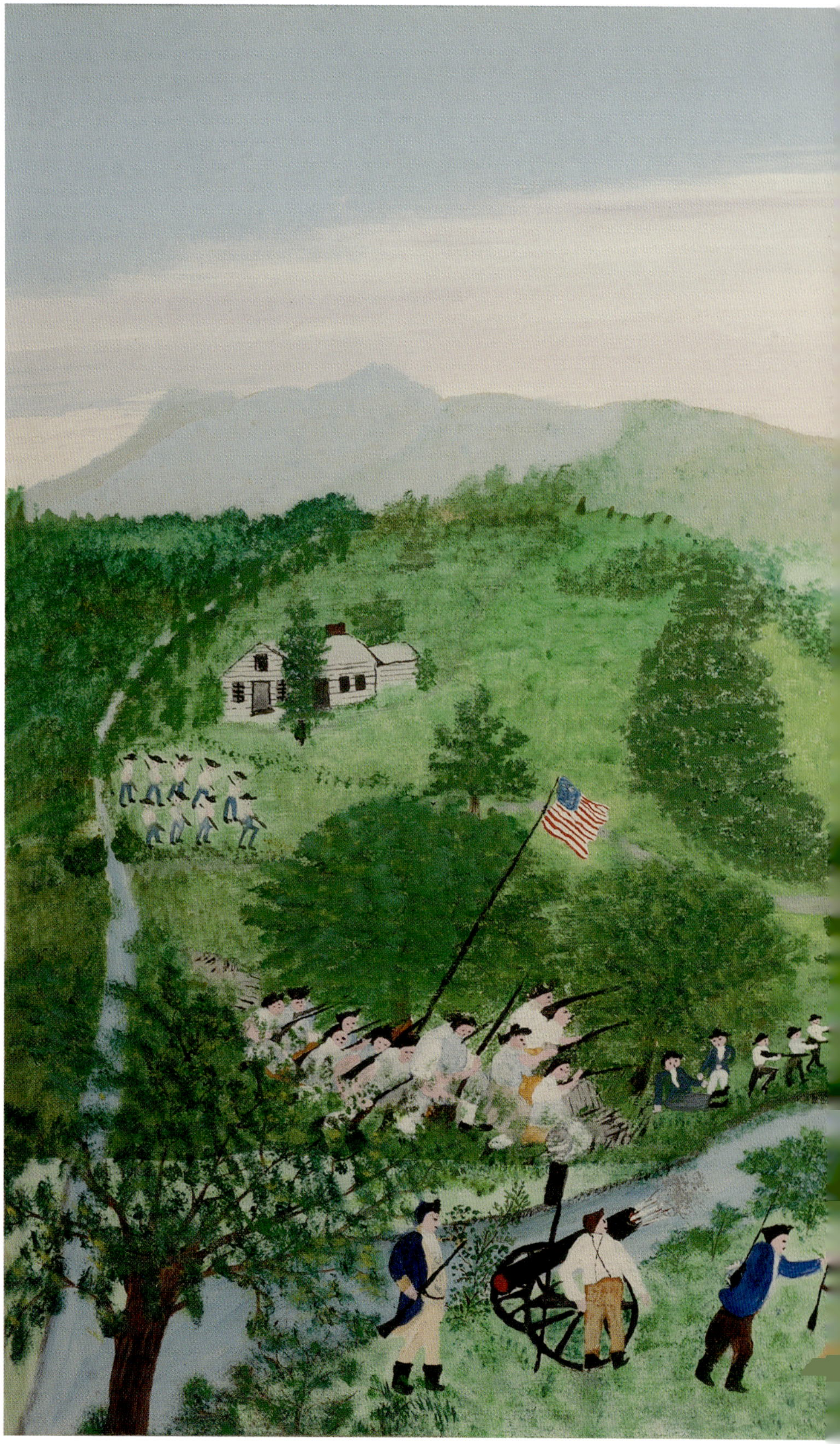

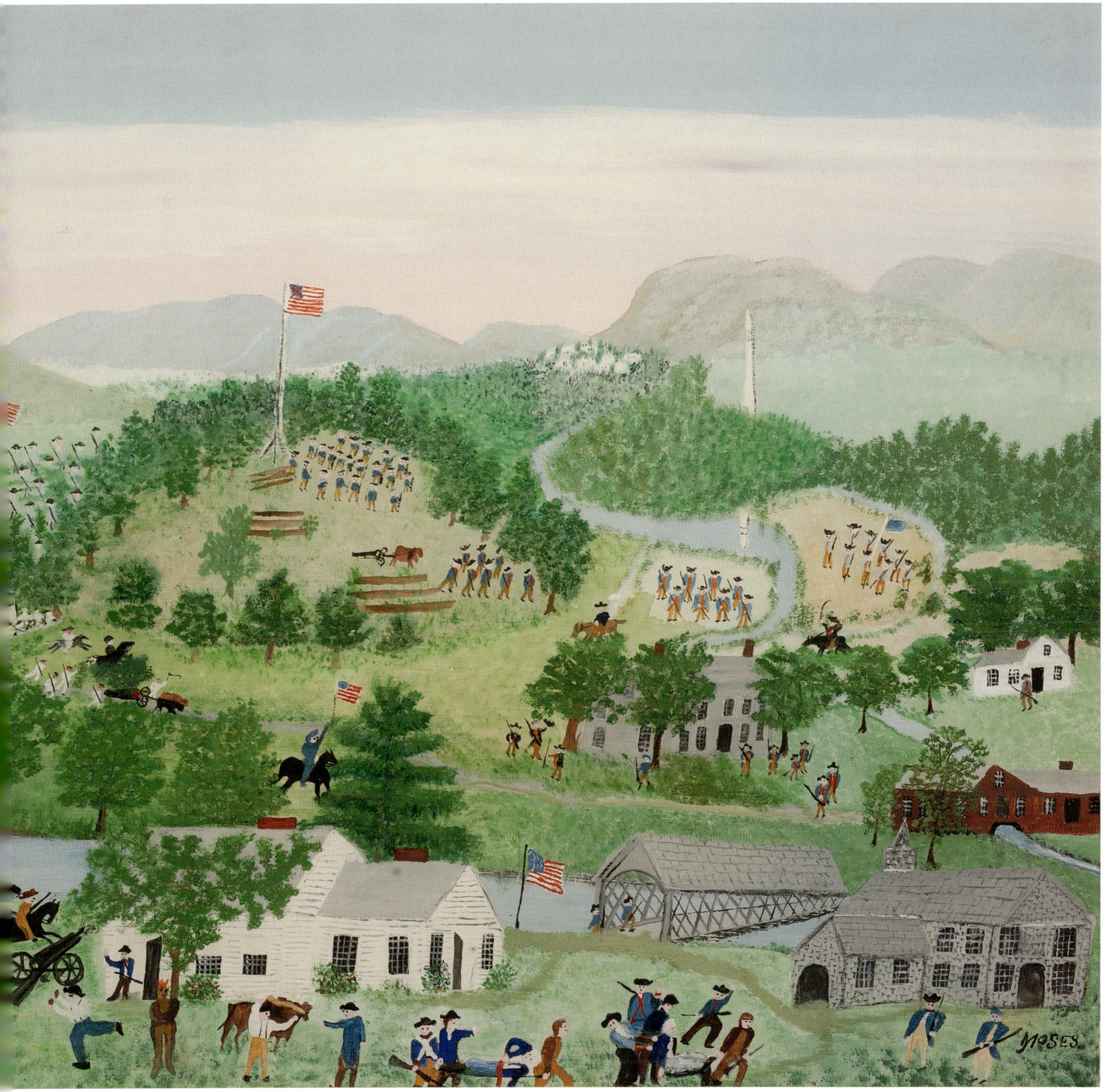
MOSES.

PLATE 26

Anna Mary Robertson ("Grandma") Moses

THE POND

1957. Oil on pressed wood, 7 ⅞ × 11 ⅞ in.

Bennington Museum, Bequest of Margaret M. Carr, Bennington, Vermont, 1998.5

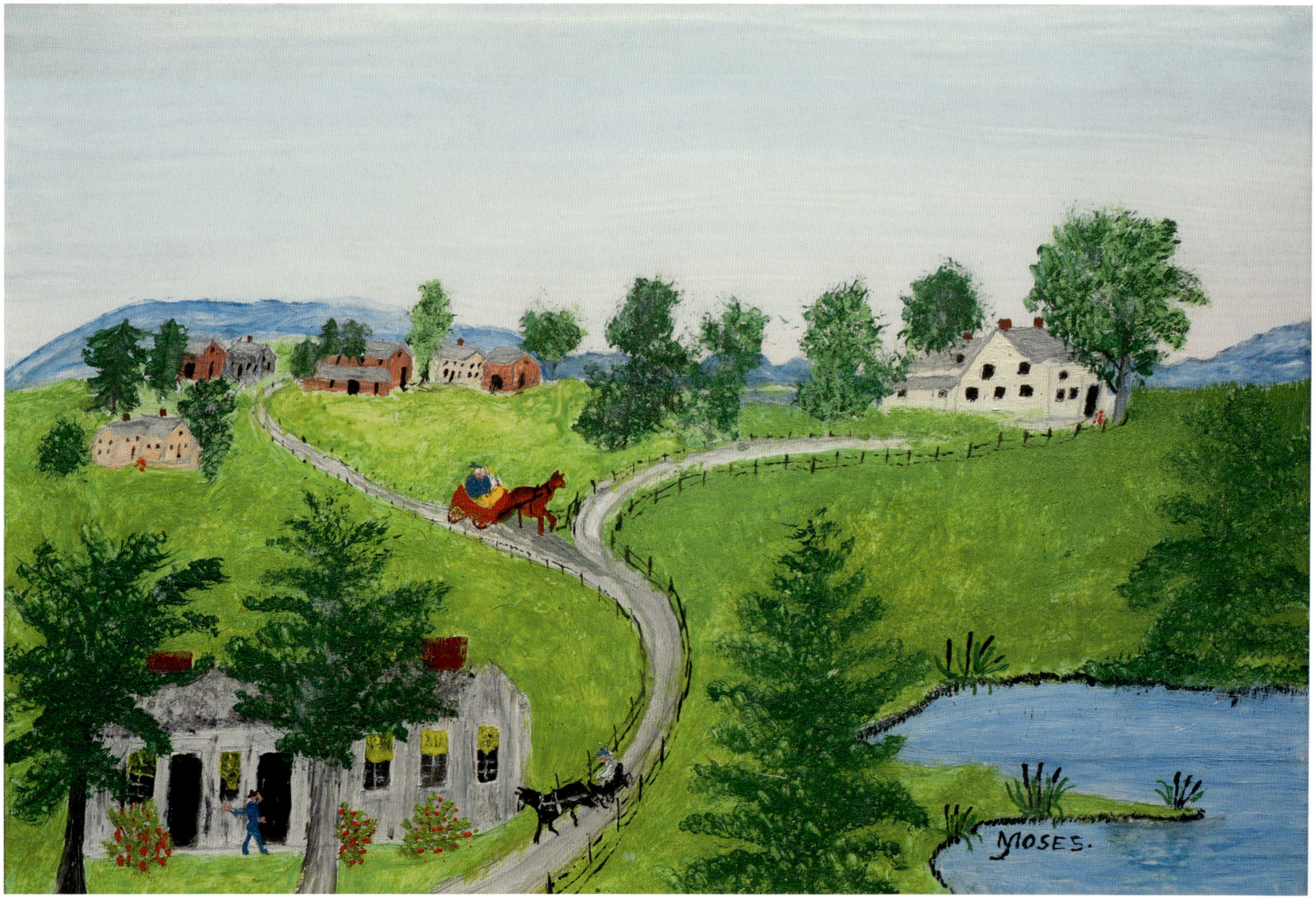

PLATE 27

Anna Mary Robertson ("Grandma") Moses

PULL BOYS

1957. Oil on pressed wood, 8 × 13 in.

Bennington Museum, Bequest of Margaret M. Carr, Bennington, Vermont, 1998.4

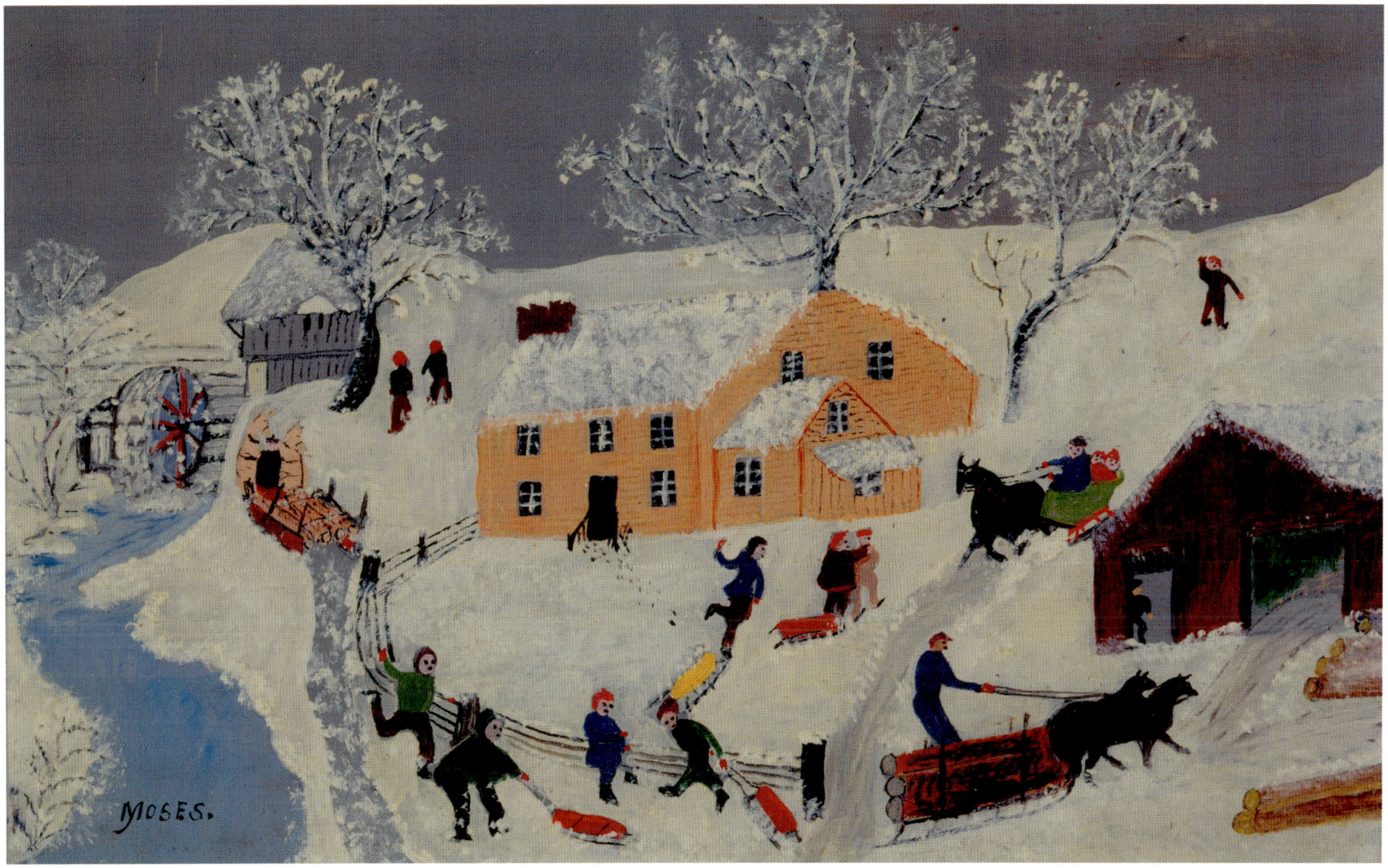

PLATE 28

Anna Mary Robertson ("Grandma") Moses

FIRST SNOW

1957. Oil on pressed wood, 8 × 12 in.
Bennington Museum, Bequest of Beatrice the Countess Gosford, Bennington, Vermont, 2003.133

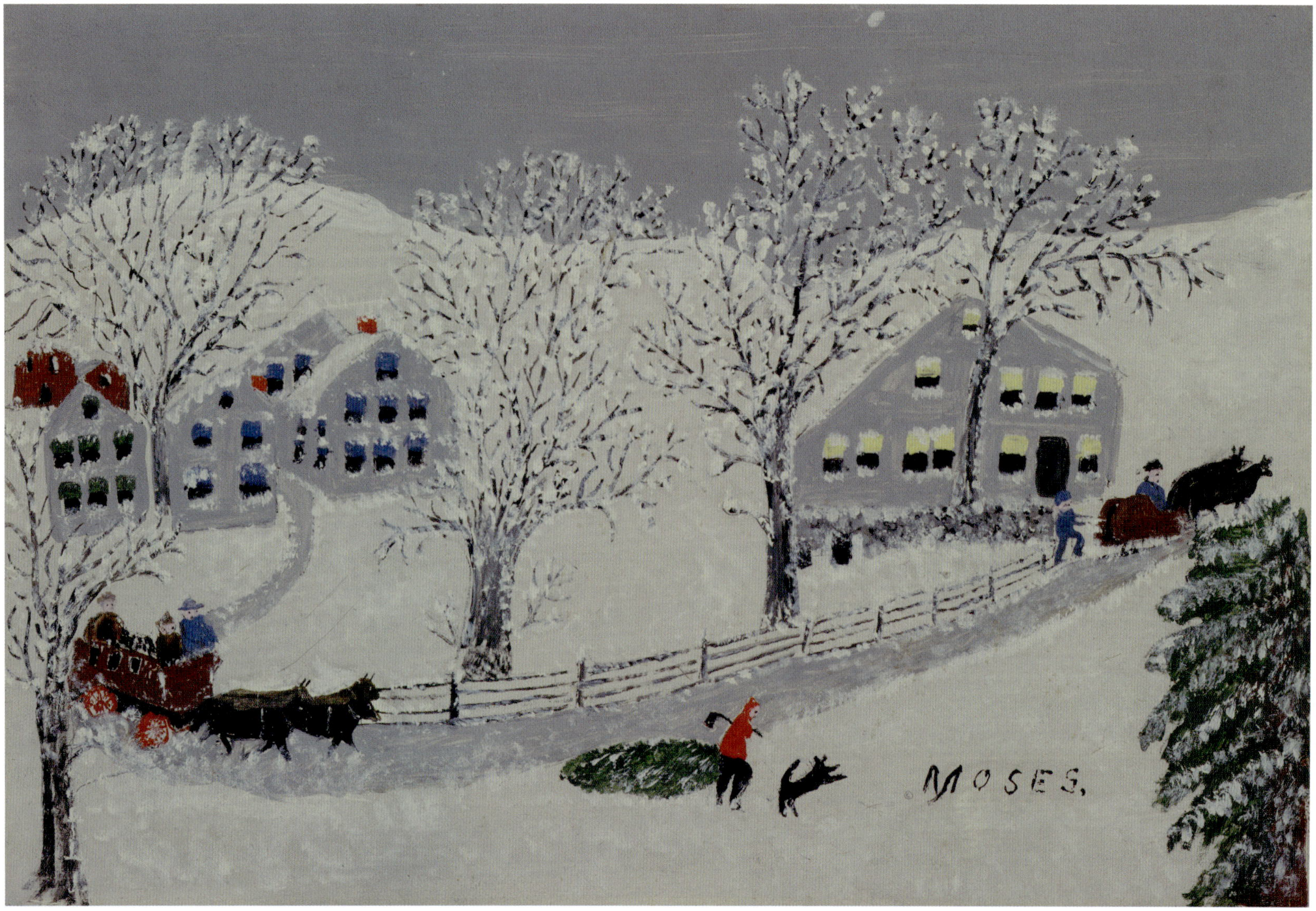

PLATE 29

Anna Mary Robertson ("Grandma") Moses

AUTUMN

1959. Oil on pressed wood, 8 × 12 in.

Bennington Museum, Bequest of Margaret M. Carr, Bennington, Vermont, 1998.3

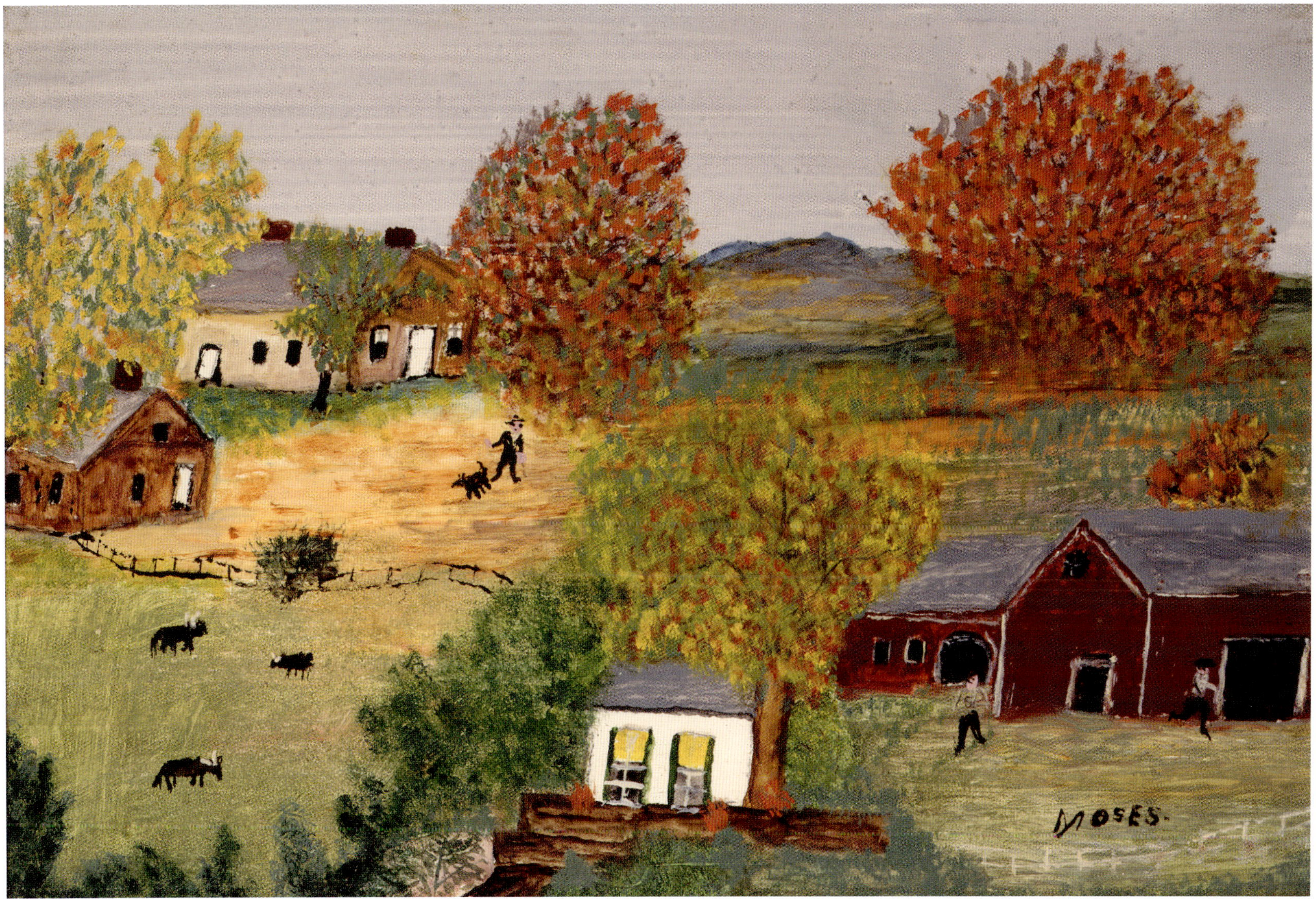

PLATE 30

Anna Mary Robertson ("Grandma") Moses

ONE HORSE SLEIGH

1959. Oil on pressed wood, 16 × 24 in.

Bennington Museum, Museum purchase, Bennington, Vermont, 2003.26

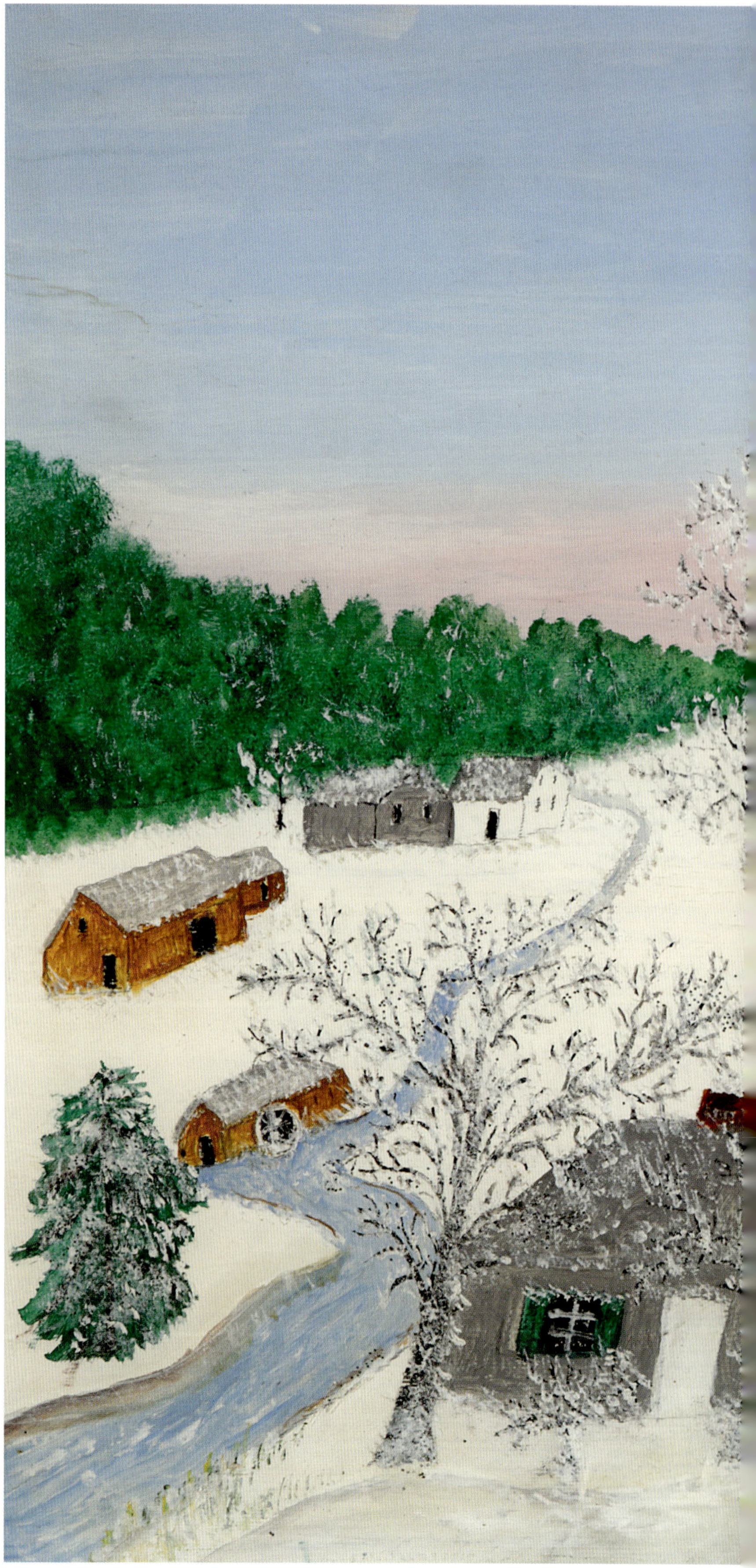

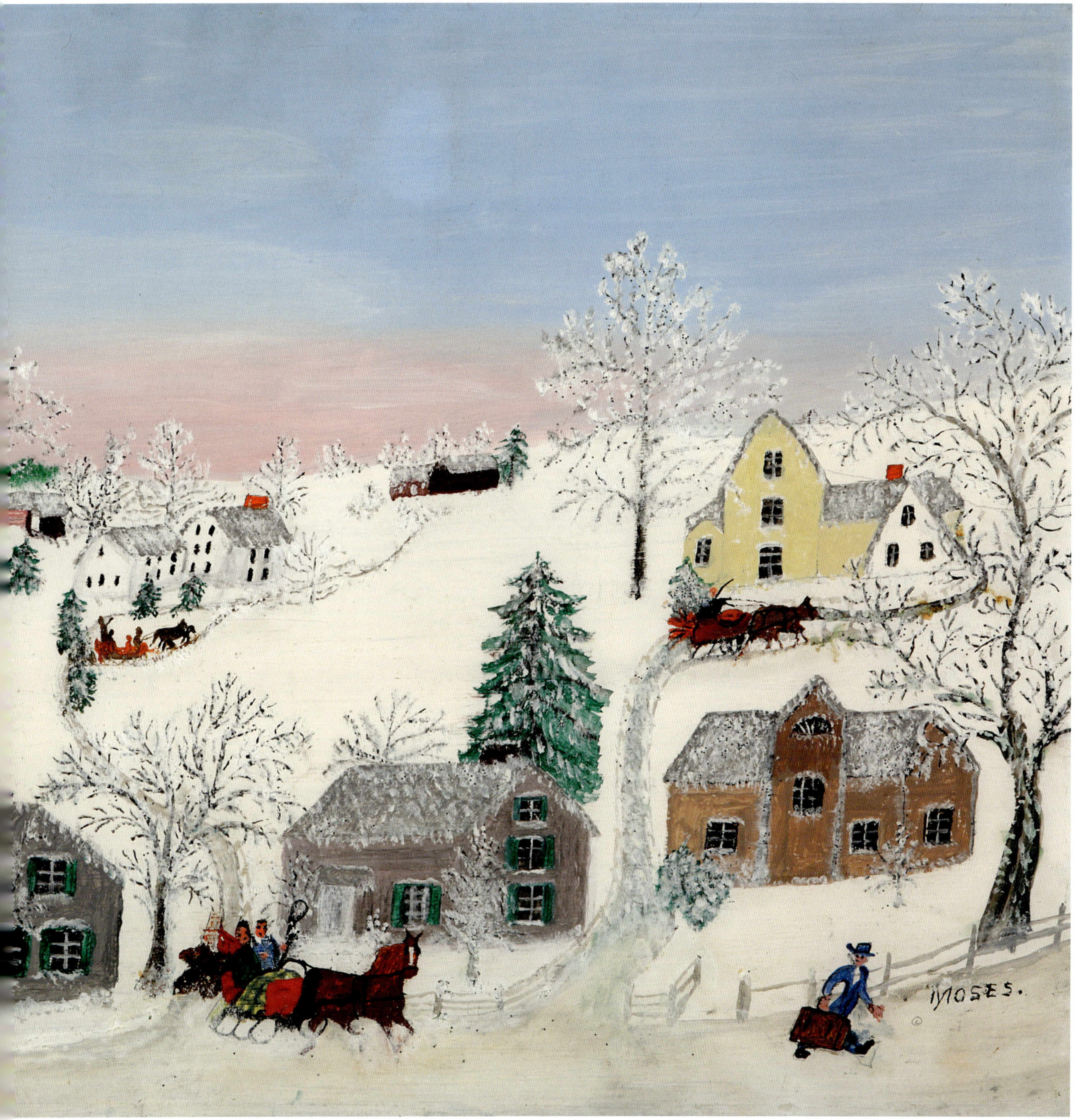
MOSES.

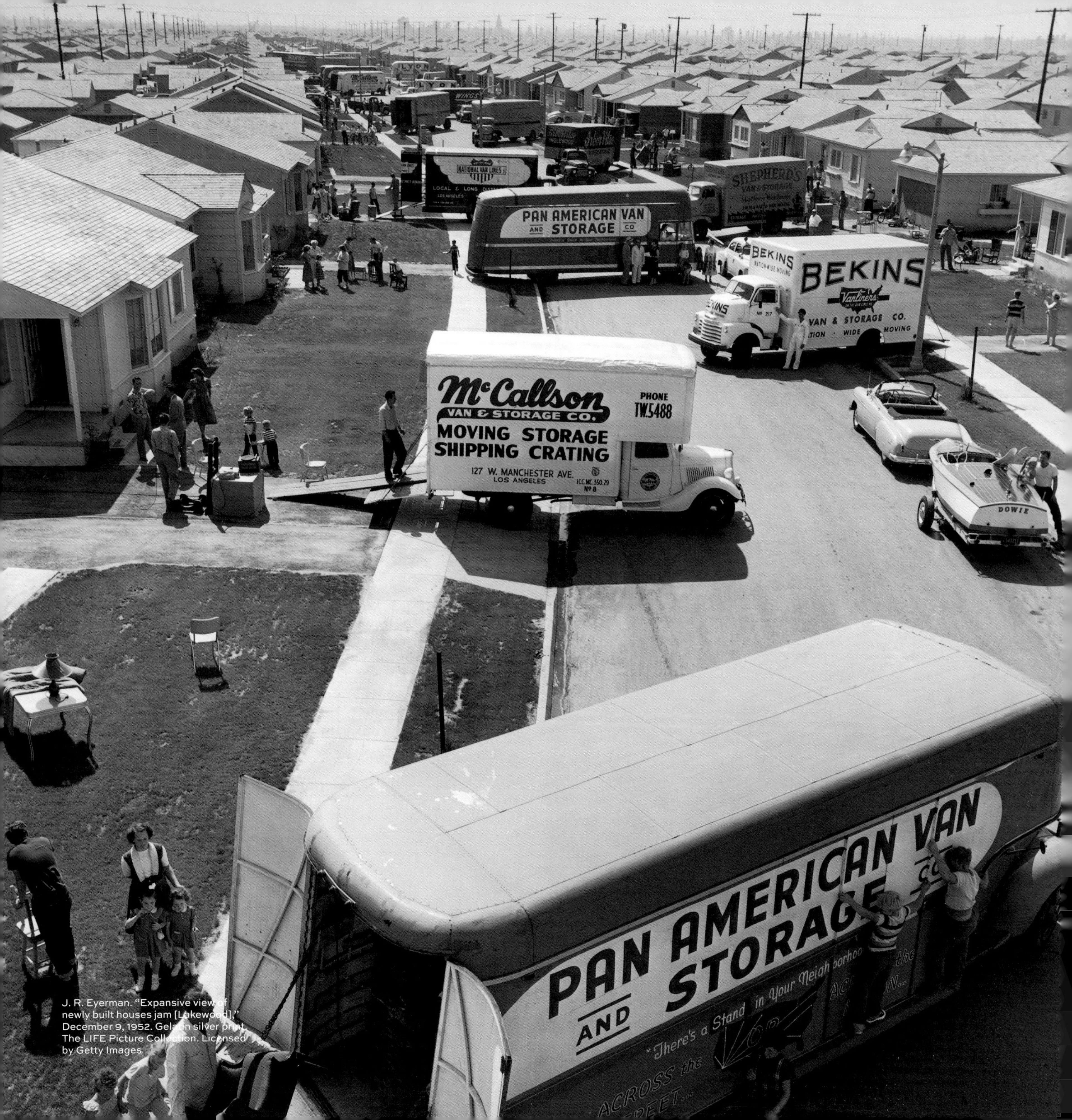

J. R. Eyerman. "Expansive view of newly built houses jam [Lakewood]," December 9, 1952. Gelatin silver print. The LIFE Picture Collection. Licensed by Getty Images

THE NEW DETACHED HOUSE: GRANDMA MOSES AND 1950s AMERICA

THOMAS DENENBERG

THE PAINTINGS OF GRANDMA MOSES engendered a sense of community in an era marked by widespread perceptions of alienation in the United States. As the "American Dream" came to be defined as life in a single-family dwelling on the outskirts of an urban center, a sentimental mythology of domesticity evolved as an answer to the pervasive anxiety engendered by the demographic relocation to the suburbs (opposite). Anna Mary Robertson Moses, understood in her lifetime as a memory painter, an artist seemingly from an earlier era and rural place, provided an ideology of hearth and home for the new patterns of life in suburban America. Often taken in her day to be *sui generis* and apart from the times in which she lived, the popularity and authority of Moses's artistic vision derived not from her singularity but rather from her role as heir to myriad traditions in American visual culture.

SMALL-TOWN AMERICA

Consider the painting *Cambridge* (fig. 42). Painted during the depths of World War II in 1944, with the United States fully mobilized to combat Fascism in Europe and Asia, *Cambridge* depicts a valley settlement in upstate New York, just northwest of Bennington, Vermont. *Cambridge,* central in what the art historian Roger Cardinal and others have called "Grandma Moses Country," is a quiescent microcosm.[1] Sheltered between the viewer and the distant mountains is a village rife with implication for the period as well as references to the American scene of the previous century. Moses invites the

FIG. 42
Anna Mary Robertson ("Grandma") Moses. *Cambridge*, 1944. Oil on pressed wood, 20 1/4 × 24 3/8 in. Collection of Shelburne Museum, Museum purchase, Shelburne, Vermont, 1961-210.1

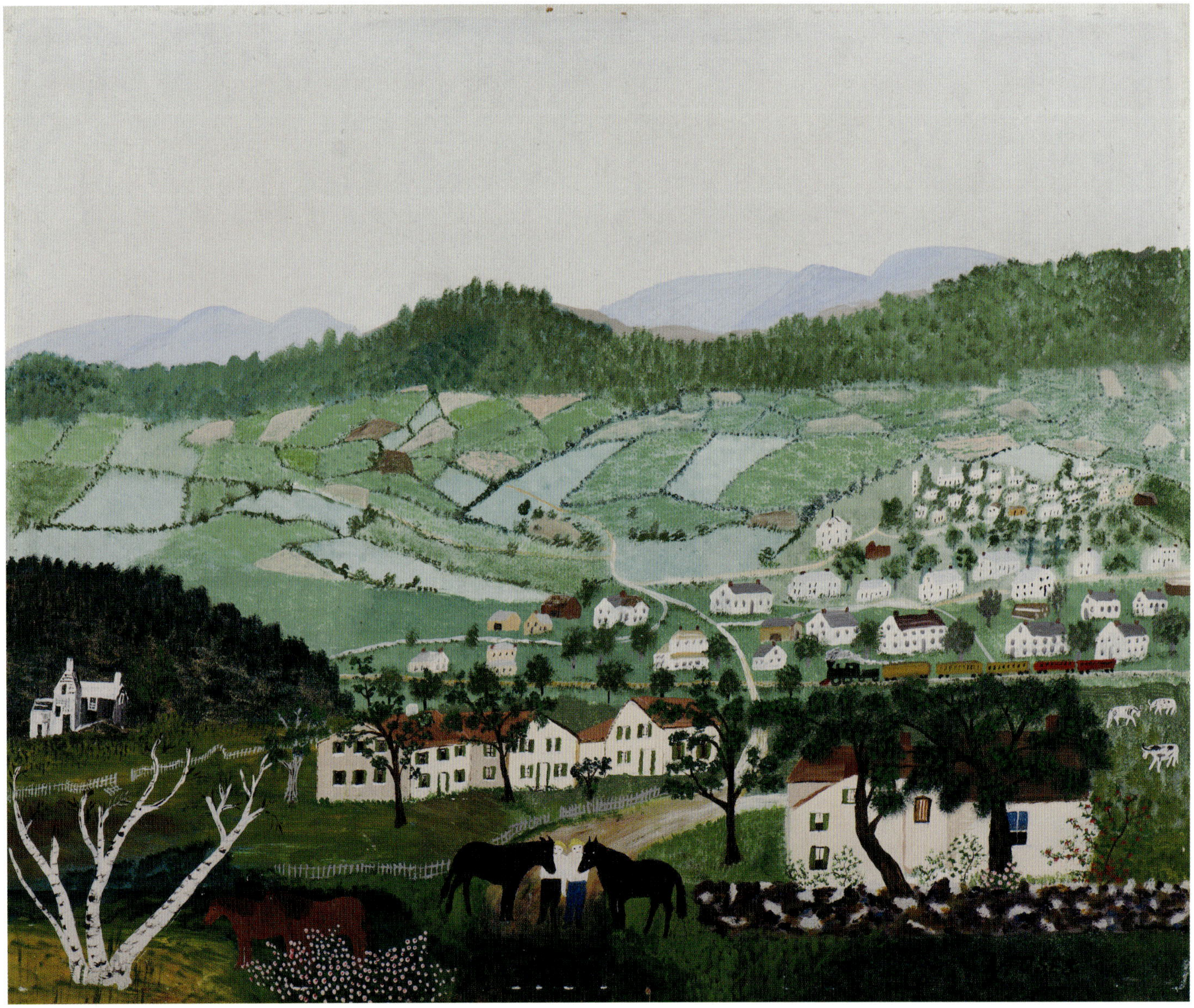

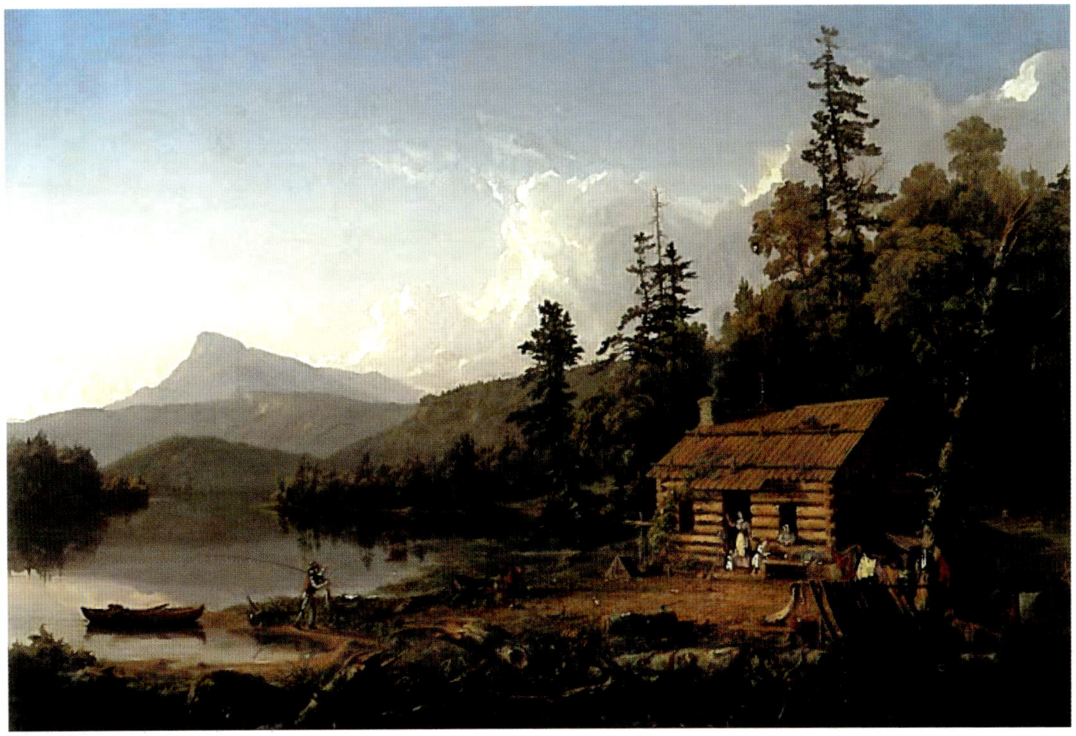

FIG. 43
Thomas Cole. *Home in the Woods*, 1847. Oil on canvas, 44 3/8 × 66 1/8 in. Courtesy of Reynolda House Museum of American Art, Affiliated with Wake Forest University, Gift of Barbara B. Millhouse, 1978.2.2

eye by creating a break in the stone wall at foreground and providing a narrative path—literally a winding road—that leads us between an evocative meeting of two black horses, their bridles held by a pair of men in straw hats. From this initial, liminal moment, Moses presents a prosperous landscape of white houses punctuated by a steam engine (yet another black horse, iron now) pulling a train, and up onto a checkerboard hillside of tidy fields. It is a scene of harmony and contentment, grounded in agriculture and architecture, with symbols of commerce readily at hand to reference larger worlds over the verdant mountains. It is the very ideal of small-town America that rose to prominence in the popular imagination in the 1930s and became institutionalized in the national landscape by the 1950s.

Idealization of small-town life has a long tradition in American culture.[2] As industrialization and urbanization transformed the American economy and dramatically altered the landscape in the course of the nineteenth century, giving rise to bustling factories in busy cities, a new ideal emerged in the collective imagination—that of the yeoman family living autonomously in a house of their own. Trading in an age-old Jeffersonian concept—witness the paintings of Thomas Cole and so many followers in the 1830s and '40s who saw the promise of the young nation realized in a land of cabins in the wilderness or the writings of Henry David Thoreau—the idea of the detached house in the country was inextricably linked to modernity (fig. 43). As city life became normative, an industry sprang up to reacquaint Americans with the virtues of country life, real or imagined. "In antebellum

FIG. 44
James Hope. *Clarendon Springs, Vermont*, 1853. Oil on canvas, 26 1/8 × 36 3/16 in. Collection of Shelburne Museum, Museum purchase, acquired from Maxim Karolik, Shelburne, Vermont, 1957-690.10

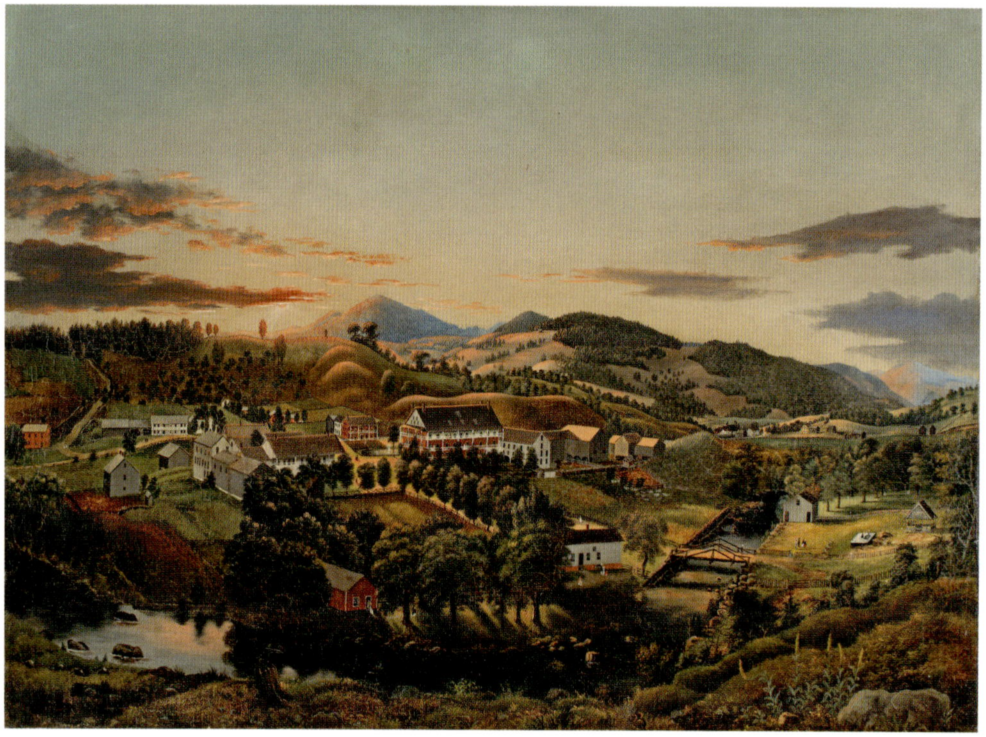

America," writes the art historian Sarah Burns, "nostalgia found expression in outpourings on the long-ago, far-away, humble cottage home."[3] Longing for the country picked up steam after the Civil War, so much so that a chromolithograph of *The Old Homestead* by Currier & Ives became de rigueur in the new middle-class interior by the turn of the century.[4] For those who could afford the investment, an oil painting of rural gentility—the old family farm—graced the walls of many who had moved off the land to find fortune in the city, ancestral portraits without the ancestor (fig. 44).

COUNTRY LIFE

This ruralizing impulse for "the country life" came to provide the background for countless back-to-the-land tales of city folk out of their element—Kate Sanborn's 1891 *Adopting an Abandoned Farm*, a how-to manual for making the move from "Gotham to Gooseville," is a harbinger of the genre, a class of narrative that perhaps found its apogee in Hollywood and the 1948 Cary Grant vehicle *Mr. Blandings Builds His Dream House*, the story of a hapless cosmopolitan couple restoring an old farmhouse. In the decades before small-town life became the stuff of humor on the big screen, however, the idea of a return to the social economy of the village held great currency in America. The privations of the Great Depression, alloyed with fears of Communism, catalyzed the widely held notions that the roots of American democracy were to be found in the vernacular settlement patterns of New England—

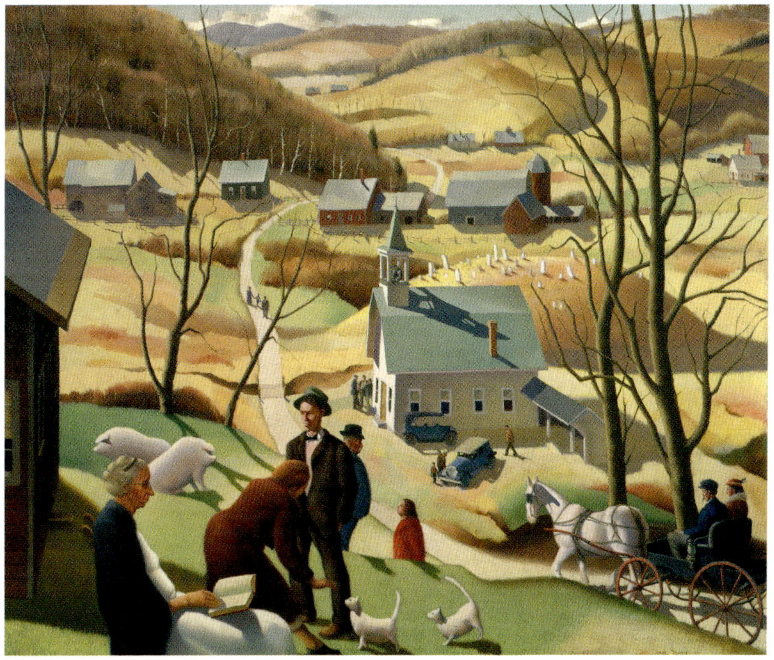

FIG. 45 (TOP)
Paul Sample. *Beaver Meadow*, 1939. Oil on canvas. Overall: 40 × 48 ¼ in. Hood Museum of Art, Dartmouth College, Hanover, New Hampshire, Gift of the artist, Class of 1920, in memory of his brother, Donald M. Sample, Class of 1921, P.943.126.1

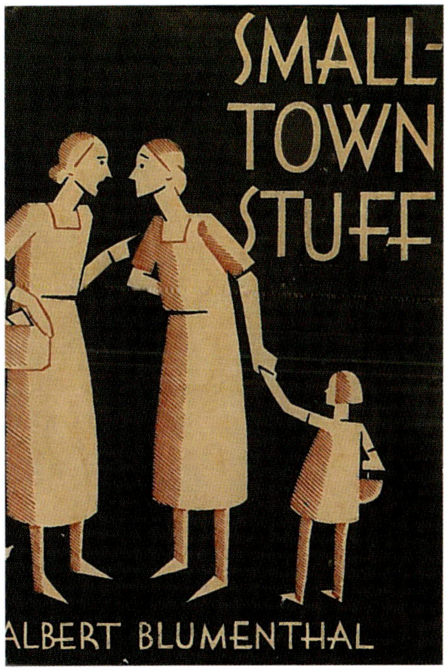

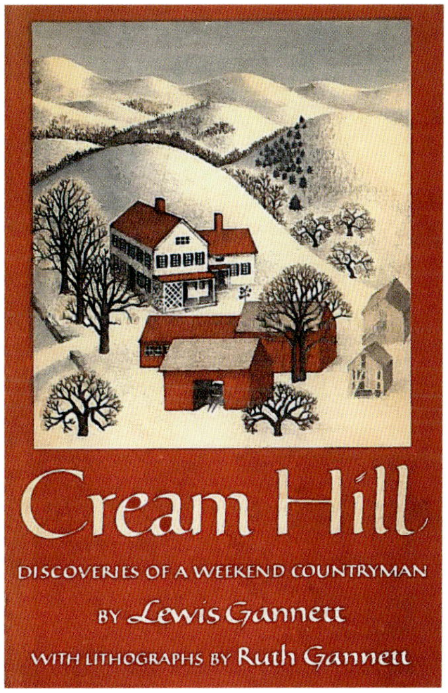

FIG. 46 (BOTTOM LEFT)
Small-Town Stuff (Cover), by Albert Blumenthal (University of Chicago Press, 1932)

FIG. 47 (BOTTOM RIGHT)
Cream Hill: Discoveries of a Weekend Countryman (Cover), by Lewis Gannett, with lithographs by Ruth Gannett (Viking, 1949)

what one author called "town meeting country."[5] The tidy village typified by Thornton Wilder's Grover's Corners, the fictional New Hampshire setting of *Our Town* as it opened on Broadway in 1938, provided an answer for the vicissitudes of modern life.[6]

The folksy drama of small-town life often took a dark turn, however. Moses's *Cambridge* becomes all the more optimistic a vision when compared to *Beaver Meadow,* a slightly earlier painting

FIG. 48
Charlotte J. Sternberg. *Connecticut,* From the "United States" series, 1946. Gouache on prepared paperboard, 18 1⁄16 × 15 in. Gift of the Container Corporation of America, Smithsonian American Art Museum, Washington, D.C./Art Resource, NY

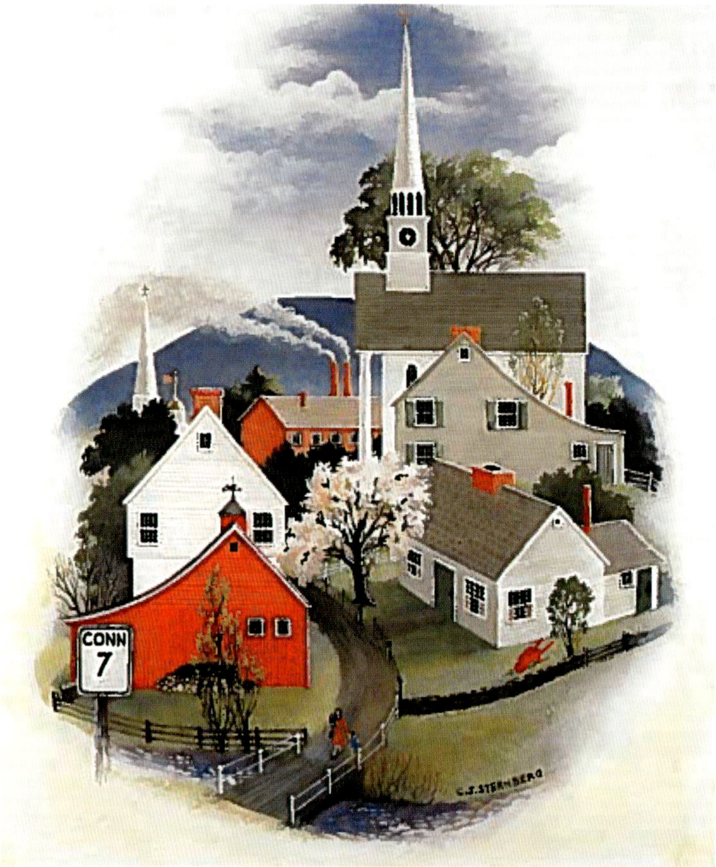

from 1939 by Paul Sample (fig. 45). Employing the icy, hard-edged precision associated with the midwestern regionalism of Grant Wood, Sample captures the isolation of hill town New England, a place where laconic Yankee "reserve" is a point of honor. The composition of *Beaver Meadow* is reminiscent of *Cambridge,* yet Moses's painting limns a positive vision of community absent from Sample's perspective. The cheerful train in *Cambridge,* emblematic of commerce and intercourse with the larger world, is somehow diminished in translation to the automobiles depicted in *Beaver Meadow.* Even the curious equine tableau in the foreground of *Cambridge* is far less ominous than Sample's vignette of a gray-haired woman in profile oddly engrossed in her book. People face one another in Sample's hermetic village, but clearly do not communicate.

By the time Sample sketched the disquiet of *Beaver Meadow,* tales of small-town life could be found at every turn in America. A cottage industry in community studies—from academic sociology to avuncular storytelling—plumbed the structures of everyday life from the 1930s through midcentury (figs. 46 and 47). "Not long since," wrote the sociologist Albert Blumenthal in the 1932 ethnography *Small-Town Stuff,* "American civilization was a small-town civilization, but time has wrought great changes."[7] *Cream Hill,* by Lewis Gannett and illustrated by Ruth Stiles Gannett, tells the story of one New York family's purchase of an old farmhouse in the northwest corner of Connecticut. "We were not Blandings," writes Gannett of the slapstick movie, but rusticating urban summer folk, a new class in the landscape. Comic relief in the book comes not in the misadventures of restoring an old farmhouse as it does in the Cary Grant movie but in the author's self-deprecating tale of writing an op-ed piece for the newspaper in support of the preservation of the local covered bridge, which promptly drew the attention of the highway department, which condemned said bridge, declaring it a hazard, and earning Gannett the enmity of his neighbors.[8] Gannett, the editor of *The New York Review of Books*, summed up received wisdom on small-town life: "A quaint superstition is abroad that Maine and Vermont are populated exclusively by ancient granite characters; that the rest of New England, and the Southern mountains, teem with them; and that while a few characters survive in the cow country of the West, the remainder of the United States . . . is dismally normal."[9]

Gannett's New England—the answer to an increasingly (and dismally) normal nation—is captured by illustrator Charlotte Sternberg in *Connecticut* of 1946 (fig. 48). Commissioned by the Container Corporation of America as part of a national advertising campaign, *Connecticut* provided a delivery system for the imagery and ideology of small-town New England. Set on State Route 7, a principal north–south artery, the image trades in the traditional symbols of multiple church spires, garrison and Cape Cod–style small houses, a blossoming apple tree, and billowing smoke stacks from a productive mill discreetly tucked into the background, *Connecticut* is a harbinger of the postwar built environment.

THE EARLY AMERICAN SUBURB

"Ownership of single-family homes," writes the historian Lizabeth Cohen, "grew more in the decade following World War II than it had in the previous 150 years."[10] No single design more completely captures the postwar suburb than the modest and efficient Cape Cod as designed by Boston architect Royal Barry Wills (fig. 49). Wills, the "most popular architect among the American middle class after World War II," according to the architectural historian Richard Guy Wilson, came to prominence in a competition staged by *Life* magazine in 1938 that pitted his designs for a home of the future against those of Frank Lloyd Wright.[11] Wills won, and the nation would never be the same. By the time of his death, his firm had completed more than 2,500 "colonial" houses and inspired countless others from coast to coast. Indeed, by 1958 the *Saturday Evening Post* remarked that "Many a would-be homeowner, surveying the infinite variations of Mr. Wills's Cape Codders in plan books and magazines, has concluded that he is the man who somehow invented the design."[12] A more

FIG. 49
Charles Crombie. *House in Duxbury, Mass.*, c. 1950. Graphite on paper, 16 × 24 3/4 in. Published in *Living on the Level: One-Story Houses*, by Royal Barry Wills (Houghton Mifflin, 1954). Royal Barry Wills Associates Archive Courtesy of Historic New England, Boston, MA

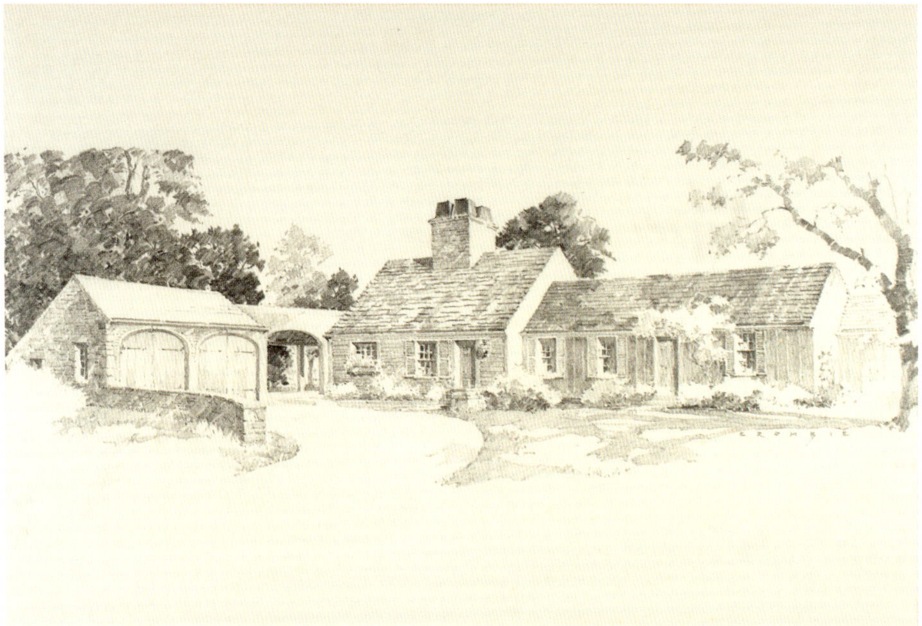

accurate measure of Wills's influence, however, can be found in the architect's prolific writings. *Life* magazine, profiling Wills again in 1946, noted that his five books had reached some 520,000 copies in print, making him the most published architect of the modern era.[13]

The styles and types of architecture in the colonial revival suburb reflect the inherent tensions of the era. The United States, a world power and nation of plenty under persistent threat of nuclear destruction during the Cold War, transitioned from what the sociologist David Riesman termed the "inner-directed" to the "other-directed" self in the wildly popular 1950 book *The Lonely Crowd*.[14] The other-directed American identified with reflected definitions to create a sense of self; institutions become paramount, according to Riesman, appearances everything. In this new society of conformity, organizing myths take on new meaning. The invented traditions of a genteel colonial America become the national idiom in a landscape of small capes, garrisons, and gambrel-roof houses from coast to coast. By the 1950s, life in the modern colonial house not only comprised a consumer culture built on "early American" design, but offered a pilgrimage route to idealized notions of a glorious past in the form of museum villages.

HOUSING HISTORY

Old Home (fig. 50) by Grandma Moses reveals a close relationship to one such museum. A diminutive work in oil on Masonite, *Old Home* is the product of Moses's mature style—if we can call the effort of a ninety-seven-year-old painter mature—and it is a paradigm of her oeuvre. A small, vernacular

FIG. 50
Anna Mary Robertson ("Grandma") Moses. *Old Home*, 1957. Oil on pressed wood, 11 ¼ × 15 ¼ in. Collection of Shelburne Museum, Gift of Anna Mary Robertson Moses, Shelburne, Vermont, 1957-697

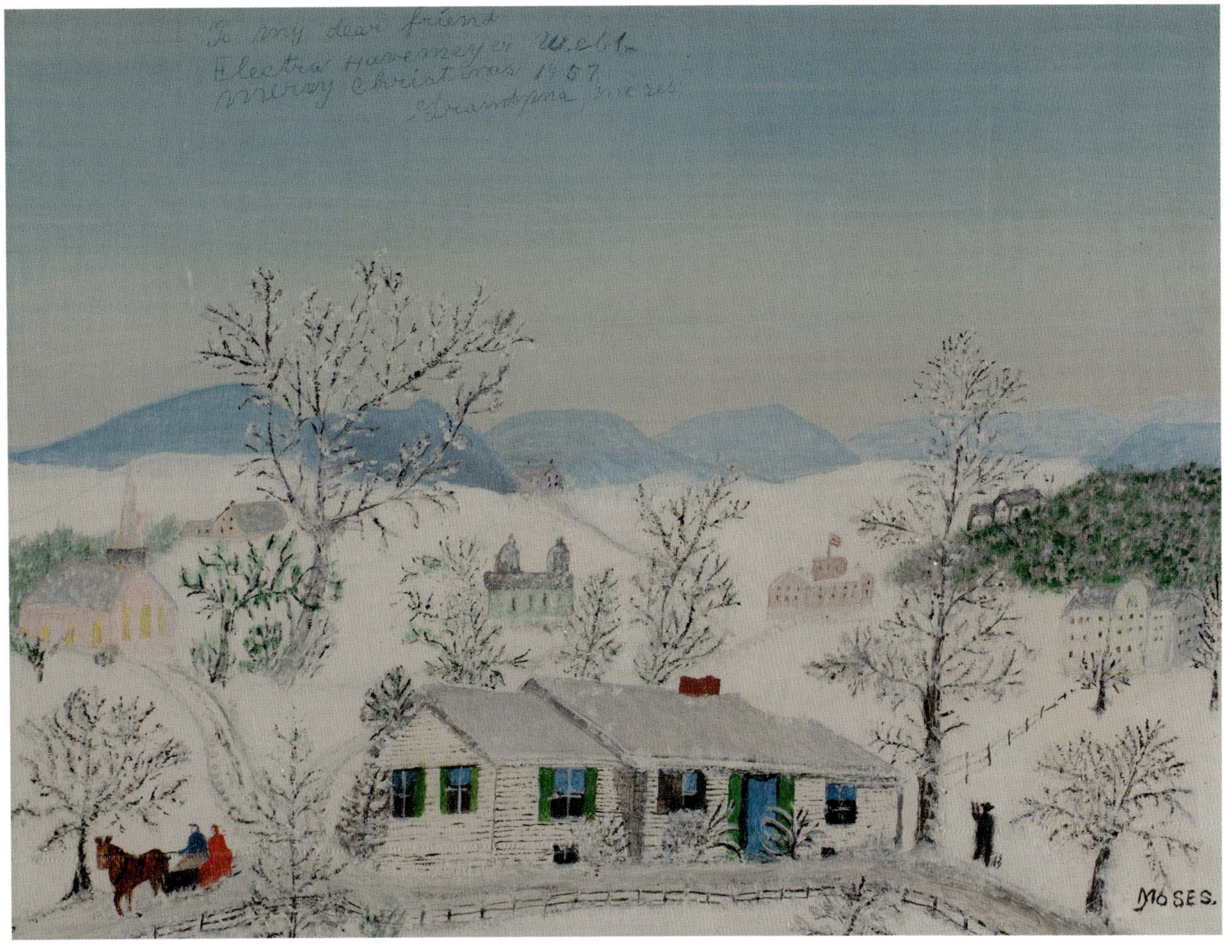

house with flanking additions presents a symmetrical vision of domestic order in a winter landscape. Whitewashed, the house recedes into the snowy scene and anchors a composition that includes a church, school, and mill—building types easily read as representing religion, learning, and commerce. Far-off hills bisect the composition, and Moses's application of glitter into the pigment activates the painting—creating a shimmering, festive effect. The latter gesture comes into sharp focus in light of the inscription in the sky: "To my dear friend / Electra Havemeyer Webb / Merry Christmas 1957, / Grandma Moses."

Not only does *Old Home* trade on the long tradition of sentimental imagery of house and home in American visual culture—a category of representation that held sway in Moses's youth and

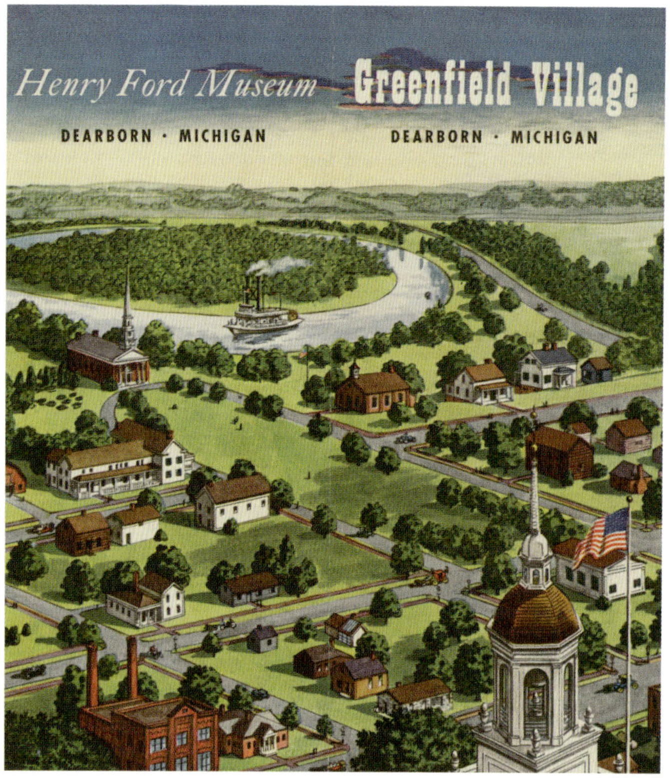

FIG. 51
"For a Memorable Holiday Journey into Yesterday," brochure for Henry Ford Museum and Greenfield Village, Dearborn, Michigan, c. 1956. Ink on paper, 9 × 8 in. (folded). The Henry Ford Museum, Dearborn, Michigan, EI.225.2

maintained authority well into the twentieth century—but it also alludes to the artist's facility with the art of cultivating relationships that result in a network of patronage. In the case of *Old Home*, the painting is a testament to Moses's friendship with the collector and heiress Electra Havemeyer Webb (1886–1960) who founded Shelburne Museum a decade earlier.

Webb, daughter of Louisine and H. O. Havemeyer, the Gilded Age collectors responsible for bringing French impressionism to the United States in the last quarter of the nineteenth century, played a key role herself in defining American folk art as a field worthy of investigation and investment in the 1920s. An ecumenical collector, she dramatically renovated a Vermont farmhouse into a colonial revival mansion that served as the laboratory for the display of her many and varied acquisitions. In 1947 she incorporated Shelburne Museum, in Shelburne, Vermont, to create a permanent home for her endeavors and, in doing so, participated in a movement that served as the genesis for museum villages throughout the country, with Colonial Williamsburg, in Williamsburg, Virginia (1926), Greenfield Village, in Dearborn, Michigan (1929), and Old Sturbridge Village, in Sturbridge, Massachusetts (1947), being archetypes (fig. 51). Loosely following a master plan penned by the New York landscape architecture firm of Innocenti and Webel, Webb moved a series of historic structures from Vermont and upstate New York onto land near her in-law's Gilded-Age estate, Shelburne Farms.

FIG. 52
Edward Sanborn. *Shelburne Museum* [map of Museum's grounds for visitor's brochure], 1965. Ink and gouache on paperboard, 14 × 29 ¼ in. Collection of Shelburne Museum. Shelburne, Vermont, 1965-352. Photography by Andy Duback

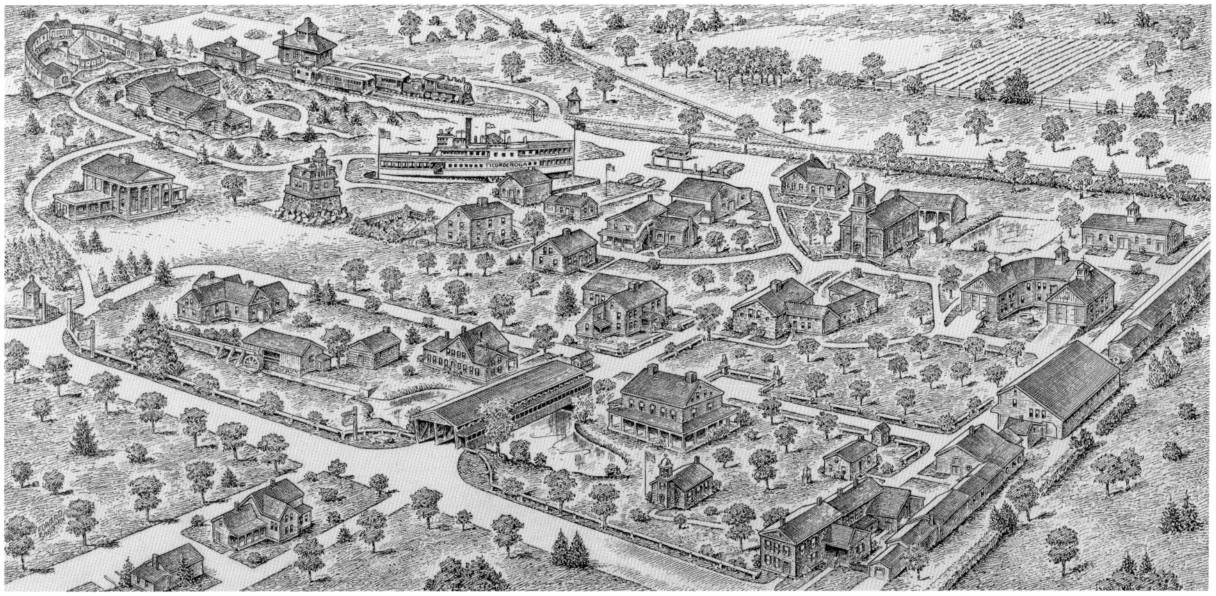

Shelburne Museum opened to the public in 1952 with nine buildings, and Webb added twelve more structures before 1955 (fig. 52). In 1960, a modern gallery building was added to house Shelburne Museum's burgeoning American paintings collection. A gathering of by-then canonical American artists such as John Singleton Copley, Thomas Cole, Fitz Henry Lane, Eastman Johnson, Winslow Homer, Martin Johnson Heade, the collection was shaped by individuals such as the Boston connoisseur Maxim Karolik from whom Webb purchased the majority of the paintings. Tellingly, Webb opened her new museum that summer with an exhibition celebrating the 100th birthday of Grandma Moses.

The rise of museum villages in the United States played a key role in enchanting the postwar American suburb. Not only did they provide a sense of authenticity as Americans consumed their past by collecting antiques or decorating with a palette prescribed by Colonial Williamsburg, but they carried a call to action, occasionally clarion, to view the small town as a bulwark against the growing threat of Eastern Europe. The preservationist Henry Flynt organized Historic Deerfield, in Deerfield, Massachusetts, as a museum in 1952, publishing *Frontier of Freedom*, a profile of the restored village, with the artist Samuel Chamberlain that same year. "In this tenuous and murky mid-century," wrote Flynt, "when our young and powerful nation finds itself engaged in an ideological conflict with Communism," an answer can be found in "the New England Village," an institution he considered

FIG. 53 (BELOW)
Brochure for Grandma Moses dinnerware. Courtesy of Galerie St. Etienne, New York

FIG. 54 (RIGHT)
Brochure for Grandma Moses tiles, 1952. Courtesy of Galerie St. Etienne, New York

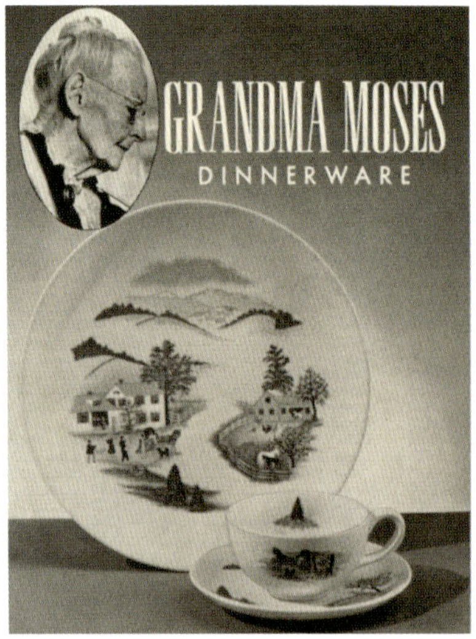

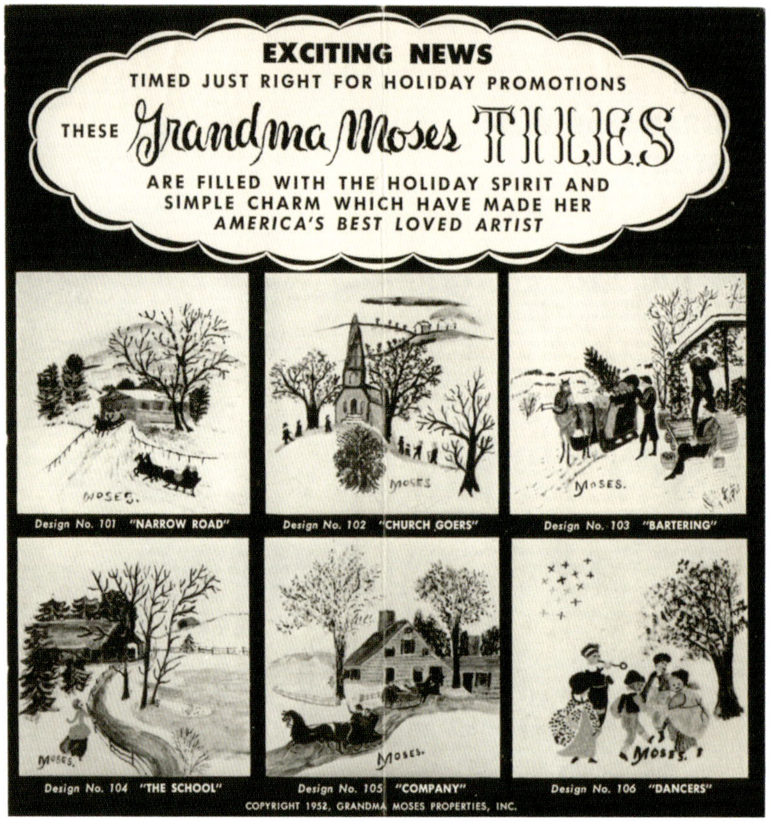

coequal with "state university, model factory, and western farm" as cornerstones of American democracy.[15] Flynt's "model factory" represents the faith that many Americans held in the economic power of the United States in the decade after World War II.

Consumer culture, a vehicle challenged by the same economic downturn that focused attention on small-town life in the 1930s, allowed the new middle class to construct their identities as latter-day Pilgrims in the 1950s. Grandma Moses, playing the role of personal advisor seen throughout the golden age of advertising, quickly achieved a larger-than-life presence in the marketplace. Although artists have long sought to secure an income by moving horizontally into related media, few struck as resonant a chord as Moses in the 1950s (figs. 53 and 54). In 1947 Hallmark Cards began issuing Grandma Moses Christmas cards, and from this stream a river of product soon flowed. By 1950, the art historian Karal Ann Marling points out, "a well-coordinated national ad campaign announced a new line of licensed Grandma Moses fabrics."[16] Yard goods were soon joined by ceramic tiles and, eventually, china for the table (figs. 55A–55D). These intertwined product lines reinforced each other in the marketplace, and in this way, Grandma Moses (the artist) became Grandma Moses (the brand).

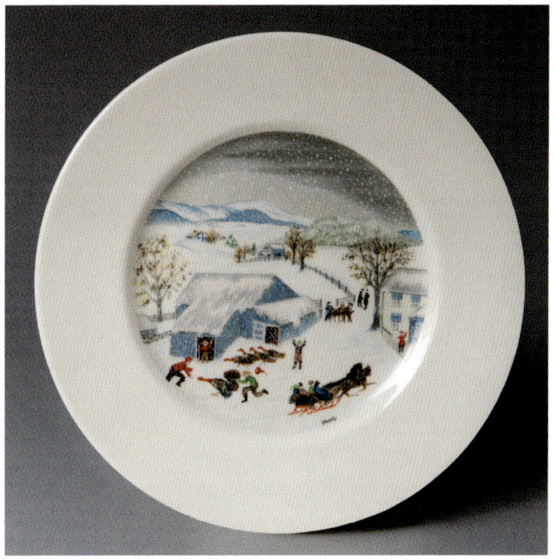

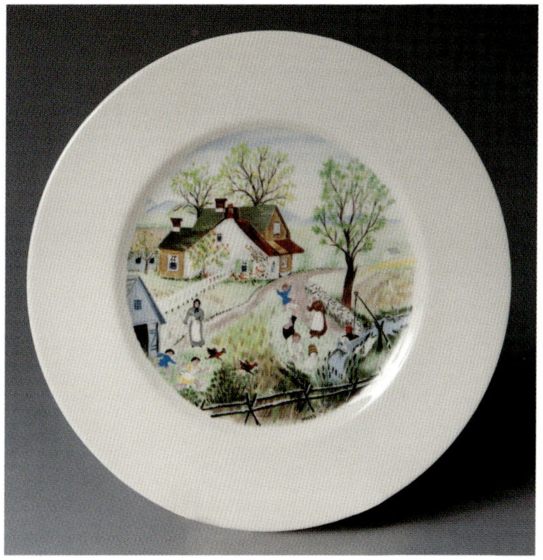

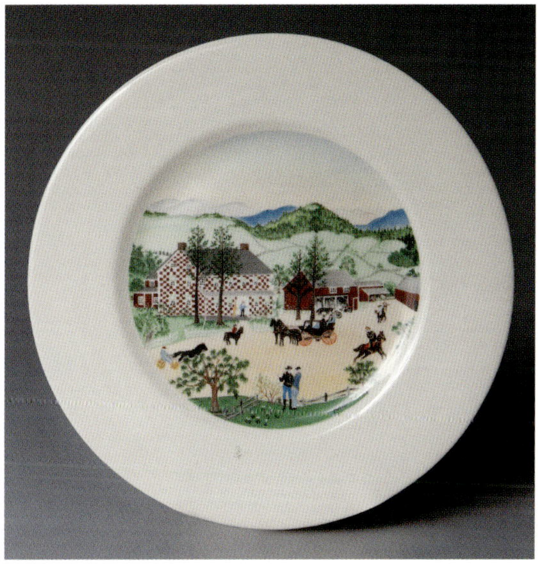

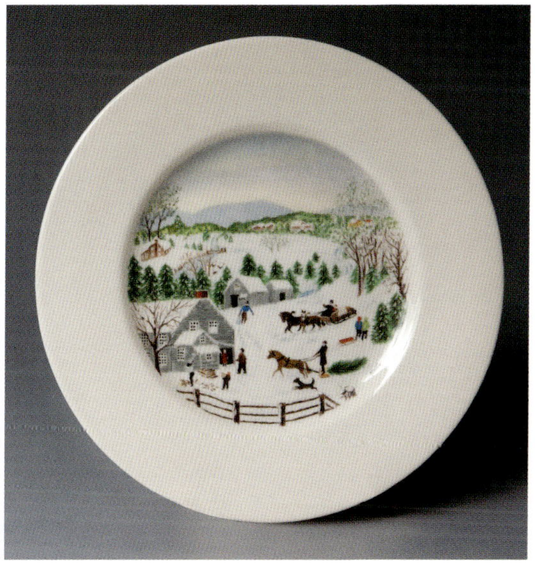

FIG. 55A (TOP LEFT)
Atlas China. "Catching the Thanksgiving Turkey" Grandma Moses series, c. 1950–60. 10 in. diameter. Bennington Museum, 2003.30.2

FIG. 55B (TOP RIGHT)
Atlas China. "Jack and Jill" Grandma Moses series, c. 1950–60. 10 in. diameter. Bennington Museum, 2004.578

FIG. 55C (LOWER LEFT)
Atlas China. "The Red Checkered House" Grandma Moses series, c. 1950–60. 10 in. diameter. Bennington Museum, 2003.30.3

FIG. 55D (LOWER RIGHT)
Atlas China. "Out for the Christmas Tree" Grandma Moses series, c. 1950–60. 10 in. diameter Bennington Museum, 2003.30.1

A BRIDGE TO THE PAST

On the occasion of the opening of her exhibition in 1955, Grandma Moses sat down with the actress Lillian Gish in the IBM Gallery on East Fifty-Seventh Street in Manhattan to discuss painting (see page 8). Two years earlier Gish had portrayed Moses in a biographical movie; now she interviewed the artist on national television. The occasion, organized by IBM chairman Thomas J. Watson and broadcast on NBC, celebrated the artist's ninety-fifth year in an exhibition that concretized the myth of her unlikely rise and set the stage for her final chapter as a celebrity in postwar American culture. Although other television appearances would follow, notably Edward R. Murrow's long-format

FIG. 56
Anna Mary Robertson ("Grandma") Moses.
Covered Bridge with Carriage or Black Buggy,
1946. Oil on pressed wood, 29 × 22 3/8 in.
Collection of Shelburne Museum, Museum
purchase, Shelburne, Vermont, 1961-210.3

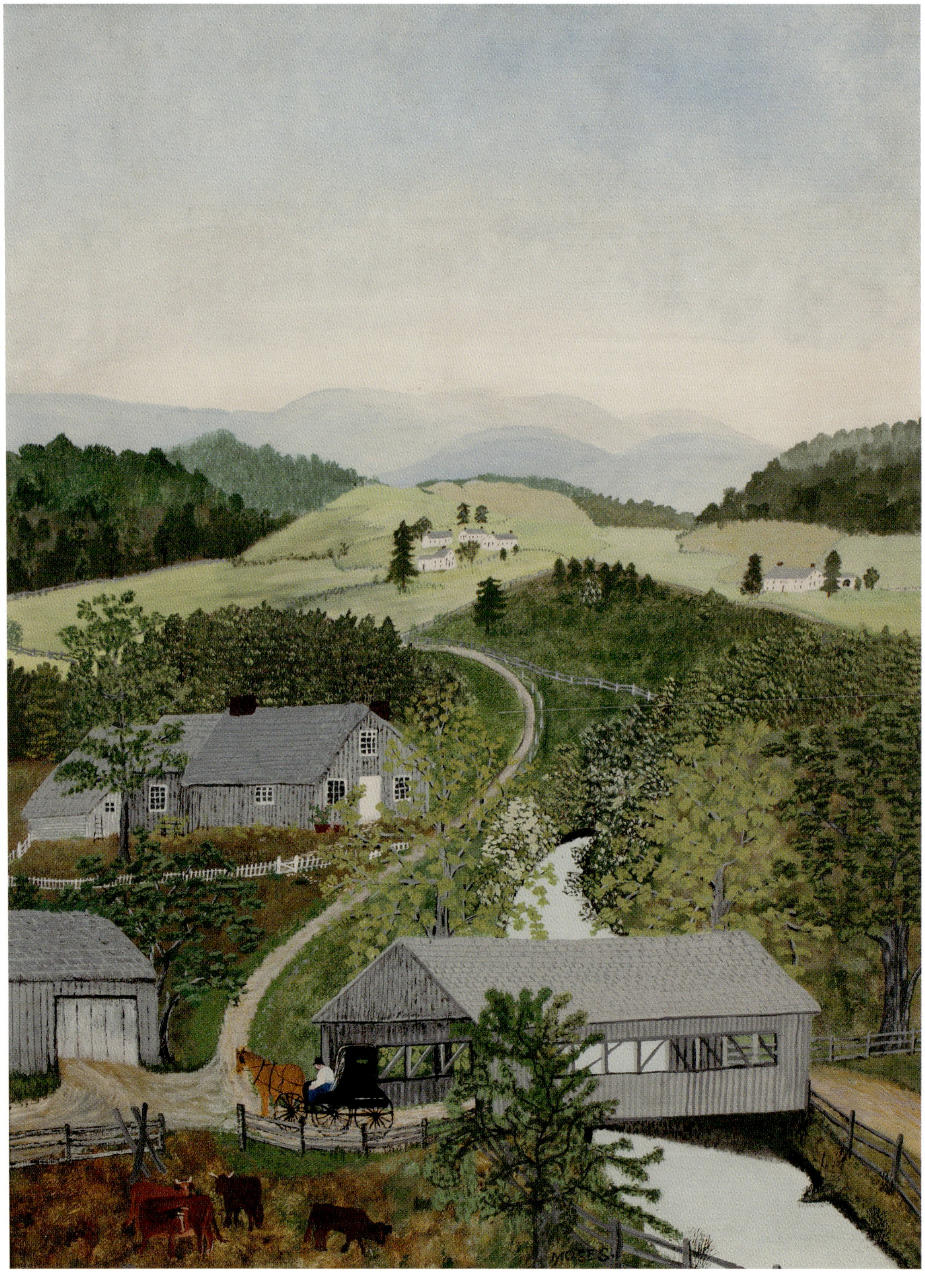

interview on "See It Now," the IBM celebration is a watershed moment, for it offers a clear view of the artist's role as an icon of popular culture in the post–World War II era.

Grandma Moses, through her creative work and carefully constructed personal narrative as a farmer's wife from a halcyon moment in American history, provided life lessons for an anxious nation embracing new patterns of domestic organization in the 1950s. As suburbia shifted from idealization to actuality in the United States and contributed to a moment of alienation and anxiety, Moses offered a mythology that animated life in the detached house and participated in the creation of an operating system for the American dream. The painting over her shoulder in the IBM Gallery, a covered bridge rendered in an unusual vertical composition from 1946 (fig. 56), is symbolic of the journey that the viewing audience took with Grandma Moses to an America of small towns, historic homes, and pastures forever green.

NOTES

1. Roger Cardinal, "The Sense of Time and Place," in *Grandma Moses in the 21st Century*, ed. Jane Kallir (New Haven, CT: Yale University Press in association with Art Services International, 2001), 80–105.

2. One of the best discussions of the topic is William H. Truettner, "Small-Town America," in *Picturing Old New England: Image and Memory*, ed. William H. Truettner and Roger B. Stein (New Haven, CT: Yale University Press in association with National Museum of American Art, Smithsonian Institution, 1999), 111–42.

3. Sarah Burns, *Pastoral Inventions: Rural Life in Nineteenth-Century American Art and Culture* (Philadelphia: Temple University Press, 1989), 125.

4. Peter C. Marzio, *The Democratic Art: Pictures for a 19th-Century America: Chromolithography, 1840–1900* (Boston: D. R. Godine in association with Amon Carter Museum of Western Art, 1979).

5. Clarence M. Webster, *Town Meeting Country* (New York: Duell, Sloan & Pearce, 1945).

6. Joseph S. Wood, "New England's Legacy Landscape," in *A Landscape History of New England*, ed. Blake Harrison and Richard W. Judd (Cambridge, MA: MIT Press, 2011), 251–68.

7. Albert Blumenthal, *Small-Town Stuff* (Chicago: University of Chicago Press, 1932), xv.

8. Lewis Gannett, *Cream Hill: Discoveries of a Weekend Countryman* (New York: Viking, 1949), 155.

9. Ibid., 157.

10. Lizabeth Cohen, *A Consumer's Republic: The Politics of Mass Consumption in Postwar America* (New York: Alfred A. Knopf, 2003), 196.

11. "Eight Houses for Modern Living," *Life* 5, no. 13 (Sept. 26, 1938): 44–67; and Richard Guy Wilson, *The Colonial Revival House* (New York: Harry N. Abrams, 2004), 179.

12. Arnold Nicholson, "Big Man in Small Houses," *Saturday Evening Post* 230, no. 39 (Mar. 29, 1958): 36, quoted in Wilson, *Colonial Revival House*, 179.

13. David Gebhard, "Royal Barry Wills and the American Colonial Revival," *Winterthur Portfolio* 27, no. 1 (Spring 1992): 45–74.

14. David Riesman, *The Lonely Crowd: A Study of the Changing American Culture* (New Haven, CT: Yale University Press, 1950).

15. Samuel Chamberlain and Henry N. Flynt, *Frontier of Freedom: The Soul and Substance of America Portrayed in one Extraordinary Village, Old Deerfield, Massachusetts* (New York: Hastings House, 1952), 1.

16. Karal Ann Marling, *Designs on the Heart: The Homemade Art of Grandma Moses* (Cambridge, MA: Harvard University Press, 2006), 195.

PLATE 31

Anna Mary Robertson ("Grandma") Moses

HOOSICK VALLEY (FROM THE WINDOW)

1946. Oil on pressed wood, 19 1/4 × 22 in.

Private Collection, courtesy of Galerie St. Etienne, New York

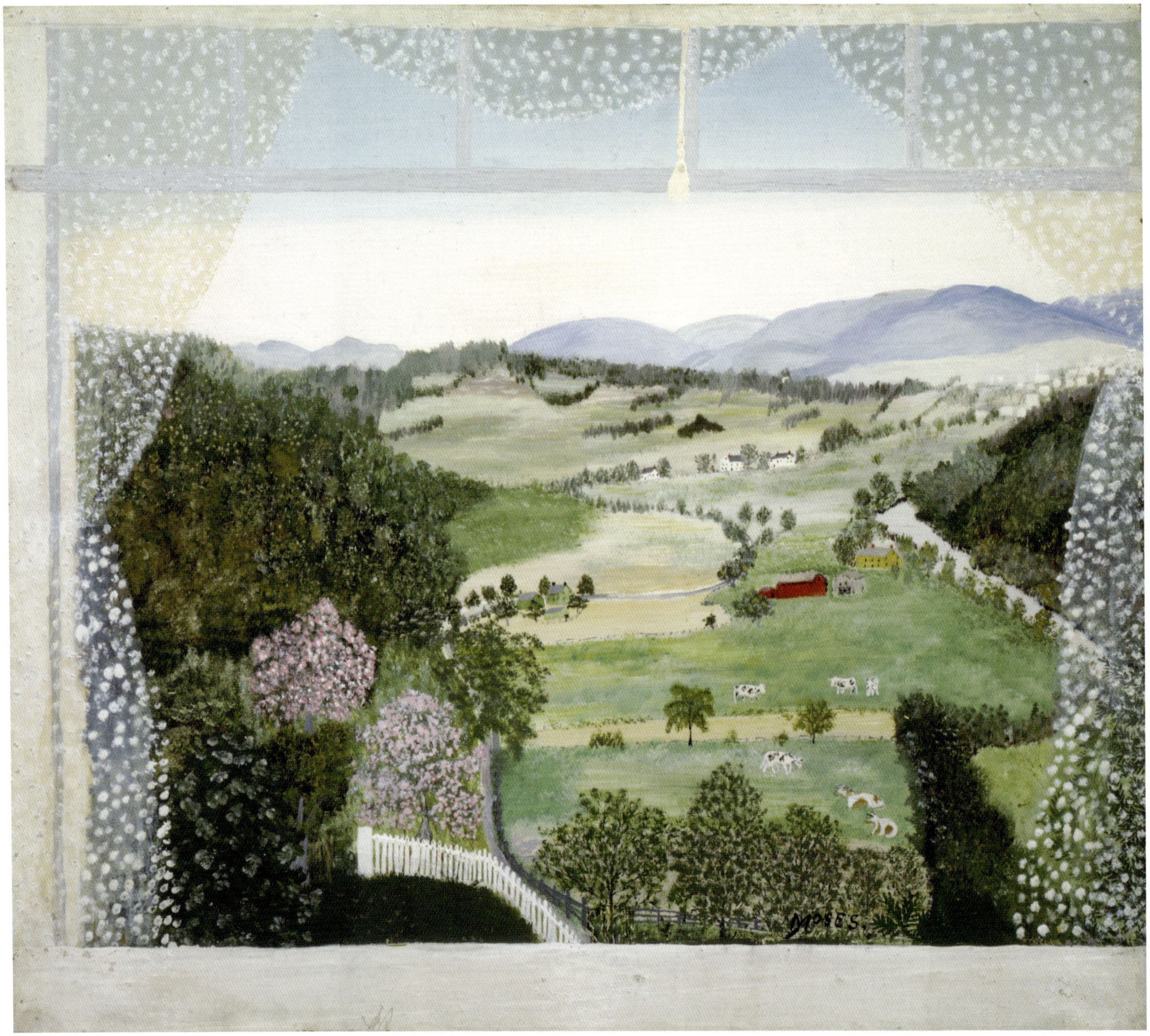

PLATE 32

Anna Mary Robertson ("Grandma") Moses

STAGE STOP

1958. Oil on pressed wood, 16 × 24 in.

Bennington Museum, Bequest of Margaret M. Carr, Bennington, Vermont, 1998.7

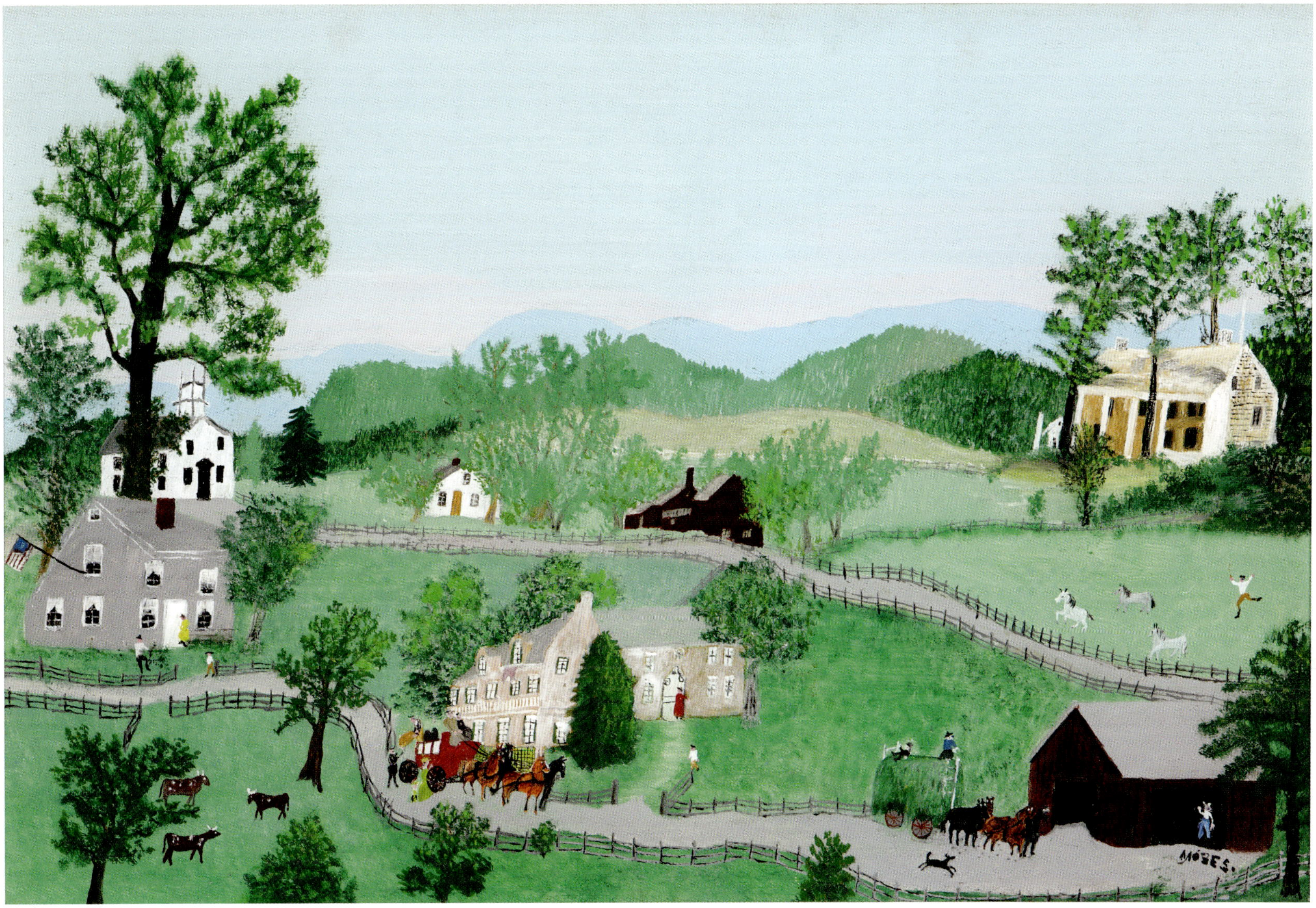

PLATE 33

Anna Mary Robertson ("Grandma") Moses

VERMONT

1958. Oil on pressed wood, 16 × 24 in.

Bennington Museum, Bequest of Margaret M. Carr, Bennington, Vermont, 1998.8

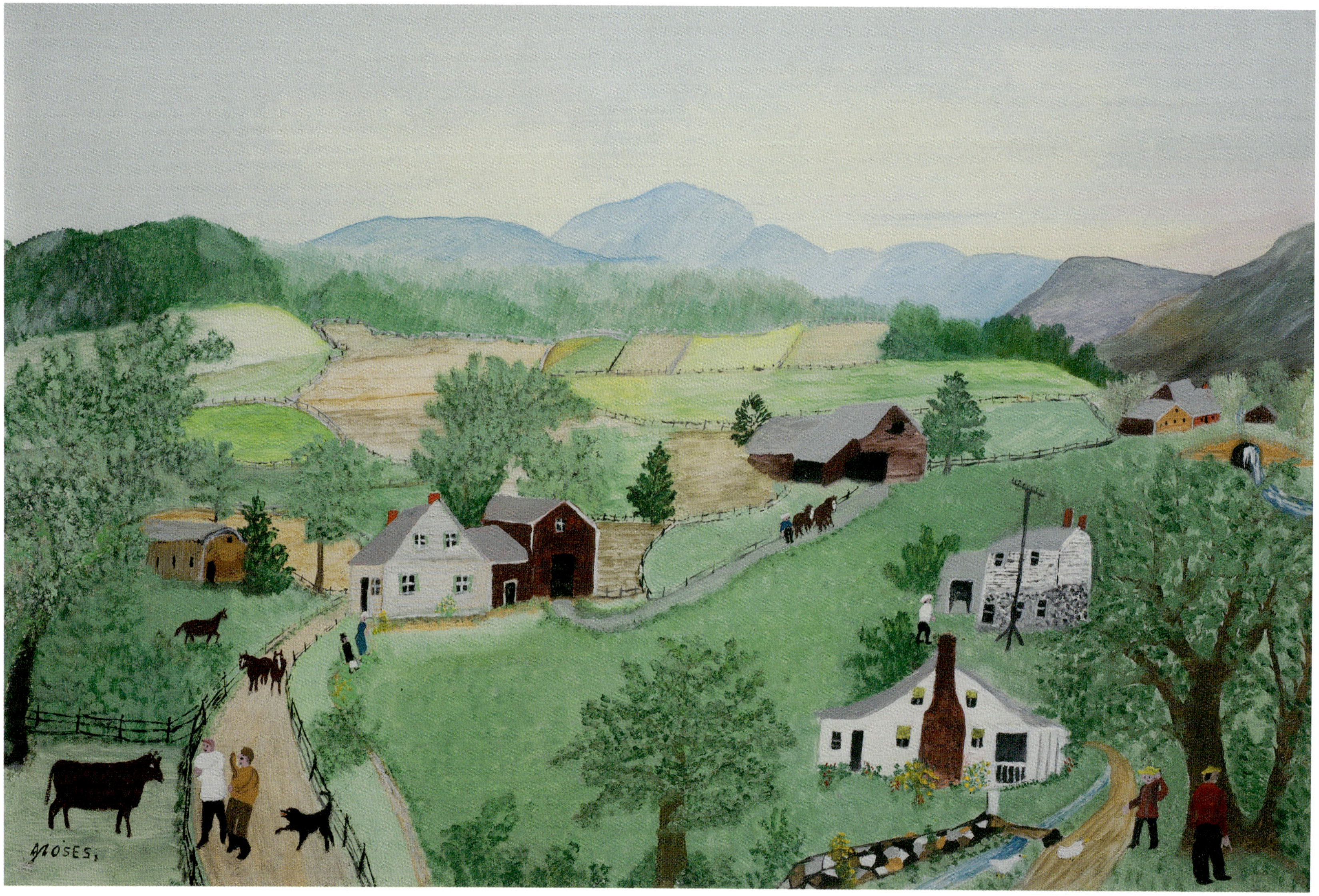

PLATE 34
Anna Mary Robertson ("Grandma") Moses
THE BAKER HOME
1954. Oil on pressed wood, 12 × 18 in.
Bennington Museum, Gift of Rachel Wilkins Baker Cottrell,
Bennington, Vermont, 2003.27

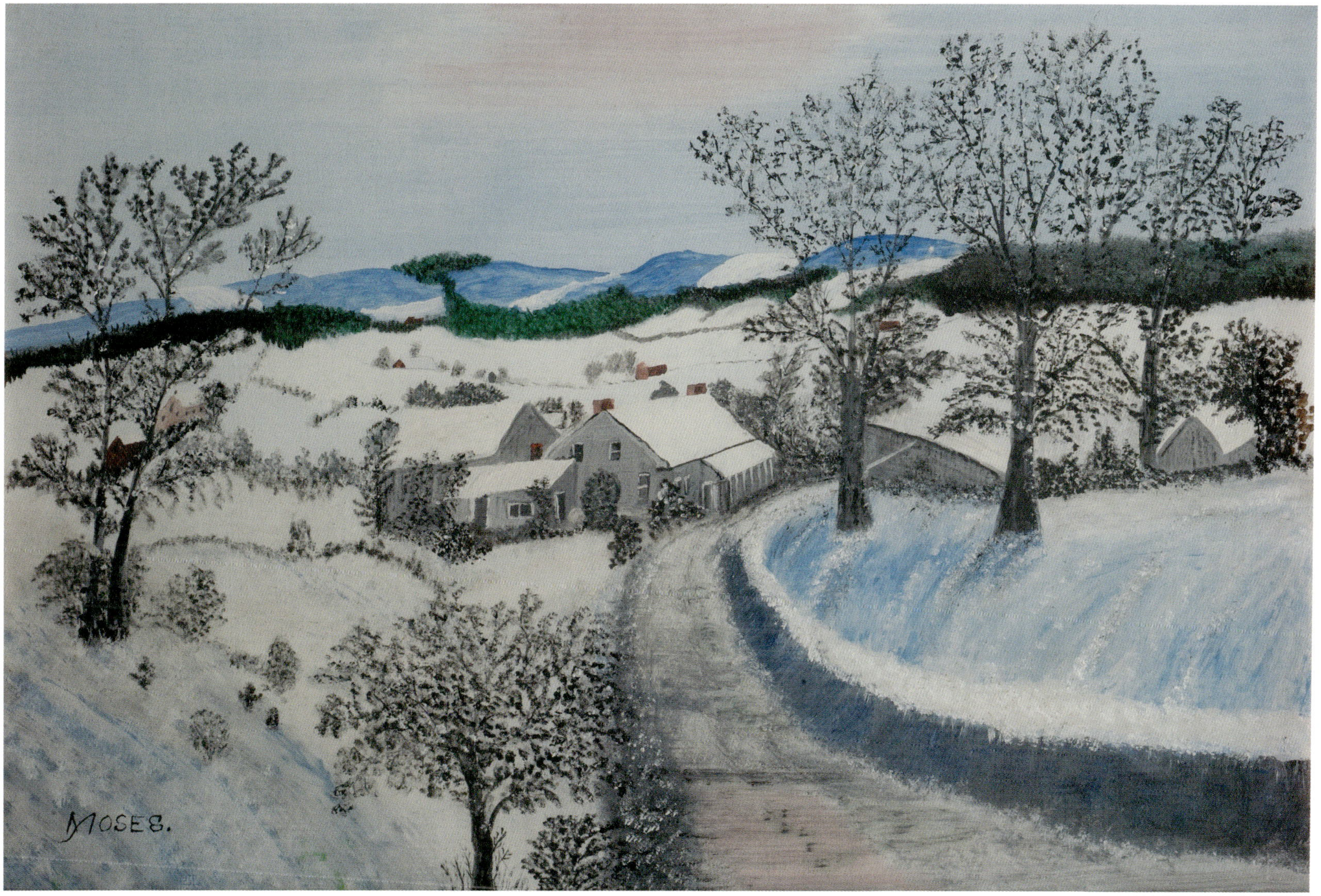

PLATE 35

Anna Mary Robertson ("Grandma") Moses

EAGLE BRIDGE HOTEL

1959. Oil on pressed wood, 16 × 24 in.

Private Collection, courtesy of Galerie St. Etienne, New York

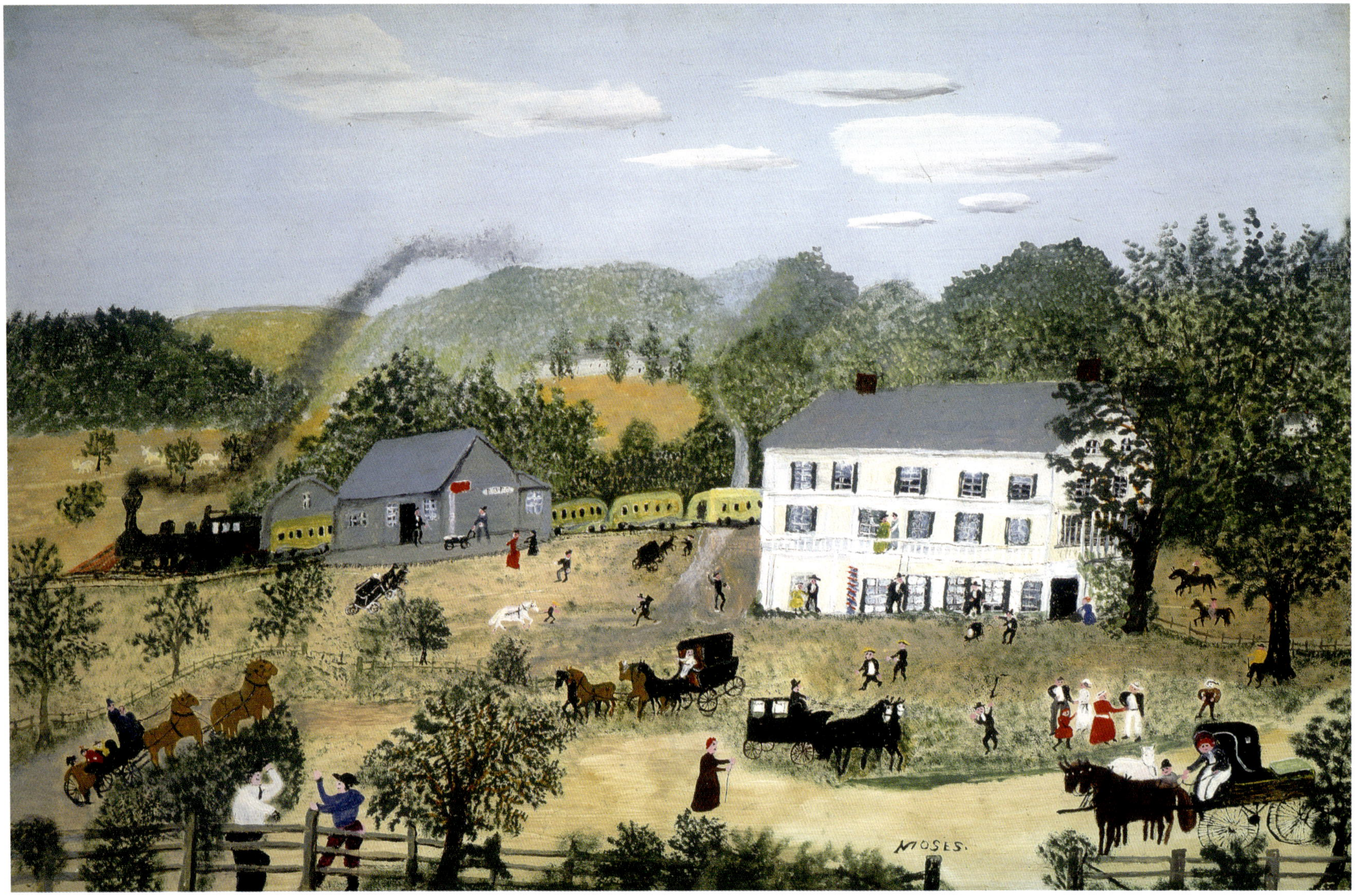

PLATE 36

Anna Mary Robertson ("Grandma") Moses

COUNTRYSIDE

1959. Oil on pressed wood, 8 × 12 in.

Bennington Museum, Bequest of Margaret M. Carr, Bennington, Vermont, 1998.6

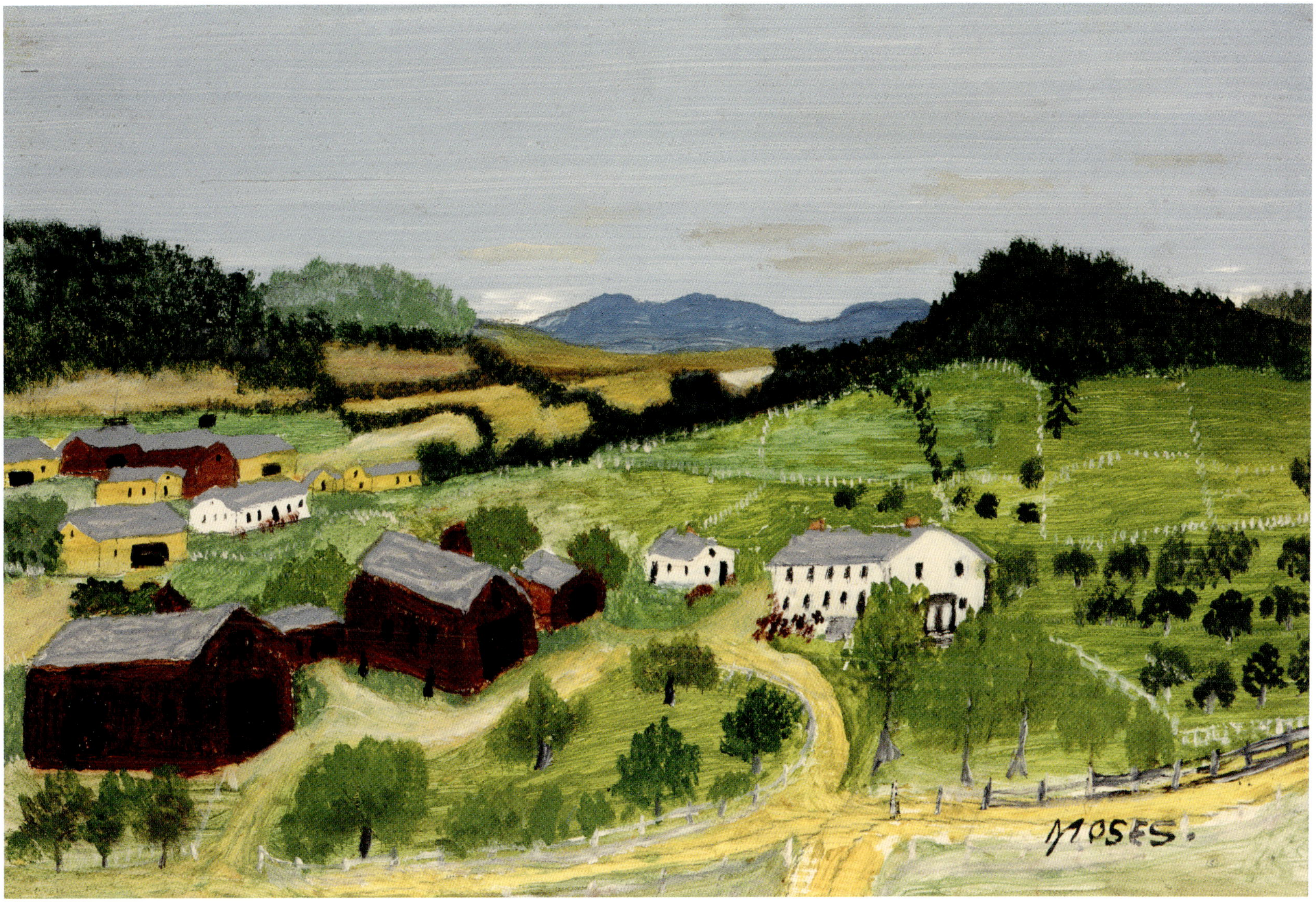

PLATE 37

Anna Mary Robertson ("Grandma") Moses

THE OLD CHECKERED HOUSE, 1853

1944. Oil on pressed wood, 20 ¾ × 28 in.

Bennington Museum, Museum purchase, Bennington, Vermont, 2000.2

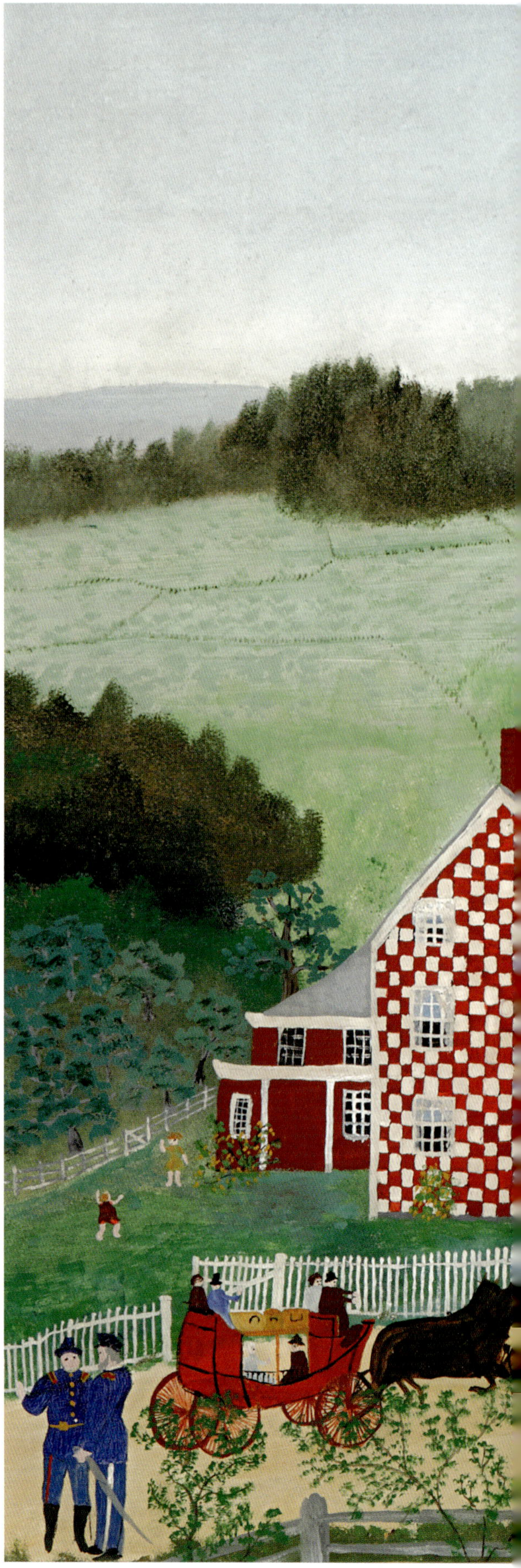

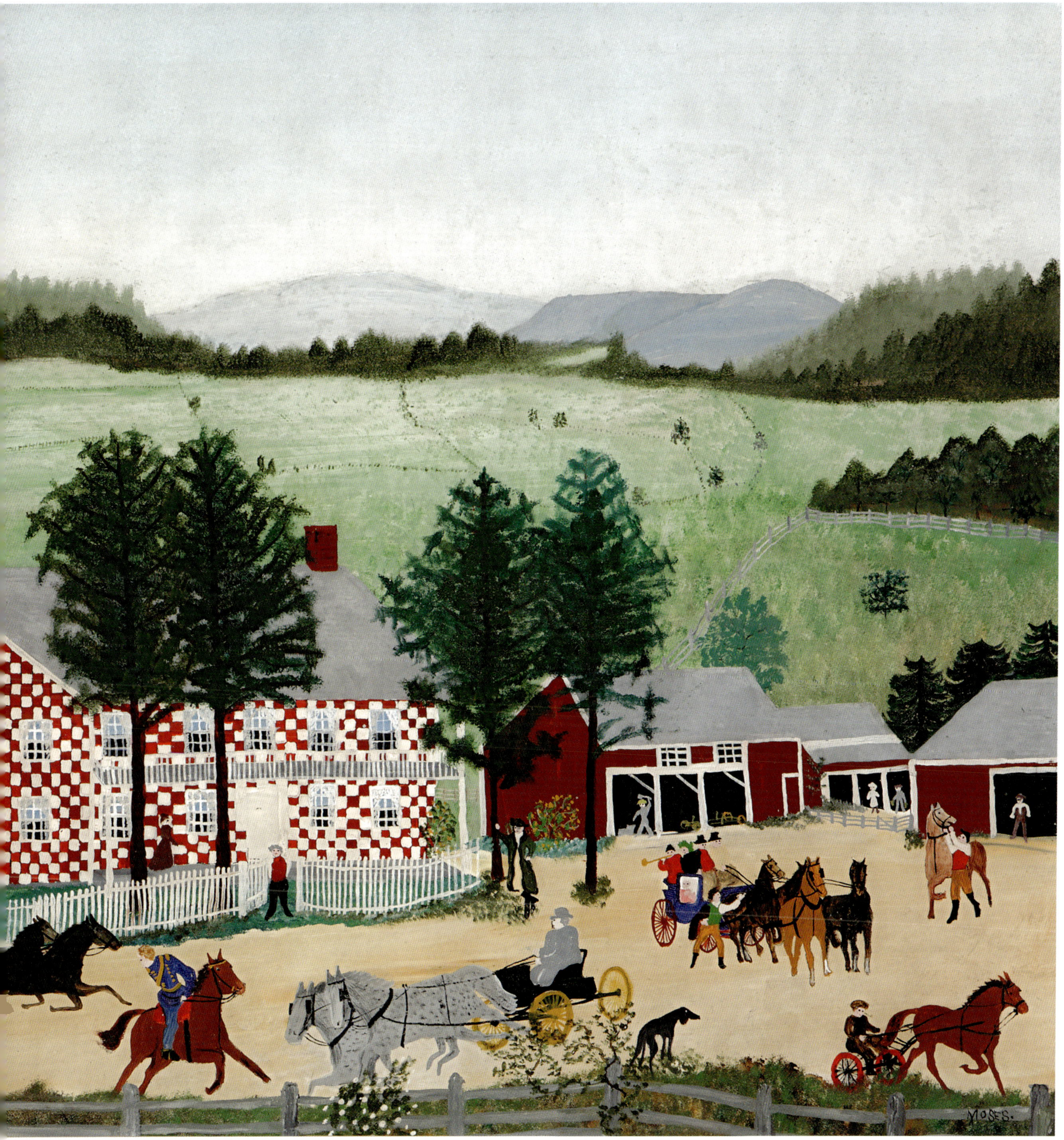
MOSES.

PLATE 38

Anna Mary Robertson ("Grandma") Moses

GRIST MILL

1959. Oil on pressed wood, 7 3/4 × 12 in.

Bennington Museum, Given in memory of Ilse Baum, Bennington, Vermont, 2011.152

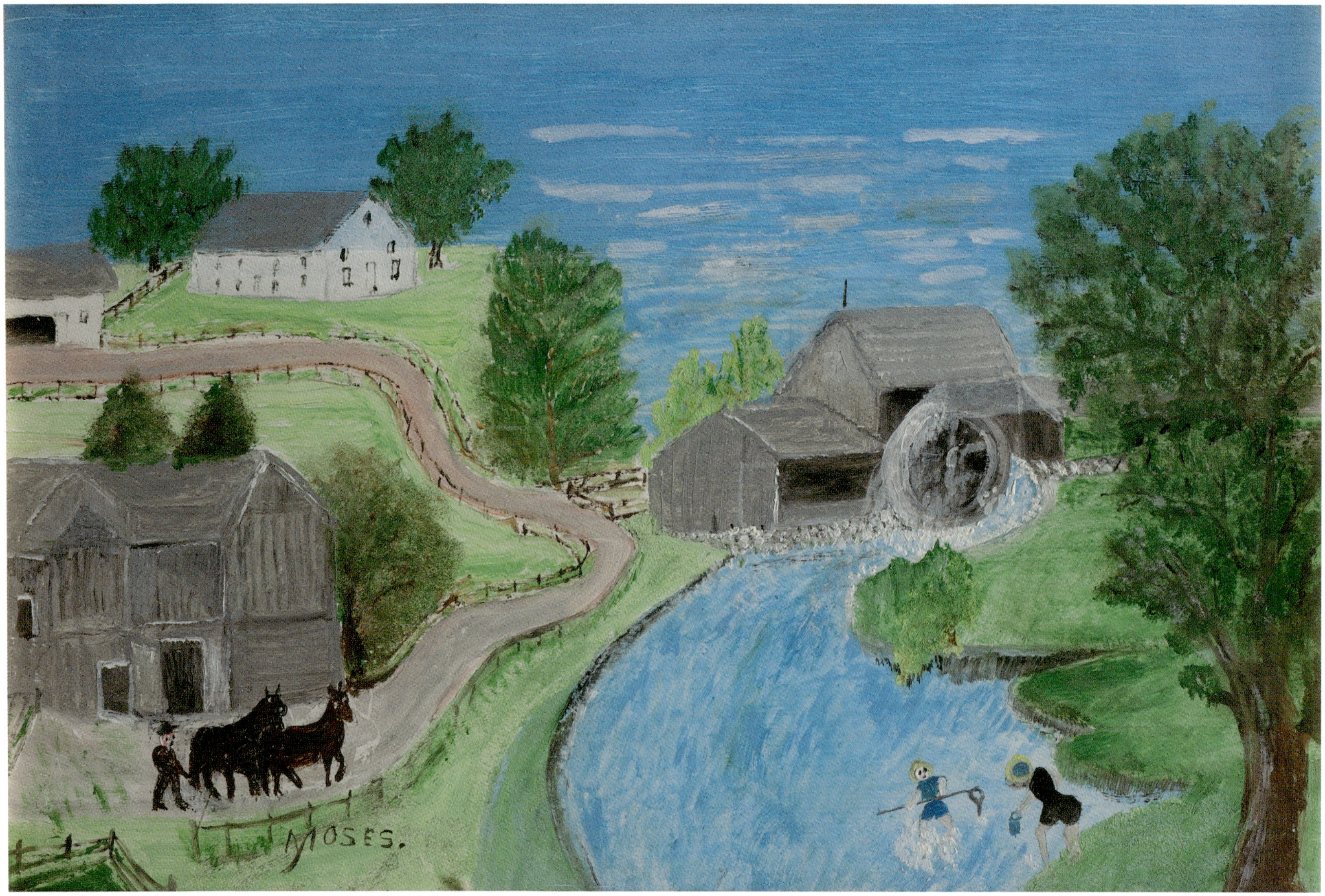

PLATE 39

Anna Mary Robertson ("Grandma") Moses

HAYING TIME

1959. Oil on pressed wood. 16 × 24 in.

Bennington Museum, Museum purchase with funds provided by Josephine Hartford Bryce, Bennington, Vermont, 2003.135

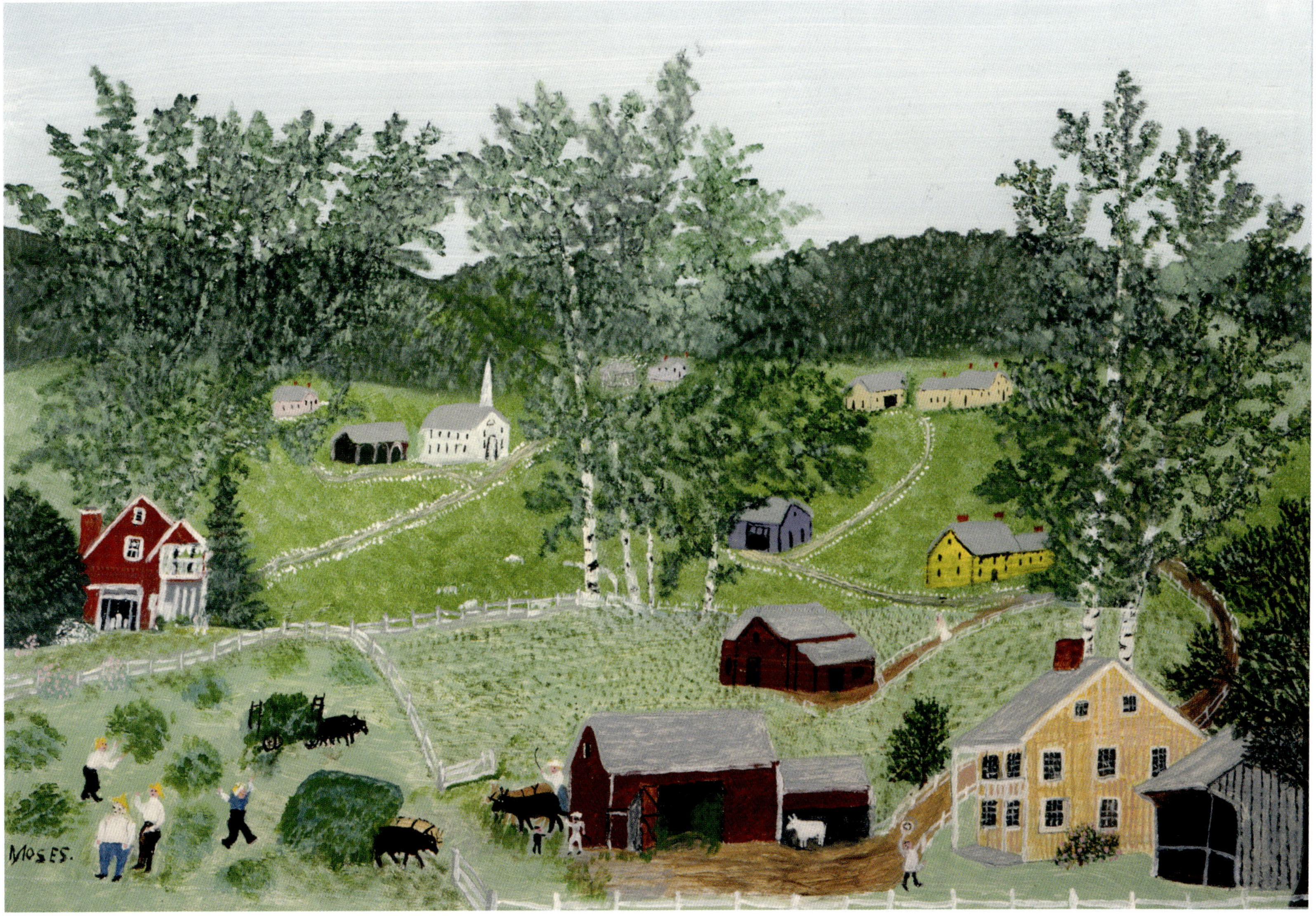

PLATE 40

Anna Mary Robertson ("Grandma") Moses

HORSESHOEING

1960. Oil on pressed wood, 16 × 24 in.

Collection of Harry L. Moses and the estate of Roy W. Moses

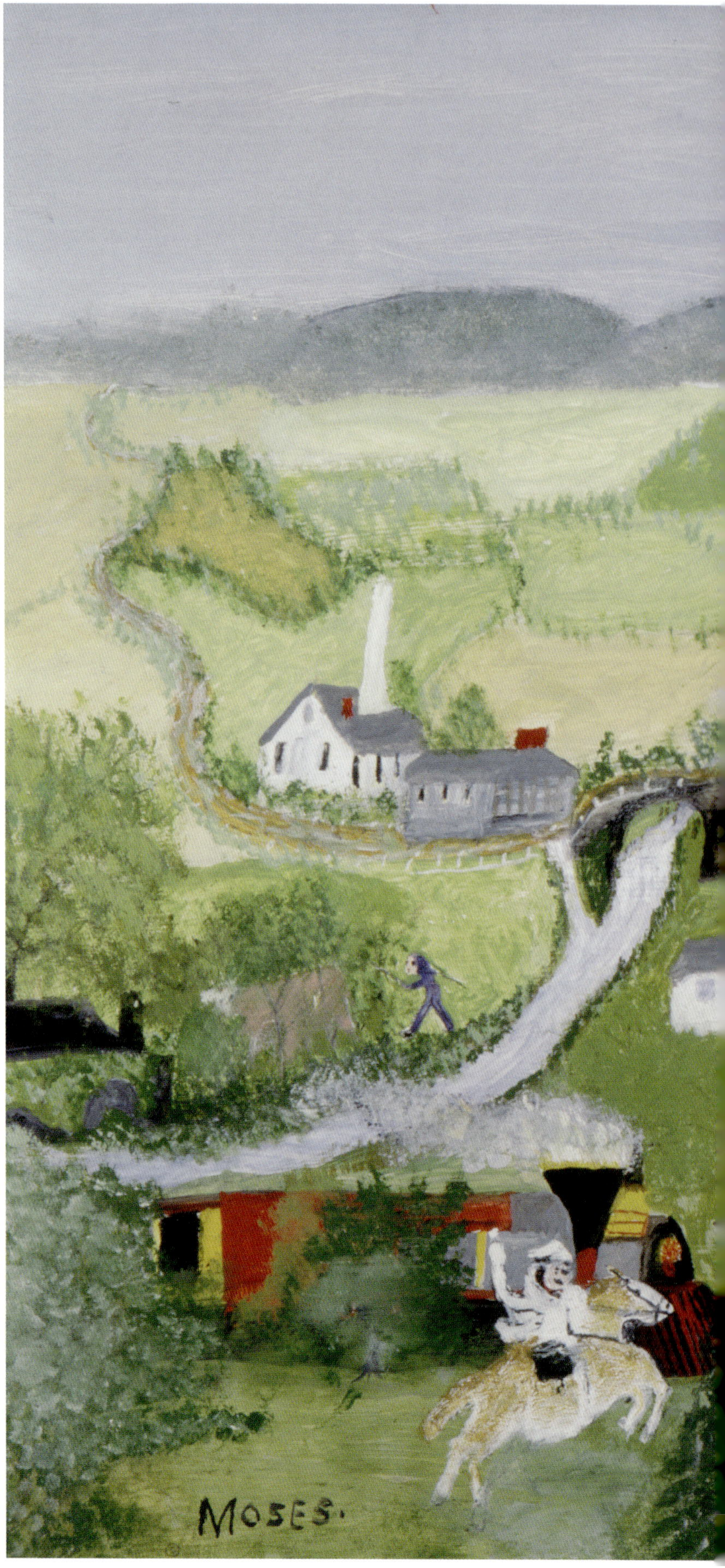

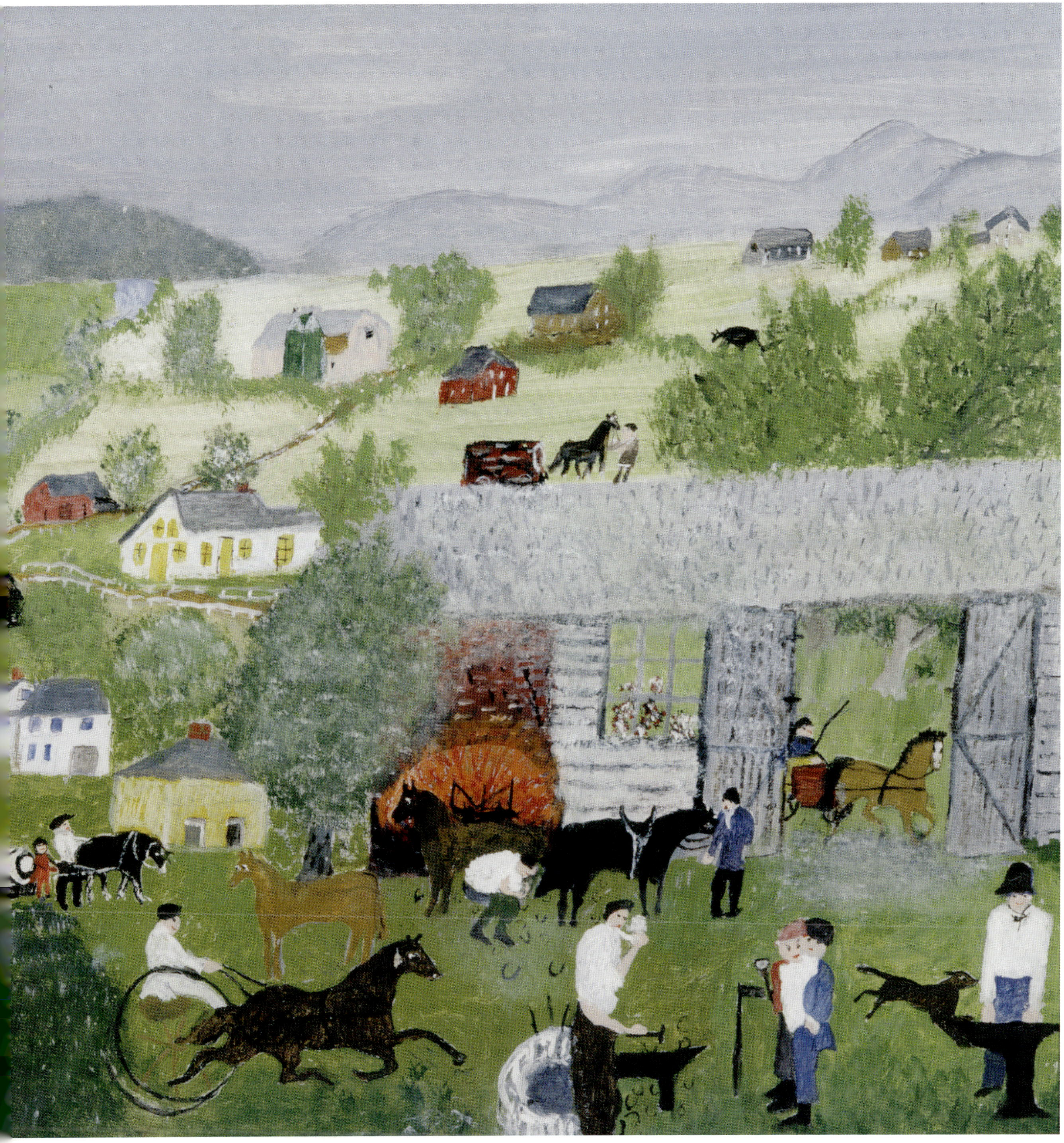

PLATE 41

Anna Mary Robertson ("Grandma") Moses

RIVER

1960. Oil on pressed wood, 16 × 24 in.

Collection of Harry L. Moses and the estate of Roy W. Moses

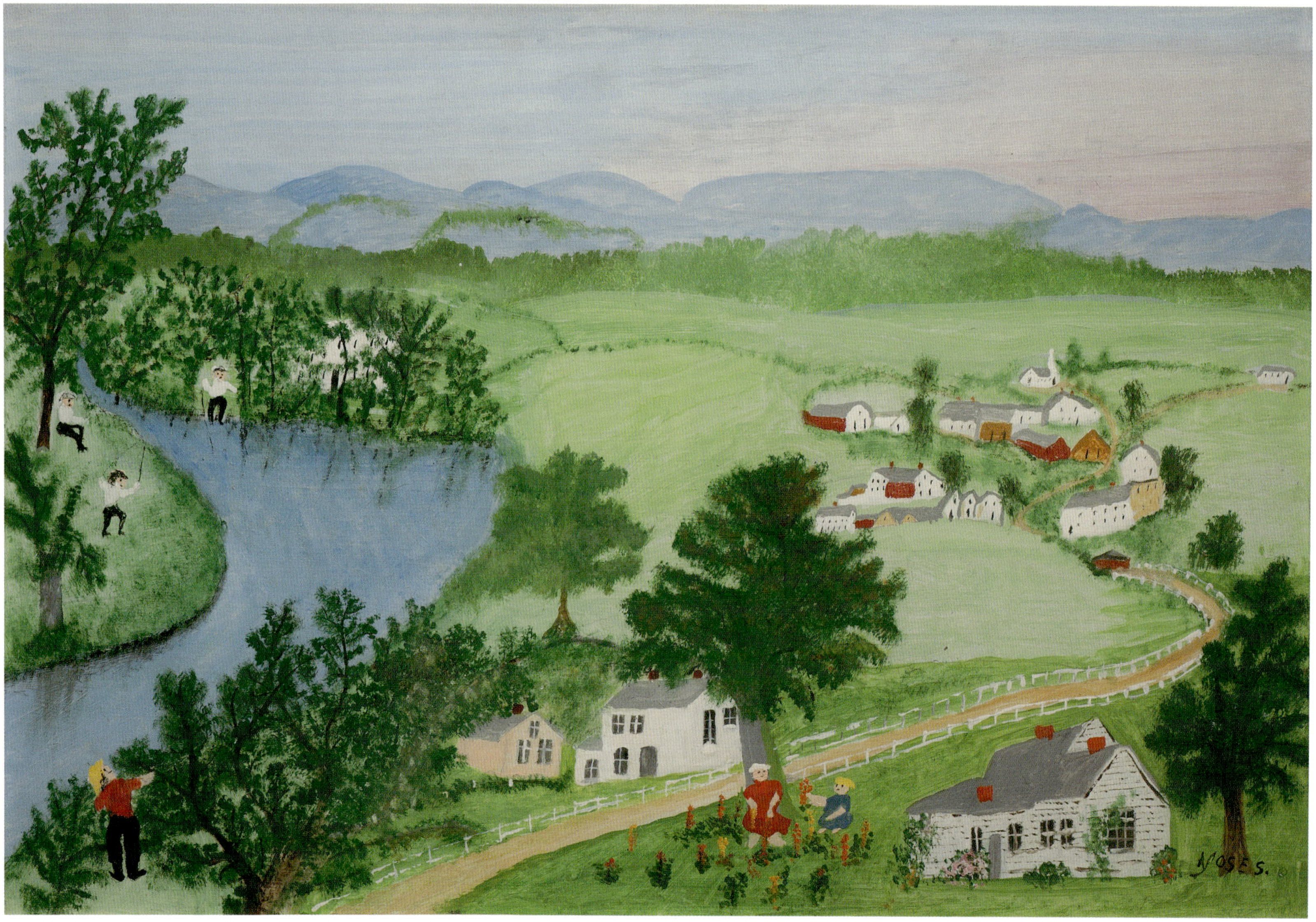

PLATE 42

Anna Mary Robertson ("Grandma") Moses

WAGON REPAIR SHOP

1960. Oil on pressed wood, 16 × 24 in.

Bennington Museum, Museum purchase, Bennington, Vermont, 2003.134

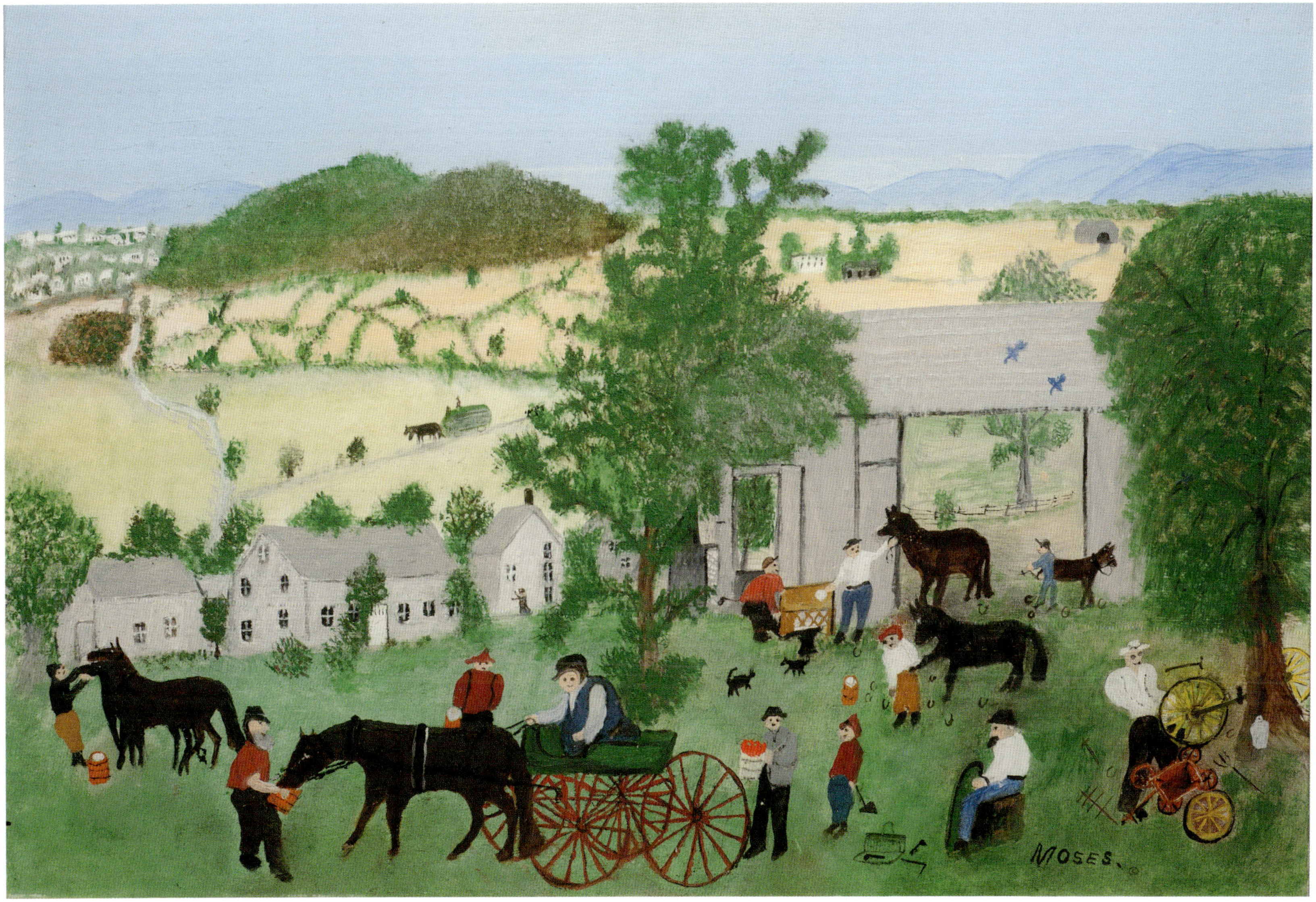

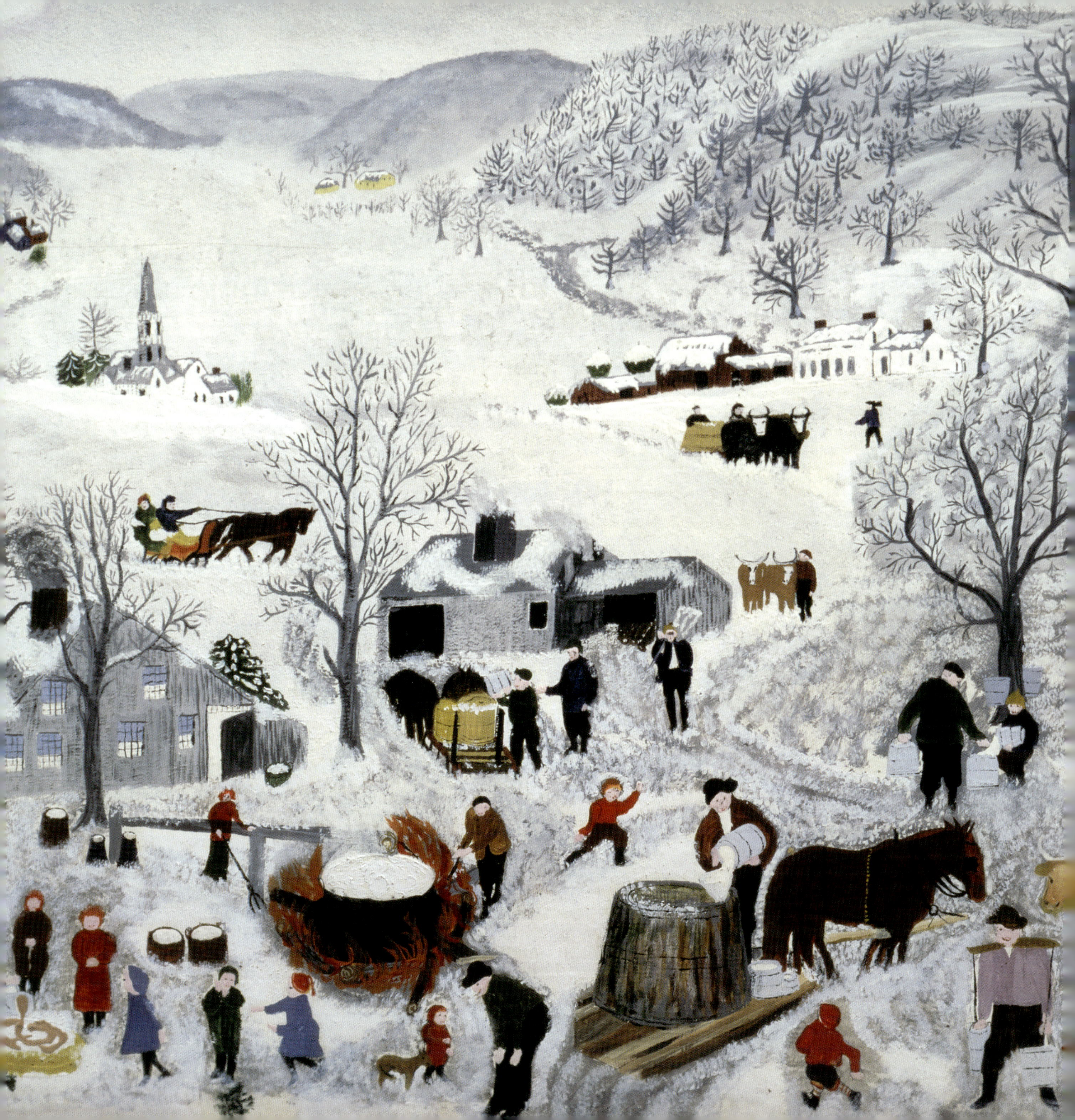

GRANDMA MOSES: AMERICAN MODERN

BIBLIOGRAPHY

Biracree, Tom. *Grandma Moses, Painter*. New York and Philadelphia: Chelsea House, 1989.

Cleary, Margot. *Grandma Moses*. New York: Crescent Books, 1991.

Janis, Sidney. *They Taught Themselves: American Primitive Painters of the 20th Century*. New York: Dial Press, 1942. Reprint, New York: Hudson River Press, 1999.

Kallir, Jane. *Grandma Moses in the 21st Century*. New York: Art Services International, 2001.

———. *Grandma Moses: The Artist Behind the Myth*. New York: Clarkson N. Potter, 1982.

Kallir, Otto. *Grandma Moses*. New York: Harry N. Abrams, 1973.

———. *Grandma Moses: American Primitive*. New York: The Dryden Press, 1946; 2nd ed. Garden City, NY: Doubleday, 1947.

Kallir, Otto, ed. *Art and Life of Grandma Moses*. Exh. Cat. Gallery of Modern Art, New York (20 February–30 March 1969). South Brunswick and New York: L A.S. Barnes, 1969; London: Thomas Yoseloff, 1969.

Marling, Karal Ann. *Designs on the Heart: The Homemade Art of Grandma Moses*. Boston: Harvard University Press, 2006.

Moses, Anna Mary Robertson. *The Grandma Moses Storybook*. Illustrated by Grandma Moses, edited by Nora Kramer. New York: Random House, 1961.

———. *My Life's History*. Edited by Otto Kallir. New York: Harper and Row, 1952.

Nikola-Lisa, W. *The Year with Grandma Moses*. New York: Henry Holt, 2000.

Oneal, Zibby. *Grandma Moses: Painter of Rural America*. New York: Viking Penguin, 1986.

INDEX

Note: Page numbers in *italic* type indicate illustrations.

Published on the occasion of the exhibition *Grandma Moses: American Modern*, organized by Shelburne Museum and Bennington Museum

EXHIBITION ITINERARY
Shelburne Museum, Vermont
June 18–October 30, 2016

Bennington Museum, Vermont
July 1–November 5, 2017

Exhibitions at Shelburne Museum are generously supported by Donna and Marvin Schwartz.

FIRST PUBLISHED IN THE UNITED STATES OF AMERICA IN 2016 BY
Skira Rizzoli Publications, Inc.
300 Park Avenue South
New York, NY 10010
www.rizzoliusa.com

IN ASSOCIATION WITH
Shelburne Museum
P.O. Box 10
Shelburne, VT 05482
www.shelburnemuseum.org

AND
Bennington Musuem
75 Main Street
Bennington, VT 05201
www.benningtonmuseum.org

2016 2017 2018 2019 / 10 9 8 7 6 5 4 3 2 1

Designed by McCall Associates

FOR SKIRA RIZZOLI PUBLICATIONS, INC.
Charles Miers, Publisher
Margaret Rennolds Chace, Associate Publisher
Ellen Cohen, Editor

LIBRARY OF CONGRESS CONTROL NUMBER:
2016932213

ISBN: 978-0-8478-4923-9 (hardcover)
ISBN: 978-0-8478-4762-4 (paperback)

Printed in China

PAGE 2
Anna Mary Robertson ("Grandma") Moses. *Bennington* (detail), 1953. Oil on pressed wood, 18 × 24 in. Bennington Museum, Museum purchase, Bennington, Vermont, 1986.347

PAGE 4
Grandma Moses with a sample of Riverdale's "Williamstown" fabric, based on one of her paintings, c. 1951–52.